METHODISTS & MOONSHINERS

Another
PROHIBITION EXPEDITION THROUGH THE SOUTH
...with Cocktail Recipes

KATHRYN SMITH

Published by Evening Post Books, Charleston, South Carolina

Copyright © 2023 by Kathryn Smith
All rights reserved.
First edition

Editor: Elizabeth W. Hollerith
Design and composition: Kim Scott/Bumpy Design

No part of this book may be reproduced or transmitted in any form or by any means, electronic or mechanical, including photocopying, recording or by information storage and retrieval system—except by a reviewer who may quote brief passages in a review to be printed in a magazine, newspaper, or on the web—without permission in writing from the publisher. For information, please contact the publisher. First printing 2021 Printed in the United States of America

A CIP catalog record for this book has been applied for from the Library of Congress.

ISBN: 978-1-929647-89-7

For Susan

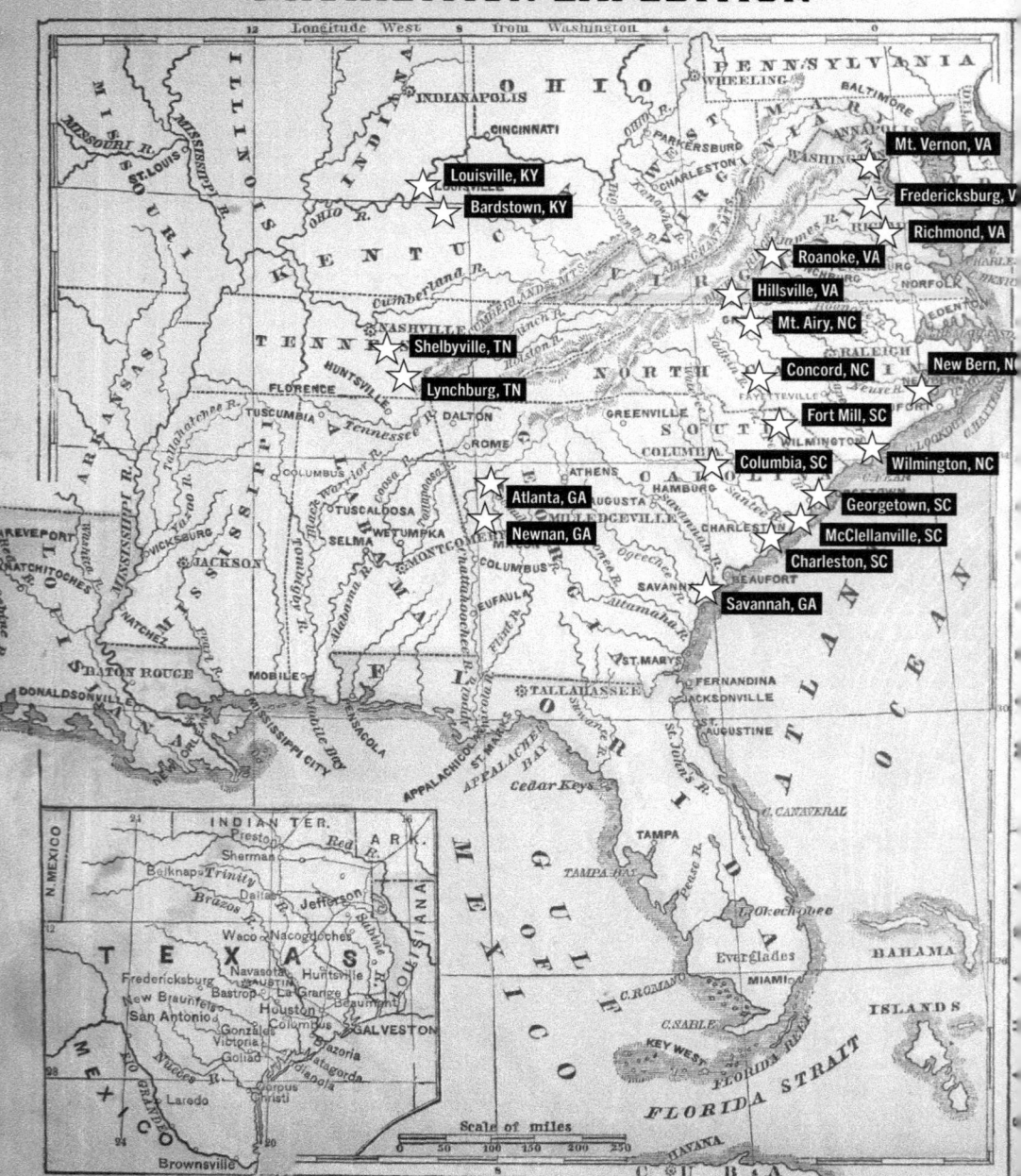

Table of Contents

Introduction 1

CHAPTER ONE
    Travels with My Aunt 9

CHAPTER TWO
    George Washington Drank Here 29

CHAPTER THREE
    An Inauspicious Beginning 49

CHAPTER FOUR
    Mt. Airy and Thereabouts 69

CHAPTER FIVE
    The Anti-Saloon Juggernaut 87

CHAPTER SIX
    The Department of Easy Virtue 107

CHAPTER SEVEN
    The Worm Turns 125

CHAPTER EIGHT
    The Crème de la Crime 149

CHAPTER NINE
    Whiskey Tourism 179

CHAPTER TEN
    In Search of Sobriety 201

Acknowledgements 211
Photo Credits 213
Notes 215
Index 235
About the Author 242

Introduction

How can you tell the difference between a Methodist and a Baptist?
The Methodist will speak to you in a liquor store.

YOU'VE PROBABLY HEARD THIS JOKE, which always gets a laugh, even from the Baptists. But you must admit that the idea of a Methodist being caught dead in a liquor store, much less meeting the eye of anyone else in one, is a fairly recent phenomenon. When we look back at the history of drinking in America and the people trying to control it, the Methodists were much more gung-ho than the Baptists.

John Wesley, the founder of Methodism, was a Church of England minister who came to America in 1736 with James Oglethorpe, who established the colony of Georgia three years before. John and his brother, Charles, arrived as spiritual leaders to Savannah and the new settlement of Fredericka, a hundred miles south on the Georgia coast.

John was so abstemious that when their ship arrived, he swore off wine and "flesh" (as in meat), and, with two accompanying like-minded men, for a time tried to live on dry bread and water alone, declaring that the three of them "were more vigorous and healthy than while we tasted nothing else." (Obviously he had never heard of scurvy or typhoid, or paid close attention to Matthew 4:4: "Man shall not live on bread alone." Or maybe he was just taking that passage too literally, as he spent most of his waking hours in prayer and Bible reading.)[1] No wonder then, that members of the church he

John Wesley preaches to Native Georgians in this mural at Atlanta's Ansley Park Hotel. He actually had very little interaction with them. *Postcard from author's collection.*

established in America in 1784 were among the leading proponents of temperance, heading up such dauntless nineteenth century anti-alcohol groups as the Chautauqua Institution, the Women's Christian Temperance Union, and the Anti-Saloon League.

I hope that if you have picked up this book you are already familiar with *Baptists and Bootleggers*, my previous book about Prohibition in the South. It was inspired by a book with a similar title written by my father, Bruce Yandle, and son, Adam C. Smith, both Ph.D. economists. Their book *Bootleggers and Baptists* covers the strange political bedfellows that influence government regulation, while mine is a response to the many people who, hearing the first book's title, responded, "That sounds like a fun book!"[2] I wrote a fun book, but give me a break. I have only a bachelor's degree in journalism from the University of Georgia, which was voted the country's No. 1 party school the year I matriculated.

Since *Baptists and Bootleggers*' release in 2021, I have learned much more about Prohibition and the history of drinking in the South, both prior to 1920 and after 1933, when the "noble experiment" was in place. People kept sharing great stories and suggesting locales with terrific true crime histories that I had neglected in *B&B*. This was partly because I did all the research on *B&B* in the midst of the covid-19 pandemic and had to dodge outbreaks as I traveled and researched. So, I readily admit I didn't do justice to North Carolina and Virginia, which were hotbeds of illegal alcohol activity, and gave just a lick and a promise to the story of the German brewers and their role in the whole debacle, as well as beer in general because I don't drink it much.

I also wanted to give a harder look at America's founding years and the drinking habits of the colonists and the citizens of the newly minted country, as that history explains much of what followed. That meant checking into a little-known aspect of the life of George Washington—founding father, father of our country, social drinker—and, incidentally, one heck of a distiller of rye whiskey. He is thoroughly covered in the first two chapters, **"Travels with My Aunt"** and **"George Washington Drank Here."**

The full story of John Wesley, his hymn-writing brother Charles, and how they were chased out of Georgia for stirring up so much trouble with their holier-than-thou ways is told in Chapter Three, **"An Inauspicious Beginning."** That chapter covers the story of the Methodists and the nineteenth century temperance movement, including the tradition of drinking grape juice—or "unfermented wine," as a certain Dr. Welch called it—instead of wine at communion.

With drink getting the reformers' boot, tobacco worried if it was next in this undated cartoon from the collection of the Calhoun County Museum and Cultural Center, St. Matthews, South Carolina.

Chapter Four brings us to **"Mt. Airy and Thereabouts,"** the North Carolina home of actor Andy Griffith and the model for the fictitious town of Mayberry on the beloved television series. You will remember the town drunk Otis Campbell was a regular visitor to the jail, and there were several episodes in which moonshine making was played for laughs. In the nineteenth century, however, that part of North Carolina and adjoining Virginia were embroiled in illegal moonshining activity, feuds, and even a deadly courthouse shoot-out that took out the judge, the prosecuting attorney, the sheriff, the jury foreman, and a witness. There is also an intriguing side story here about the original Siamese twins, Chang and Eng Bunker, who farmed and raised their families near Mt. Airy, and the problem that ensued when one conjoined twin is an alcoholic and the other is not.

By the late nineteenth and early twentieth centuries, covered in Chapter Five, **"The Anti-Saloon Juggernaut,"** the temperance movement was making great gains, especially in the South, where most of the people were members of the Methodist, Baptist, or Presbyterian churches. Even the Episcopalians got on board. The efforts of progressive do-gooders out to remake society, coupled with bigots who distrusted and outright hated Catholics, immigrants, German brewers, and minorities of all stripes—often with the Ku Klux Klan leading the charge or at least along for the ride (in white hoods and sheets, of course)—culminated with Congress voting to implement national Prohibition. I take a look at the plight of the shell-shocked veterans of World War I, accustomed to having alcohol to calm their nerves and stiffen their spines, returning to a dry America.

The policing of Prohibition was the job of the Warren G. Harding administration, infamous for its corruption. In Chapter Six, **"The Department of Easy Virtue,"** I write of Attorney General Harry Daugherty and the other political hacks and opportunists who worked for him, focusing especially on a North Carolinian named Gaston Means, one of the century's most successful con men—up to a point—who took hundreds of thousands of dollars in bribe money from bootleggers and claimed President Harding was poisoned by his wife.

Chapter Seven, **"The Worm Turns,"** brings us to the year 1926, seen by many as the turning point for the now deeply divisive ban on alcohol. Congressional hearings put the drys on the defensive, Georgia Congressman W.D. Upshaw, the "driest of the dry," lost his seat, and even former adherents jumped ship, arguing that Prohibition was the worst way in the world to reduce alcoholism and its consequences for society. But it took a major crime wave, the Great Depression, and a few more more election cycles to bring the country to its senses.

The Twenty-first Amendment, repealing the Eighteenth, was ratified in December 1933 with much celebration. But in the South, not much changed. Statewide prohibition lasted in some states for years, and the lure of illegal money led to the crime spree of a Memphis bootlegger nicknamed "Machine Gun" Kelly and a ramping up of moonshine production that continued well into the 1970s. In Chapter Eight, **"The Crème de la Crime,"** I'll take another look at the torturous road to a legal drink in the nation and the South and the wave of related crime that outlasted Prohibition.

That brings us to the present day. The South's about-face on the liquor issue became complete when some of the earliest states to ban booze, including Tennessee and Kentucky, embraced whiskey, wine, and beer "trails" as a driver of tourism dollars. In Chapter Nine, **"Whiskey Tourism,"** I visit Bardstown, Kentucky, "the bourbon capital of the world," and Lynchburg, Tennessee, home of what I like to call Jack Daniel's Land. I will also explore how states that used to spend money enforcing dry liquor laws are now spending it to encourage tourists to visit and drink, while loosening regulations and reducing taxes on the producers. Another one of the places I check out is a new distillery honoring the legacy of Nearest Green, the former slave who taught Jack Daniel the secrets of Tennessee whiskey making.

Jack Daniel is lauded in this display at the distillery visitor center in Lynchburg, Tennessee. *Author photo.*

Finally, in Chapter Ten, **"In Search of Sobriety,"** I explore the history of organizations that have tried over the years to help alcoholics and almost-alcoholics turn from drinking: the nineteenth century George Washington Society (they were uninformed about or simply ignored George's post-presidential career), Alcoholics Anonymous, founded in 1935, and today's Sober

Curious movement, which has resulted in a plethora of non-alcoholic wines, beers, and liquors and even non-alcoholic bars and bottle stores.

Along the way, I will take you to historic sites, museums, distilleries, modern-day speakeasies, and cemeteries, and share recipes for cocktails and mocktails with tie-ins to the chapters.

Two bits of housekeeping: when I refer to the national ban on alcohol ushered in by the Eighteenth Amendment, I call it Prohibition with a big P. When I refer to local or state bans, I call it prohibition with a little p. And when I refer to the South, I count the states of Alabama, Arkansas, Florida, Georgia, Kentucky, Louisiana, Mississippi, North Carolina, South Carolina, Tennessee, and Virginia. Sorry, Texas, you are a land unto yourself.

Incidentally, people have already been asking me if I have a third book in mind, one for the Presbyterians. My response so far is that the only title that comes to mind is *Presbyterians and Prostitutes*, and I don't think I want to investigate that particular sin. But you never know.

To get you started, here is a story about a famous socialite, Lady Mendl, and the cocktail she invented.

THE PINK LADY

Lady Mendl, aka Elsie de Wolfe, was America's first professional interior decorator. Born in 1859, she championed a more sleek and modern style to counter the heavy, fussy furniture of the Victorian era. She became Lady Mendl following her 1926 marriage to British diplomat Sir Charles Mendl.

Lady Mendl was among the beautiful people who popularized the French Riviera in the off-season, a trend started by Cole Porter, his friends Gerald and Sara Murphy, and the F. Scott Fitzgeralds. Heiress Gertrude Sanford Legendre, subject of my biography *Gertie*, recalled Lady Mendl

Lady Mendl in about 1920, with her dogs. *Wikimedia Commons*.

always wearing opera gloves—the type that reached up to her armpits—as protection against sunburn when she swam.[3] Not to be outdone in the elegance department, Sara Murphy wore a rope of real pearls even when sunbathing.

Lady Mendl was a practitioner of yoga and had a daily exercise regimen that included standing on her head and walking on her hands, even in her seventies. Of course, she gave fabulous parties. Among her many talents, Lady Mendl is said to have invented a beautiful and tasty drink, the Pink Lady.

Sometimes vilified as a "sissy drink," the Pink Lady, depending on the recipe you use, can certainly pack a wallop. But it is pretty, with a foamy layer on top achieved by using a bit of egg white.

A Pink Lady waits among the vintage glassware in my Prohibition-era dry bar. *Author photo.*

Here is the recipe from *The Savoy Cocktail Book*, first published in London in 1930[4]:

- the white of one egg
- 1 tbsp. Grenadine
- 1 glass of gin (1½ to 2 oz. should do it)

Shake well and strain into a medium size cocktail glass.

If you want to step it up a notch, here's the recipe from another vintage cocktail book, *The Artistry of Mixing Drinks*, written by Frank Meier, head bartender of the Ritz Bar in Paris, and published in 1934[5]:

"In shaker: half white of Egg, a teaspoon each of Grenadine, Lemon juice, and Brandy; one-half glass of gin [1 oz.] Shake well with ice, strain into a cocktail glass and serve."

CHAPTER ONE

Travels with My Aunt

IT WAS 11 O'CLOCK on a Monday morning and I was drinking rye whiskey.

But it wasn't just any rye whiskey. My aunt, Susan Middleton, and I were sipping from elegant little tasting glasses inscribed with the cypher GW, enjoying four-year-old George Washington Straight Rye Whiskey in the distillery at Mount Vernon straight out of the barrel. Our host was Steve Bashore, whose job title is director of historic trades. In other words, he makes the stuff.

Most people have no idea that George Washington was one of the largest distillers in the country. He "retired under my vine and fig tree," as he said in his farewell address, coming home to his plantation on the banks of the Potomac River in 1797. He spent the final two years of his life overseeing his farms, where hundreds of enslaved workers toiled, and entertaining a Niagara Falls-size torrent of visitors.[6] He also set up a distillery a couple of miles down the road from his house.

Mount Vernon was the first stop on a trip Susan and I made following President Washington's tour of the Southern states in the spring of 1791 and researching what the drinking was like, then and now. We are only eight years apart in age—in fact, I was born on her birthday—and we have always felt more like sisters than aunt and niece. We share not only a birthday but a

The author, left, and her aunt, Susan Middleton, during their George Washington odyssey.

tremendous curiosity about American history, so when I invited her on this trip, she didn't have to think twice to say, "Yes!"

So back to George. The president—he took office in April 1789—had already visited all the other former colonies. Leaving from Philadelphia on March 21, he traveled to Mount Vernon and then all the way to Savannah, Georgia and back, a journey of 1,900 miles that took three months.[7] He rode in a custom-built, cream-colored coach pulled by four bay horses, accompanied by a small entourage that included a baggage wagon and his stunning white charger, Prescott, which he often mounted when he arrived at his destination cities to better show himself to the people. He also brought along his favorite greyhound, Cornwallis, named for the British general he defeated at the Battle of Yorktown, Virginia in 1781.[8]

Susan and I were traveling rather more modestly in my blue Honda Fit, and we left our dogs at home, but we had a distinct advantage over Washington in that we had GPS to keep us from getting lost, paved roads, and internet booking sites to help us find places to spend the night. Washington was often at the mercy of taverns, which sometimes proved unfit for man or horse. (We ended up at one Quality Inn of which I would say the same. The water in the swimming pool was green, but at least we didn't have to worry about stabling a horse.)

By the time we got to the distillery, Susan and I had already had a flash tour of the house, which Washington's father began building in 1734.[9] Our guide, Gail Cassidy, was a seasoned one, and like everyone we met at Mount Vernon, seemed to love her job. The historic site is open 365 days a year, she said, because George Washington never turned away a visitor, even

Mount Vernon is a wooden house painted to look like sandstone. *Author photo.*

on Christmas day. In one post-presidency year, he and Martha hosted 677 guests. That is a huge number, but it pales next to the million visitors who come to Mount Vernon annually today. Gail guided us through the various formal rooms and bedrooms, including the one where Washington died of a throat ailment called "quincy," and shared the fascinating facts that he had a personal library of 1,339 books and loved ice cream, which was often served to his guests. Then she sent us down the road to the gristmill and distillery.

Steve Bashore took us into the gristmill first, explaining that Mount Vernon's original major crop had been tobacco. But it had worn out the soil, and after a couple of bad crop years in the 1760s, the fields were planted in grains, which were then milled into flour for export. Washington had a large mill built in 1771 to process rye, wheat, barley, oats, and corn. And so things continued while he led the Continental Army and served eight years as president. [10] The country's capital then was Philadelphia, so he depended on a farm manager to carry out his wishes, which were extensive and meticulous.

In 1797, Washington's old manager having retired, he hired a man named James Anderson, who quickly set about persuading him to use some of his grain for another purpose. A Scot, Anderson was quite familiar with

The Mount Vernon distillery was built on the foundation of the one George Washington had built in 1797. *Photo courtesy Steve Bashore.*

distilling, and told Washington he could make a lot more money by selling whiskey to the taverns in Alexandria than shipping flour to England.

Washington, then sixty-five years of age, agreed to give it a try. With two stills in operation under Anderson's son, John, and an enslaved man, about 600 gallons of what is called "white dog"—unaged whiskey—were turned out in six months and sold in casks to the taverns in Alexandria, Virginia. It made such a profit that Washington decided to build a large distillery and expand production, buying copper stills, worms, and a boiler.

By March 1798, he had five stills in production run by John Anderson and six enslaved men. That year, the distillery produced 4,500 gallons of whiskey. In 1799, the year he died, the distillery produced almost 11,000 gallons of whiskey, as well as smaller amounts of peach, apple and persimmon brandy, Steve said.

Washington, who had no children of his own, left Mount Vernon to family members, though, of course, Martha lived there until her death several years later. Over the years, Mount Vernon deteriorated. The distillery burned down in 1814, and it was not until 1932 that the footprint of the mill and the distillery were discovered. Because Prohibition was on its way out but still a contentious issue, it was thought best to rebuild the gristmill only and let the sleeping white dog lie. Seventy years or so later, public opinion had loosened up enough to give it another shot, and some serious archaeology provided enough information to rebuild the distillery much as it was in Washington's day. In fact, some of the large stones in the mash room floor are original. His meticulous farm records provided a recipe for the mash bill, the mix of grains used in distilling. Purchased from local farms, it is 60 percent rye, 30–35 percent corn, and the remainder malted barley, Steve said. The grain is ground in the gristmill, which is operated in the eighteenth-century manner.

Steve, one of a handful of millers in the country trained in historic methods, joined Mount Vernon's staff in 2007, the same year the distillery opened. "We never anticipated the goal was to make whiskey," he said; the idea was to give visitors an educational experience as they saw how whiskey was made in Washington's day. He readily admits that the first batch, produced in March 2009, was "not so tasty." Nevertheless, it sold out in three hours. With practice and help from distillery professionals, the runs have increased in size and the whiskey has gotten better.

The big difference is that today they only distill during two months of the year, March and November, Steve said, and, of course, the amount of whiskey made is modest, a thousand gallons or so a year.

Over at the Mount Vernon gift shop following the tour, I discovered the whiskey business is continuing to support Washington's home, which is owned and operated by the Mount Vernon Ladies' Association. (The founder was a patriotic woman from Laurens County, South Carolina named Ann Pamela Cunningham, who was appalled by the state of the house in the mid-nineteenth century. She and her team of determined women raised enough money to buy the property and take over operations in 1860, the eve of the Civil War.)

Mash rakes like these were used in George Washington's day and are still employed in making whiskey at Mount Vernon. *Author photo.*

At the shop you can not only buy GW tasting glasses like the ones Steve provided Susan and me, but rocks glasses inscribed with a Washington quote from 1783 upon the cessation of hostilities with the English: "An extra ration of liquor to be issued to every man tomorrow, to drink Perpetual Peace, Independence & Happiness to the United States of America."

You can also find a GW flask (actually, four versions), a beer bottle opener shaped like George the general, wine glasses, wine stoppers, and, of course, the products of the distillery. The four-year-old rye I tasted sells for $225 per 375 ml. bottle.

Other than the bottle opener, which was a little silly, I think George Washington would be rather pleased about the drinkers' corner of the gift shop. In his book *Founding Spirits: George Washington and the Beginnings of the American Whiskey Industry*, Dennis J. Pogue writes, "To the surprise of some, George Washington's association with alcoholic beverages was extensive. In his personal life he was a confirmed social drinker—he consumed ale and beer, cider and brandy, rum and whiskey, and an assortment of wines." His favorite was Madeira wine, a fortified wine imported from Portugal, an enthusiasm he shared with much of the gentry in early America. Pogue says Washington offered it "as an after dinner treat to the many visitors who routinely sought his company in the years following the Revolution, and he delighted in toasting the new nation that he had been so instrumental in founding."[11]

Indeed. According to the Washington Library at Mount Vernon, his fondness for Madeira was somewhat legendary, and he demanded "the best quality." Before and after the Revolutionary War, he ordered it by "the pipe," which held 126 gallons. In his retirement, his step-granddaughter, Nelly Custis, remembered him drinking three glasses of Madeira after dinner one night, but keep in mind that it was served in small glasses, like port is.[12]

He also understood the importance of alcohol as a political tool. When Washington first ran for office in 1755, seeking a seat in the Virginia Assembly, he was defeated. Two years later, he supplied the polling places with 144 gallons of booze, making sure the voters knew where it came from. As Susan Cheever writes in her book *Drinking in America*, "At 307 votes, he got a return on his investment of almost two votes per gallon."[13]

That said, Washington was famous for his reserve and rectitude, and he highly disapproved of drunkenness. "Over the course of his lifetime he was forced to endure the poor performance of valued employees, soldiers, and even their officers, as a consequence of habitual drunkenness and the erratic behavior that ensued," Pogue observes.[14] Writing on August 1, 1792 to Henry Knox, then his secretary of war, Washington opined, "So long as the vice of drunkenness exists in the army, so long, I hope, ejections of those officers who are found guilty of it will continue; for that and gaming will debilitate and render unfit for active service any army whatsoever."[15] Not to mention the fights, duels, and political backstabbing within the ranks of the Continental Army and the state militias. Early in the war Washington even had to break up a snowball fight in Boston between two militias that threatened to turn into a bloody free-for-all.

After the tour, Susan and I got back into my little blue Honda Fit and headed down the road to Fredericksburg, where George Washington's sister lived. We were listening to the soundtrack from the hit Broadway musical *Hamilton*. One of playwright Lin-Manuel Miranda's lyrics gave a hint about why Washington was so eager to make his Southern tour:

> When Britain taxed our TEA we got frisky
> Imagine what gon' happen when you try & tax our whiskey[16]

In Miranda's musical, the words come from the mouth of Thomas Jefferson, who challenged Alexander Hamilton's proposal to impose excise taxes on whiskey to raise money to pay off the individual states' war debts and put the new country on a sound financial footing.[17] Washington had signed the Duties on Distilled Spirits Act shortly before his departure for the South and one of his aims in making the trip was to take the pulse of the public on the bill. Incidentally, the act had been endorsed by the Philadelphia College of Physicians, whose members felt it would result in less consumption of a product damaging to public health.[18] Unintentionally perhaps, it was the young government's first shot across the bow for temperance.

If Washington hoped to get a coherent response from anyone on the Southern tour, he probably gave up fairly quickly. From Fredericksburg to Savannah and back, it was one long drinking party. There's no record of Washington over-indulging, but certainly the people who surrounded him were throwing down a lot of alcohol.

Fredericksburg is forty-two miles from Mount Vernon, a drive of an hour or so for us, but two days for Washington. His mother, Mary Ball Washington, spent her final years there in a house he bought for her. On this visit, he dined and lodged with his widowed sister, Betty Lewis. Perhaps he had time to make an appearance at Weedon's Tavern, a favorite gathering place for patriots plotting the revolution. Washington patronized Weedon's often for food, drink, and card games, which he said he usually lost.[19] It was also the site of a great Peace Ball after the surrender of Cornwallis at Yorktown. Washington escorted his mother to the ball that night, but at 10 p.m. she announced, "it is time for old ladies to be in the bed," and the gallant Marquis de Lafayette took her home. He returned, of course, for more partying.[20]

Weedon's Tavern burned down early in the nineteenth century, but, amazingly, another colonial tavern is still intact and open for tours. Susan and I pulled up to Rising Sun Tavern on Caroline Street late in the afternoon, just in time to take one. It turns out that George had spent time there, too, for the house was built by his younger brother, Charles, and was used as his home before he and his family decamped for western Virginia.[21]

This was according to our guide, Kelly Pedigoe, who was conducting her last tour before heading off to a new job at Winterthur Museum in Delaware. A bit of a black sheep, Charles was "very invested in drinking and gambling," she said. A couple of owners after Charles left town, the house was turned into a pub with bedrooms upstairs for up to twelve guests, "sort of like an Airbnb." At the time, there were three kinds of public houses, she explained. An inn was for lodging, an ordinary was a restaurant, and a tavern provided both services, as well as a bar.

Kelly guided us through the downstairs rooms, which were furnished with era-appropriate antiques, though none of them were original to the house. Rising Sun lost its liquor license for unknown reasons in 1820, Kelly said, and has been a museum for 113 years. One of the most successful operators of the Rising Sun was a woman, which was not unusual at

Rising Sun Tavern has occupied the same lot on Fredericksburg's Caroline Street since 1760. *Author photo.*

the time. During her ownership, women were welcome to dine, drink, and play the popular card games poker, blackjack, and whist in the banquet room. For quieter pursuits, such as reading and conversation, there was a drawing room.

The dining table held a huge bowl of faux punch. I asked Kelly about Washington's preference for punch, and she said it was reputed to be a version of Fish House Punch containing three bottles of peach brandy. Regretfully, no drink is sold at the tavern today, except on special occasions such as the ticketed "Whiskey, Taxes and Federalists," an educational event and whiskey tasting held the week after we visited. A Bourbon & Boxwood fundraiser in May raised over $135,000 for the organization that owns the tavern and three other historic properties in Fredericksburg.[22]

Kelly said, in Washington's day, it took sixteen hours to travel from Fredericksburg to Richmond, and that meant an overnight stay along the way. Fortunately, we got there in about an hour, and checked into The Commonwealth, a historic hotel facing the Capitol Square. We got a warm welcome at our hotel, especially from the ebullient, history-loving valet, who was eager to point out the landmarks of his city, but it was nothing like Washington's welcome. He was met with cannon fire.

PROHIBITION EXPEDITION: MOUNT VERNON

George Washington's Mount Vernon offers educational fun for all ages, every day of the year, with the house where George and Martha entertained being only one of many attractions.

3200 Mount Vernon Highway, Mount Vernon, Virginia • www.mtvernon.org

---

From there, head down to Fredericksburg to the **Rising Sun Tavern**, 1304 Caroline Street, and its sister museums. www.washingtonheritagemuseums.org

CEMETERY SIDE TRIP

In his will, **George Washington**, requested that a new tomb be built of brick to hold "my remains, with those of my deceased relatives (now in the old Vault) and such others of my family as may chuse to be entombed there, may be deposited."[23] A new tomb was finally built in 1831. George and Martha, "Consort of Washington," rest in marble sarcophagi in the tomb, where brief wreath-laying ceremonies are now held each day at noon.

A vintage postcard shows Washington's tomb at Mount Vernon. *Author's collection.*

Ann Pamela Cunningham, founder of the Mount Vernon Ladies' Association, is buried in the churchyard of First Presbyterian Church in Columbia, South Carolina in a lovely tomb provided by a nephew. The marker is inscribed with a poignant reminder of the crippling fall from a horse that plagued her with pain all her adult life: "It is good that I have been afflicted. I shall be satisfied when I awaken with thy likeness." The parents of President Woodrow Wilson are also buried in the churchyard.

We're getting ahead of ourselves here, but George Washington did visit Columbia for a few days during his return trip in 1791. The house on Gervais Street

Ann Pamela Cunningham's tomb is located in the churchyard of First Presbyterian, Columbia. *Author photo.*

where he was entertained is long gone, but walk over to the nearby State House grounds to see a bronze copy of the marble Washington statue that stands in the capitol building in Richmond. It's one of six copies cast in bronze in 1857, and it was was purchased by the South Carolina General Assembly the following year for display at the State House. According to a plaque added to the base some years later, the statue's cane was vandalized by Union soldiers during the occupation of Columbia in February 1865, the lower part snapped off, never to be replaced.[24]

FISH HOUSE PUNCH

- One pint lemon juice
- One pint each Jamaica rum, brandy, and peach brandy
- Four pounds sugar
- Nine pints of water
- Make lemonade first, then add the liquors

—Recipe adapted from Eat, Drink and Be Merry in Maryland by Frederick Philip Stieff[25]

Richmond was the largest city in the most populous state in the young United States in 1791, and many of its four thousand residents came out to greet President Washington. The capitol building, designed by Thomas Jefferson, was almost completed, but it was formed of brick. The stucco layer that makes it so spanking white today had not been applied. The president wrote in his diary, rather snarkily, "The buildings in this place have increased a good deal since I was here last, but they are not of the best kind."[26] I assume he kept this opinion to himself.

By the way, Washington and Jefferson were two of the eight presidents born in Virginia. For extra credit, can you name the other six?[27]

Washington arrived in Richmond around 2 p.m. on April 1, and the festivities began in earnest that afternoon with cannon fire and continued that evening when the city was "illuminated." That meant lots of candles in windows, and in the streets flaming torches and tar barrels. During his three nights in Richmond, he was tossed about from banquets to fetes but managed a private conversation with the man in charge of federal revenues for that district (i.e. the tax collector). This fellow assured the president there would be no problem collecting the new excise tax on whiskey—indeed, that "it will become popular in a little time."[28] This opinion was not shared by a bunch of roustabouts in Pennsylvania, who would rise up against it three years later in what became known as the Whiskey Rebellion.

This painting attributed to Frederick Kemmelmeyer depicts George Washington and his troops near Fort Cumberland, Maryland before their march to suppress the Whiskey Rebellion in western Pennsylvania. *Collection of the Metropolitan Museum of Art, New York.*

THE WHISKEY REBELLION

Washington was right to be concerned about the reactions to the new excise tax on liquor dreamed up by his secretary of the treasury, Alexander Hamilton, who had a deep abhorrence of drunkenness. (This may come as a surprise to *Hamilton* fans, who recall the scenes in the musical in which he swigs from a pewter mug.) At one point during his time as an artillery commander during the Revolutionary War, his inebriated soldiers' mishandling of a cannon resulted in an explosion, killing six and wounding several others.[29] Susan Cheever writes in *Drinking in America* that the stills springing up on farms all over the young country "struck Hamilton as a great opportunity to levy taxes and, perhaps, punish drinkers."[30]

In the bigger cities and at larger distilleries, the tax of seven-and-a-half-cents a gallon plus sixty cents a year on each gallon of capacity was accepted without much complaint. But out in the boonies, it was a different story.[31] One of Washington's biographers, James Thomas Flexner, describes the rough characters who settled the Pennsylvania frontier as "often misfits, sometimes psychopaths, but always self-reliant, warlike, physically active."[32] These were the men who didn't cotton to paying taxes on the liquor they produced in their itty-bitty stills.

They began by terrorizing federal tax collectors and advanced to destroying the stills of people who were known to pay their excise taxes. How did they know? They stole mail bags and read their neighbors' mail! Terrorism ran rife, with the residents of the small city of Pittsburgh petrified that their homes were going to be burned down by marauding distillers. Small distillers in Kentucky got riled up and joined the protest. Things got so bad that in 1784, George Washington called out the militias, donned his general's uniform, and led an army of 15,000 armed men against the troublemakers. That's more soldiers than ever fought in a single Revolutionary War battle. [33] And the hated Hamilton rode by his side.

The rebellion was quashed much as a cannon ball might smash an outhouse, with minimum violence (unless someone is inside). Washington pardoned the two rebellious distillers convicted of treason. It was an important moment, as the rebellion was the first challenge to the taxing authority of the new federal government.

Thomas Jefferson, who disagreed with Hamilton on most things, had found a winning campaign issue. Writing snidely to James Monroe, he said, "An insurrection was announced and proclaimed and armed against, but never could be found." He was elected president in 1800 and Congress repealed the whiskey tax in 1802.[34] It didn't rear its ugly head again until Abraham Lincoln needed money to pay for the Union Army in 1862.

As Susan and I had only one night in Richmond, we put on our finery and walked nine blocks from The Commonwealth to the Jefferson Hotel, a fully restored and modernized Victorian treasure that opened in 1895.[35] It would have knocked Washington's eyes out with its hand-carved mantels, stained glass windows, marble columns, and bronze alligators scattered about.

What? Alligators? Yes, the Jefferson once had fishponds in its palm court where live alligators resided. Richmond residents would vacation in Florida, bring home cute baby alligators as pets, then realize a growing alligator could have serious repercussions for family life, especially if there were pets or small children around. They would bring the reptiles to live at the Jefferson. The last of the alligators, Old Pompey, did a see-ya-later in 1948 and joined his buddies in that great Okefenokee Swamp in the sky, but the gators are memorialized by several life-size replicas, jaws agape.[36] Guests entering the rotunda lobby are met with an equally life-size marble statue of Thomas Jefferson under a stained-glass ceiling worthy of the Vatican, or at least a fancy Belle Epoque bistro in Paris.

Susan and I headed to the bar, where we found two comfortable chairs beside a small table and perused the menu. The special drink the Lemaire restaurant was promoting was the French Traveler, named not for Lafayette, as I supposed, but for American artists such as Mary Cassatt and James McNeill Whistler who traveled to France and whose works were currently featured at the Virginia Museum of Fine Arts. We ordered the drink, a refreshing blend of gin, berry liqueur, lemon juice, and sparkling wine served in a coupe glass. Next, we decided to split a few appetizers for dinner, ordering oysters on the half shell and a cheese board and finished up with Manhattans for dessert. Over the Manhattans, we had a serious history discussion, focusing on which founding father we would most like to have dated. Susan said Hamilton ("Sorry, Eliza") and I said Jefferson, because I am also a Francophile, and he had such a great wine cellar.[37] We strolled back to The Commonwealth and slept well.

The French Traveler, a specialty of the Jefferson Hotel in Richmond. *Courtesy RVA Imaging.*

> ### The French Traveler
>
> - 1 oz. Citadelle Gin
> - ½ oz. Chambourd (or another berry liqueur)
> - ½ oz. lemon juice
>
> Add ingredients to shaker of ice, shake and strain into a coup glass. Top with champagne and garnish with lemon peel and a blackberry.
>
> —*Recipe courtesy the Jefferson Hotel*

The next morning, we walked across the street and up the hill to Capitol Square. To our dismay, we saw that the equestrian statue of George Washington and much of the capitol building were in the middle of a construction site. The Washington memorial, erected just a few years before Richmond became capital of the Confederacy, was surrounded by a high fence with canvas panels sharing significant local history but obscuring the view. I could see Washington on his horse, with his tricorn hat, and I was glad that at least this part of the monument was clearly visible, as were the Virginia notables clustered at the base of the pedestal—fiery orator Patrick Henry, Thomas Jefferson, Chief Justice John Marshall, Andrew Lewis, Thomas Nelson, and George Mason.[38]

We picked our way through the construction debris to a side door of the capitol and soon found ourselves in the rotunda gazing at a life-size statue of George Washington. The Virginia capitol rotunda isn't nearly as fancy as the one at the Jefferson Hotel, but the knowledge and enthusiasm of the docents and the capitol historian, Mark Greenough, more than made up for it. The statue of Washington was commissioned by the Virginia General Assembly in 1784. The sculptor was a Frenchman,

The George Washington equestrian statue is on the grounds of the state house in Richmond. *Author photo.*

Jean-Antoine Houdon, who came to Mount Vernon the following year to study Washington, take measurements of all his body parts, and make a plaster cast of the fifty-three-year-old general's face. Houdon sailed back to France, and nobody heard anything for three years. Finally, Thomas Jefferson, who had engaged him for the job, wrote to inquire if he had begun to "attack the marble." Houdon replied that he had yet to receive any money from the General Assembly. When the legislators finally coughed up the funds, Houdon got rolling and the sculpture arrived in 1796. Although Washington himself never saw it—his 1791 visit to Richmond would be his last—many of his contemporaries did and "attested that it was a perfect likeness," Mark said.

The historian pointed out some interesting details, such as missing buttons on the general's uniform, that showed just how lifelike it was. While reflecting that the fastidious Washington would likely be mortified, I thought this added to his humanity, as did the fact that Houdon gave him a bit of a spare tire around the middle.

The Houdon sculpture of Washington is in the capitol rotunda. *Author photo.*

Mark said there are "at least" thirty-seven bronze or plaster copies of this statue in the United States and in six foreign countries. (I mentioned the one in Columbia, South Carolina in the previous chapter.) But he points with pride to the fact that Virginia has the original—sculpted in white marble, no less—and the only statue of Washington made from life.

He also shared an interesting tidbit about drinking in Washington's day. The capital of Virginia was moved to Richmond from Williamsburg in 1780, and almost immediately, fifteen applications were made for new taverns in Richmond.

Several of the female docents we met in the capitol building reminded us to stop by the Virginia Women's Monument, located halfway down the hill. Dedicated in 2019, it contains bronze sculptures of twelve noteworthy women, all but Martha Washington being fairly obscure to people unschooled in Virginia history—rather like George Mason, Andrew Lewis, and Thomas Nelson.[39] But I was struck by the sculpture of Adèle Clark, a young suffragist holding a large "Votes for Women" banner. Clark, a native of Montgomery, Alabama, was a tireless worker for suffrage and became the president of the Virginia League of Women Voters once the Nineteenth Amendment was passed in 1920. (Virginia and eight other Southern states voted it down.) An accomplished artist, Clark was active in arts education and advocacy throughout her long life and worked for universal voting rights, though she opposed the Equal Rights Amendment.[40]

The sculpture of Adèle Clark is at the forefront of the women's monument on the capitol grounds. *Author Photo.*

I could find no reference to Clark or her suffrage organization being in favor of Prohibition, but I would be surprised if it was not. As you will learn in a future chapter, the temperance and suffrage movements were intertwined from their outset, which began before the Civil War.

PROHIBITION EXPEDITION: RICHMOND

Susan and I stayed at **The Commonwealth**, located at the foot of Capitol Square. Our stay was so enjoyable that for the rest of the trip, we'd say, "That was nice, but it wasn't The Commonwealth!"

901 Bank Street • www.commonwealthsuites.com

Reaching the **Jefferson Hotel**, where we had drinks and dinner, was a pleasant stroll through downtown Richmond.

101 W. Jefferson Street • www.jeffersonhotel.com

Information about Richmond's **Capitol and Capitol Square** can be found at www.virginiacapitol.gov. The **Virginia Museum of History and Culture** tells the state's story with artifacts and documents from ancient times to the present day.

428 N. Arthur Ashe Boulevard • www.virginiahistory.org

CEMETERY SIDE TRIP

Adèle Clark is buried at the Emmanuel Episcopal Church Cemetery 1214 Wilmer Ave, Brook Hill, Henrico County, Virginia.

Adèle Clark, far left stands with other members of the Suffrage League of Richmond at the base of the George Washington statue in this photo appearing in the Richmond *Times-Dispatch* in 1915. *Wikimedia Commons*.

RECOMMENDED READING

Founding Spirits: George Washington and the Beginnings of the American Whiskey Industry by Dennis J. Pogue (Harbor Books, 2011) is an interesting look at Washington's initial distillery as well as the modern efforts to reactivate it. Pogue, an archaeologist, was involved in the project as vice president for preservation at Mount Vernon.

George Washington's 1791 Southern Tour by Warren L. Bingham (History Press, 2016) gives a stage-by-stage account of the president's trip. It is well illustrated with both historic paintings and prints and current photographs.

President Washington's Diaries 1791 to 1799, transcribed and compiled by Jos. A. Hoskins (Big Byte Books, 2016) covers the last eight years of Washington's life, but the most detailed entries are about the 1791 tour and the Whiskey Rebellion.

CHAPTER TWO

George Washington Drank Here

FROM RICHMOND, Susan and I drove to New Bern, North Carolina, skipping Washington's next overnight stops in Petersburg, Virginia, and Halifax and Tarboro, North Carolina. (We did take a coffee break in Tarboro, whose pretty village commons boasts a historic marker about Washington. He wrote in his diary that he was received "at this place by as good a salute as could be given by one piece of artillery."[41] Indeed, there is a single piece of artillery on display on the commons today, but it dates from the twentieth century, not the eighteenth.

On the way to New Bern, Washington and his entourage "lodged at one Allan's...a very indifferent house without stabling which for the first time since I commenced my Journey [the horses] were obliged to stand without a cover."[42] Remember, horses were the combustible engines of the day, and Washington took the health of his animals seriously.

Throughout his trip, Washington insisted on paying his way, first to avoid putting anyone to expense, but also to keep people from fighting over who would honor him in their homes. Despite his unhappy experience at the first Allan's (actually, it belonged to one Shadrach Allen), he stopped for breakfast at what he thought was another public place, the home of Colonel John Allen, who may have been Shadrach's brother. Think

An early twentieth century postcard shows a lady toasting Washington with a wineglass of punch. He looks aghast. *Author's Collection.*

of Mrs. Allen's consternation when the most famous man in the country turned up in her yard with a small entourage, expecting to be fed. She set to work and managed to turn out a huge spread: "a young pig, a turkey, fried chicken, country ham, sausages, eggs in every style, waffles, batter-cakes, and hot soda biscuits," according to historian Archibald Henderson's exhaustive account of the trip.[43] Apparently President Washington's experience of the previous night was souring his stomach, so he asked for just "one hard-boiled egg and a cup of coffee with a little rum in it." His men dug in and did justice to the rest. When the meal was over, Washington asked for the bill and learned to his embarrassment that he had breakfasted in a private home. Allen refused compensation, and the family dined out on the story for the rest of their lives.

Another thing that may have contributed to Washington's abstemiousness that morning was his teeth, which bothered him most of his life. If you don't know anything else about George Washington, you probably know he had false teeth, which his jaws always seem heroically clinched around in his later portraits (but not in the Houdon sculpture). He was just trying to keep his dentures in place, poor guy. I am sure the extra gritting of his teeth that went along with those miles of jolting over bad roads in his carriage couldn't have helped.

Although some of Washington's partials are still chattering and clattering about the country, Mount Vernon boasts the only complete set, where manager of visual resources Dawn Bonner confided, a bit abashed, that it is the most requested photo from the archives. Washington would probably be humiliated, she said, because he was so dignified and conscious of his appearance. The teeth, which were set into lead plates with gold wire hinges joining top and bottom, were a combination of human and animal. Dentists of the day kept collections of teeth they had pulled or purchased—you'd

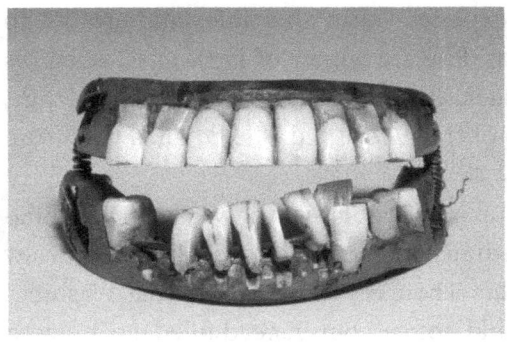

Seeing this picture of Washington's dentures, you have to know why he seldom smiled. *Courtesy Mount Vernon Ladies' Association*

have to be desperate to sell a healthy tooth, but a lot of people were—and they could also carve the teeth of horses or hippopotamus ivory to human size and shape.[44] It is also sad but true that enslaved people were asked to donate their healthy teeth for usually unsuccessful tooth implants. They were paid, but at a significantly lower rate than Whites.[45]

But I digress. Susan and I drove a few miles out of the way to visit the first town in America named after George Washington. The elders of Washington, North Carolina took the name the same year the Declaration of Independence was signed, 1776. And as the nice lady at the visitors' center reminded us, it was named for *General* Washington, not President Washington.

This brings us to the subject of booze and the Continental Army. First of all, the American colonists , especially men, were drinking an astounding amount of alcohol by the time America declared independence from England. Susan Cheever devotes a chapter of her book *Drinking in America* to the gradual substitution of profits for piety among the colonists (Pilgrims and Puritans alike), the discovery that the climate in America was much more conducive to growing the ingredients for distilled liquors than for the less potent beer, and the plans hatched by patriots in taverns, well-lubricated with booze. "A few drafts of rum could make a man powerfully convincing no matter what the odds," she writes. "Rum can also make you brave, confident, and scornful of conventional obstacles." Liquor fueled Paul Revere's ride, she asserts, as well as the famous Vermont patriot (and drunkard) Ethan Allen's capture of Fort Ticonderoga.[46]

While George Washington was well aware of the problems drunkenness caused in the ranks of his offices and soldiers, he also knew the value of a stiff drink in stiffening the spine. "The benefits arising from the moderate use of strong liquor have been experienced in all armies and are not to be disputed," he declared. In that desolate winter of 1777–1778, when his soldiers were suffering from hunger, illness, and exposure at Valley Forge, Pennsylvania—more than 2,000 of them perished—he doubled their rum rations.[47]

When the British finally gave up in 1783 and the war was won, Washington had an emotional reunion with his officers at Fraunces Tavern in New York in early December. Biographer Thomas Flexner writes that Washington was so worked up that he could not eat, but instead filled a glass with wine and asked for his officers to join him in a toast: "With tears streaming down his own face, Washington embraced each separately, and then, the height of emotion having become unbearable, walked out of the room."[48]

A Nathaniel Currier print, issued in 1848, captured this moment with Washington holding his glass and wine bottles evident on a nearby table. As the temperance movement caught hold later in the century, the print was re-issued by Currier and Ives in 1876 with Washington's hand slipped, Napoleon-like, inside his tunic and his tri-corner hat lying on the table.[49]

The original version of "Washington Takes Leave of the Officers of His Army" shows the general holding a wineglass. Notice how small it is. *Courtesy Library of Congress.*

Washington's surrender of his commission to Congress a few weeks after the gathering, along with his decision to limit his presidency to two terms, were significant acts for democracy. A monumental painting of the former by John Trumbull is displayed in the Capitol rotunda in Washington.[50] Congress was meeting at the state house in Annapolis, Maryland at the time of Washington's act, and a huge "entertainment" was held to honor him the night before. Catered by Mann's Tavern, it ran up a bill that included ninety-eight bottles of wine and two and a half gallons of spirits, not to mention eight pounds of candles and twelve packs of cards.[51]

During his tour of the South, Washington had many reunions with his men, and was entertained at lavish dinners by former officers who had formed a somewhat controversial fraternal and charitable organization in 1783 called the Society of the Cincinnati.[52] You can be sure much alcohol was involved. Such was the case in New Bern, his next major stop.

We arrived too late in the afternoon to tour the Tryon Palace, where Washington was entertained on his second night in town. Located on Front Street, the palace had been built for the colonial governor William Tryon when New Bern was the North Carolina capital, but it had since been demoted and the state had not decided on a permanent capital when Washington arrived. He enjoyed a dinner and dancing assembly there—pointedly mentioning in his diary that there were about seventy ladies present at the dance—and observed that the palace was "a good brick building but now hastening to Ruins." He was right; the original burned down in 1798 and the Tryon Palace tourists visit today was built in the 1950s.[53]

The surrounding neighborhood is full of charming historic homes, some of which were standing during Washington's visit. (New Bern has four separate districts on the National Register of Historic Places.) He spent the night in the John Wright Stanly House, which was vacant because the Stanlys had succumbed to yellow fever two years before. In preparation for the visit, the leadership in New Bern got permission to use it, cleaned it, and even borrowed furnishings from the well-to-do towns people.[54] Washington was pleased, writing that he was provided "exceeding good lodgings" in New Bern, although he did complain that he had been deprived of his favorite breakfast of griddle cakes.[55] The two-story Georgian-style Stanly House has been moved twice since Washington slept there and is now kitty-corner to the Tryon Palace. I was interested to learn that when the Union Army captured New Bern in 1862, the house was the command post

The John Wright Stanly House in New Bern was Washington's temporary home. *Author Photo.*

for General Ambrose Burnside, whose bad-ass facial hair inspired the name "sideburns."[56] I bet even Elvis didn't know that.

I hope Washington got his appetite back by the time he arrived in New Bern, because he would have needed a full belly to soak up all the booze served at the banquet at the Tryon Palace. In addition to the beverages offered with dinner, the good folks of New Bern downed their after-dinner drink fifteen times with formal toasts, each of which was followed by cannon fire. It sounds to me like a sure recipe for a hangover.

Archibald Henderson lists the toasts in his book about Washington's Southern tour:

- The United States
- The Congress
- The State of North Carolina (offered by Washington and met with "stentorian cheers")
- The Patriots of America who fell in her defense

- The late American army (as the Continental Army had been disbanded after Britain's surrender)
- The King of France

(Okay, this one may be a head scratcher unless you are really on top of your Revolutionary War history or have recently seen *Hamilton*. The young Marquis de Lafayette convinced King Louis XVI to support the patriots in the war and fight France's old enemies, the British, as a bonus. He sent money and warships but would lose his head a couple of years later in the French Revolution. Lafayette barely escaped this fate himself.)

- The National Assembly of France (which soon stripped Louis of his titles and sent him to prison)
- The memory of Dr. [Benjamin] Franklin (who had died barely a year before)
- The Marquis de Lafayette
- The commerce of the United States
- The friends of America in every part of the world
- The agricultural interests of the United States
- The Nations in alliance with us
- Universal peace and liberty

At this point President Washington excused himself, and all present raised their glasses one last time in a rousing toast to him.[57] We can assume that the president staggered off to the Stanly House where he would sleep without the hope of griddle cakes in the morning.

Susan and I were strolling down Pollock Street, admiring the lovely houses, when I noticed a sign hanging beside a porch. It said, "Savi's Wine Shop." Within seconds we were on the doorstep, where a lively little dog welcomed us inside. Just a step behind was Cammie Lassiter Lee, the broadly smiling owner of the shop and resident of the house, built in 1778.

Cammie Lassiter Lee welcomes friends and customers alike to her home and wine shop. *Author photo.*

Cammie, a lifelong resident of New Bern, bought the house in 2008. She said it was in very bad shape at the time and she renovated it from top to bottom. A few years later she was outsourced from her job and decided she would combine her love of wine and entertaining by turning her dining room into a wine shop and her backyard garden into an event space. It seemed quite fitting, as she had discovered the original builder of the house was a merchant named John Horner Hill who sold rum. She named the shop for Savannah, a little girl who lived in the house who, Cammie is convinced, haunts the place.

Back at our hotel, the friendly clerk advised us to try a restaurant downtown called MJ's Raw Bar and Grille that had good seafood. Word had gotten around about just how good the place was, because all the tables were taken, but we seated ourselves at the horseshoe-shaped bar and ordered drinks and dinner there. The customers at the bar were awfully nice and friendly—one guy even offered to share his appetizer—and as we were finishing up someone mentioned that there was a speakeasy just around the corner, down an alley, and up the back stairs.

What a delight! Tonic Parlor not only had a great speakeasy vibe and locally sourced ingredients, but a three-piece blues band, the Honey Badgers, that was soon wailing away at T-Bone Walker's "Call it Stormy Monday (But Tuesday's Just as Bad)," the song popularized by the Allman Brothers. I knew the band was legit when I noticed the singer was missing a front tooth. I was pleased to see that this bar had a drink that paid tribute to New Bern's claim to fame as the birthplace of Pepsi-Cola; the restaurant where we had eaten had only served Coca-Cola products, even though it was next door to the former drugstore of Caleb Bradham, the pharmacist who invented Pepsi in 1898.

A Pepsi bottle circa 1955, a New Bern postcard and a Carolina Libre. *Author photo.*

THE TONIC PARLOR

Tonic Parlor LLC • 218 Middle Street • https://www.tonicparlor.com

They serve spirits at the Tonic Parlor. Literally.

Leigh-Ann Sullivan, one of the owners, said she realized even before the bar opened that it was haunted. She was coming up the stairs and saw the figure of a woman, which quickly disappeared. Later, their security cameras caught odd orbs of light and free-floating voices. "The whole time we've been here it's like ghost central," she said. They were all friendly…until one morning.

Tonic Parlor had opened just before the covid-19 pandemic hit and was struggling to stay in business. Paper supplies were almost impossible to find and being sold at exorbitant prices. Leigh-Ann had placed a case of precious paper towels on the bar one night and came in the next day to find the towels scattered all over the floor.

That's when she realized the ghosts were thirsty. So ever since, her bartenders have been told to leave some sweet drinks behind on the bar when they close for the night. Maybe a customer returned a drink because it wasn't to their liking, or there was a bottle of wine open that wouldn't be good the next day. Anything to placate the ghosts. And as a bonus, the drinks also attract and kill fruit flies.

Tonic Parlor focuses on North Carolina beers, liquors, wines, and other products. It is located above Nautical Star Coffee & Staat's Bakery but when the coffee shop is closed downstairs, find the backdoor, just like Susan and I did. As one of their tee shirts says, "If you can't find the back door, you don't belong here." ■

THE CAROLINA LIBRE

In a nine-ounce rocks glass with ice:

- 1½ ounces Kill Devil pecan-flavored rum (from Outer Banks Distillery, available from cellar.com)
- Pepsi-Cola (the kind made with sugar)

Garnish with a wheel of orange. If you are feeling extra fancy, you can muddle the orange in the bottom of the glass first.

We slept well that night and, unlike George Washington, avoided being escorted out of town by "many of the principal Gentlemen of New Bern" on horses kicking up dust, plus we got to eat griddle cakes for breakfast. Well, the closest thing to it offered at a Waffle House, which is a waffle. Our waitress, Pickle ("It's a third-shift thing"), a twelve-year veteran of Waffle House, offered us a tip for keeping our coffee hot at home. Put water in your mug and heat it up in the microwave, then dump it out and pour in the coffee. The mug will hold the heat, she said.[58]

PROHIBITION EXPEDITION: NEW BERN

The Tryon Palace, a replica of the one where George Washington was entertained, offers daily tours except on Thanksgiving, Christmas, and New Year's Day. The grounds include a kitchen office and the palace gardens as well as the N.C. History Center.

529 S. Front Street • www.tryonpalace.org

Across the street is the **John Wright Stanly House**, where Washington slept.

307 George Street • www.tryonpalace.org.

Savi's Wine Shop is located down the street from the palace in a row of historic homes. Stop by for a bottle and say hello to Cammie Lee Lassiter and her pups.

713 Pollock Street • www.saviwine.com

Susan and I enjoyed our dinner and drinks around the horseshoe bar at **M.J.'s Raw Bar and Grille**, a casual dining spot downtown.

216 Middle Street • www.mjsrawbar.com

Next door is the **Birthplace of Pepsi** museum, the former drugstore where Caleb Bradham developed his refreshing soft drink. Initially called "Brad's Drink," he renamed it Pepsi-Cola because he thought it settled the stomach. Dyspepsia is another word for indigestion.[59] Anyone who has ever drunk Pepsi or Coke after a night of partying probably knew that!

256 Middle Street • www.pepsistore.com

Wilmington, North Carolina was Washington's next major stop. He arrived April 12 and got the usual warm welcome. The only trace Susan and I could find of his visit, though, was a rather stained stone marker between two garbage cans and a fire hydrant on Front Street, which marks the place where the house he slept once stood. There's a restaurant a block away called The George, which uses a bird's eye view of a martini glass with an olive in it for the "O," but I don't think it is named for *that* George.

This coastal city was where my father the economist—Susan's older brother—spent much of his youth during the Great Depression and World War II. So, we did a quick Bruce Yandle Tour, finding his high school and Grace United Methodist Church, which his family attended. The church's roots date to 1795, just a few years after Washington left town, when a missionary from England came to preach to the enslaved people there.[60] It grew and prospered over the years, spawning five other Methodist churches, while the emancipated slaves formed their own church. We'll learn more about the spread of Methodism in the next chapter.

George Washington's travels took him down the South Carolina coast, where he rode Prescott on Myrtle Beach and was rowed into Georgetown for several days of festivities. "George Town seems to be in the shade of Charleston—It suffered during the War by the British, having had many of its Houses burnt," he observed in his diary.[61] Nevertheless, it is a charming small city, chock full of historic sites, and has a museum devoted to rice, South Carolina's principal chief export at the time of Washington's visit, as he mentioned in his diary. The Stewart-Parker House, where he is said to have spent the night, still stands at 1019 Front Street. Another claim to fame, at least as far as we are concerned, was that Georgetown was home to the first Methodist church in South Carolina, established in 1785.[62]

As he drew closer to Charleston, Washington stopped for overnight visits or meals at several plantations, including Hampton Plantation, near present-day McClellanville. His hostesses for a late breakfast and mid-day meal there were Harriot Pinckney Horry, widow of a Revolutionary War cavalryman, and her celebrated mother, Eliza Lucas Pinckney, a member of one of the state's most distinguished families. Mrs. Pinckney, the widow of South Carolina Chief Justice Charles Pinckney, had introduced successful indigo cultivation to South Carolina as a young woman. The Pinckney men numbered among their members revolutionary officers, signers of the Constitution, members of Congress and the Senate, ambassadors, and South Carolina governors. She so impressed Washington during his visit that he asked to serve as a pallbearer at her funeral when she died two years later in Philadelphia, where she had traveled for treatment of breast cancer.[63]

Susan and I both got a shivery feeling of stepping back in time as we traveled in my blue Honda Fit down the sandy driveway into Hampton Plantation, imagining George Washington's carriage rolling down the same path. The stately two-story white house and grounds are maintained by the state of South Carolina as a historical site, open for self-guided tours most days, but with only limited admission to the house itself.[64] We parked and walked the rest of the way down the driveway, listening to the birds in the large oak and magnolia trees and noticing the animal tracks in the sand. ("Is that a snake track?!") The biggest tree of all is a towering oak that legend says was standing when Washington visited. Mrs. Horry was thinking of having it cut down because she had recently changed the orientation of the house to face the driveway and she feared it would ruin the view. Her mother disagreed, and Washington sided with Mrs. Pinckney. The tree still stands, 220 years later. It is called the George Washington Oak.[65]

Hampton Plantation house, with branches of the George Washington Oak in the foreground, looks much as it did in 1791. *Author photo.*

President Washington arrived in Charleston for a week of eating, drinking, dancing, toasting, and shooting off artillery on May 2, having been rowed across the Cooper River by a crew of sea captains in matching uniforms. It was just a short distance from the wharf where he landed to the Exchange Building, completed twenty years before. It was there that the Declaration of Independence had been read from the portico facing Broad Street, and there that the state's ratification of the Constitution was signed. As Charleston's grandest public building, over the next week it was the site of banquets, concerts, and balls, all attended, in Washington's own words, by "ladies in the number and appearance of wch [which] exceeded any thing of the kind I had ever seen."[66] At one ball, he counted 256 women, at another, 400. Not only were the women dressed to the nines,

The Old Exchange hosted dinners and dances for Washington. *Author photo.*

but they wore ribbons in their mile-high hair that were painted with Washington's portrait and sentiments such as "Long Live the President."[67] Charleston was America's richest city, and the excesses of New York in the 1980s didn't hold a candle to the excesses of Charleston in the 1790s.

The Exchange still stands where Broad Street intersects with East Bay, handsomely restored and maintained by the Daughters of the American Revolution. Tour guides dressed in authentic period costume (if you don't look too closely at their shoes) usher visitors around the three floors, including the dungeon, which was used as a jail during the British occupation of 1780–1782. On the second floor, guide Richard W. Hatcher III explained to me how Washington's hosts were able to cram so many people into a building that, though big, isn't *that* big.

Richard is a George Washington-sized man—that is six-foot-two—but he noted that the average man in 1791 was only five-foot-six, and the average woman was barely five feet tall (not counting the hair). So they took up a lot less space than the super-sized Americans of today. Second, the first floor of the Exchange was one big open arcade, and that's where the banquets were held. After the meal was finished—and that could take four hours because of the numerous courses served, each with Madeira wine and other beverages, not to mention the toasting punctuated by deafening artillery fire from the harbor—groups of ladies and gentlemen would go upstairs to the ballroom, the timing governed by their dance cards. That way you never had hundreds of people trying to do the minuet in a space that was smaller than a church basketball court.

There are restrooms in the Exchange today, but I knew there weren't in Washington's day. I tried to phrase my question delicately. With all that eating and drinking—especially the drinking—how did the guests—including the ladies in their voluminous gowns—handle their, er, bodily needs?

That's when I learned about "the Necessary."

THE NECESSARY

As elegantly as the Charleston ladies dressed, their lavish gowns covered a secret, Richard said. Their pantalets were slit front to back to allow them to visit "the Necessary" out back of the Exchange, have a seat, and relieve themselves without disturbing their outward appearance.

I learned more about the eighteenth-century version of the porta-potty at the Heyward-Washington House on Church Street, where Washington slept for all seven nights in Charleston. This three-story brick house is another historic treasure rescued from the wrecking ball and, since 1930, has been operated as a house museum by the Charleston Museum. The original owner, Thomas Heyward Jr., was a signer of the Declaration of Independence who lived most of the time at one of his rice plantations, though he had a law office in the house. The city fathers in Charleston rented the house for the president's use, equipping it with everything from a good supply of liquor to a housekeeper, and there he was quite comfortable.

On a tour led by Jean Rivas, who retains her British accent after forty years in America, I saw the first-floor dining chamber and second-floor drawing room (where most of the dining and drinking took place) and withdrawing room (i.e. the man cave for more drinking), as well as the bedroom where Washington slept. As our little tour group ascended the stairs, she reminded us that President Washington's hand had grasped that very banister, and suggested we do the same. The furniture in the house is not original to it, though it is historic and mostly from the same period. One of the pieces in Washington's bedroom was a "necessary chair," which looks for all the world like a mahogany Chippendale potty chair for adults.

Perhaps one was provided for President Washington. Otherwise, he had the option of using a chamber pot or the necessary out back, and that's why dining was done at least a floor off the ground, Jean said. The smells coming from the kitchen and the necessary would be most unpleasant during hot weather in the dining chamber, so when guests were coming, the servants would carry tables upstairs to the second floor on the front side of the house, where all they had to deal with was the smell of manure from the horses clomping up and down the street unless someone had recently emptied chamber pots there.

A necessary chair is one of the furnishings in the bedroom where George Washington stayed in Charleston. *Author photo.*

Incidentally, the Heyward-Washington House still has a shed in the back marked "Necessary," but thankfully it contains modern plumbing. ■

As I was leaving the Exchange, I walked next door to The Tavern, which bills itself America's oldest liquor store. (There was a group of Jehovah's Witnesses trying to sign people up for free Bible classes on the other side of the Exchange, which seemed to me to provide perfect symmetry.) Since 1686, this small shop has purveyed liquor, surviving "pirate attacks, the Revolution and Civil War, earthquakes and hurricanes," not to mention fires and Prohibition, when it used a dentist's office as cover.[68]

Jesus is replaced by a whiskey bottle on this label of Ryeteous Senator. *Author photo.*

I was struck by a bottle in the window, exclusive to the shop, labeled Ryeteous Senator, with a picture of Joseph and Mary (holding a totally sacrilegious miniature bottle of the booze, complete with halo and wings, instead of baby Jesus). I wondered if the "Ryeteous" senator was named for a real senator, but the clerk inside said no, the rye whiskey is bottled by a company whose brand is The Senator, and it made this spirit in honor of Charleston's nickname the Holy City, due to its many churches.[69] (By the time George Washington arrived, these included Bethel Methodist Church, founded in 1786.)[70]

That made sense. If it were named for a real person, it would be Self-Ryeteous Senator.

But back to George Washington. The people of Charleston were so thrilled about the president's visit that while he was still in Charleston, the city council asked him to sit for a portrait to be hung in city hall. He agreed. They contacted John Trumbull, the same man who had painted the monumental portrait of Washington resigning his commission, to paint a full-length portrait. They were thinking something along the lines of a Trumbull portrait in New York, which had Washington standing with his horse in the foreground and the city skyline in the background. Apparently, they were not specific enough about their wishes. When an emissary saw Trumbull's work, which showed Washington and his horse standing against a background of a Revolutionary War battle, he told the artist the

This full-length portrait of Washington dominates the council chamber at Charleston City Hall. *Author photo.*

Charlestonians had something more peaceful in mind, perhaps something that showed Washington with the Charleston harbor in the background.

Trumbull agreed, sold the first portrait to someone else—it is now part of the art collection of Yale University—and started over. When the new portrait arrived, the figure of the president was the same, and the harbor and city were indeed in the background, but this time it was his horse's rear that dominated. Not only that, his tail was raised as if he planned to dump a load—right on a barge holding the city fathers.[71]

Charleston's leaders accepted the portrait of the president and his horse's ass, which hangs today in the council chamber of Charleston City Hall. It took a couple of centuries, but Charleston finally got a more dignified representation of Washington in 1999 when a committee led by retired General William C. Westmoreland raised the funds to erect a life-size statue in Washington Square, Charleston's first city park.[72] He stands there today, gazing out from atop a pedestal, a tall walking staff in hand. It's hard to tell since he's made of bronze, but I would bet he is wearing the black velvet evening suit that was his usual attire at formal occasions and thinking if he had to hear one more barrage of canon fire, he would lose his mind.

At the Heyward-Washington House, guests were provided with elegant rinsing beakers so they would need only one wineglass for an entire meal. *Author photos.*

PROHIBITION EXPEDITION: GEORGETOWN TO CHARLESTON

The Stewart-Parker House in Georgetown, built in 1750, is operated as a house museum by the National Society of the Colonial Dames, whose members had ancestors in America prior to the Revolutionary War. When Washington visited Georgetown, his host was the house's second owner, Daniel Tucker. The house is the only surviving pre-revolution brick house in Georgetown and adjoins the **Kaminski House**, another Colonial Dames property, which also was standing when Washington visited. Both are open for tours.

1019 Front Street, Georgetown • www.kaminskimuseum.org

Georgetown's Rice Museum, located in the historic market building in the heart of downtown, tells the story of rice cultivation in South Carolina.

633 Front Street • www.ricemuseum.org

Hampton Plantation Historic Site is open for self-guided tours during daylight hours each day of the year, with staff on the grounds four days a week. See the website for details.

1950 Rutledge Road, McClellanville • www.southcarolinaparks.com/hampton

In Charleston, you can park your car and walk to many sites associated with George Washington. **The Old Exchange and Provost Dungeon**, where Washington was wowed by the city's beautiful women, is open daily for tours and hosts many special events.

122 East Bay Street • www.oldexchange.org

Next door is **The Tavern**, where, if you're lucky, a free liquor or wine tasting will be in progress when you come by. If not, ask to see the trap door in the back room, reputed to have been used by pirates and bootleggers.

120 East Bay Street • www.charlestonspirits.com

Charleston's celebrated **Rainbow Row** is a two-minute walk away. These thirteen houses on East Bay were built in 1740 and have been painted in pretty pastel shades since the early 1930s. It is one of the most photographed sites in the city.

The **Heyward-Washington House**, where George Washington stayed during his visit, is operated by the Charleston Museum. It has the city's only 1740s kitchen house that can be toured, as well as a small formal garden.

87 Church Street
www.charlestonmuseum.org/historic-houses/heyward-washington-house

The public is admitted Mondays and Fridays during limited hours to the second floor of the **Charleston City Hall** where the portrait of George Washington and his horse is on display.

80 Broad Street • www.nps.gov/places/charleston-city-hall.htm

Washington Square, with its handsome bronze statue of the president in evening dress, is located at 80 Broad Street.

CEMETERY SIDE TRIP

The members of the illustrious Pinckney family were buried in the churchyards of Charleston's oldest Episcopal churches, St. Philip's and St. Michael's. The churchyard of St. Michael's (Broad and Meeting Street, a short walk from the Heyward-Washington House) is the final resting place of siblings Harriott Pinckney Horry, hostess to George Washington, and her brother, Charles Cotesworth Pinckney, Continental Army officer and signer of the U.S. Constitution. The wordy gravestones are well-maintained

The graves of Charles Cotesworth Pinckney, his sister Harriott and other Pinckney family members rest at the back of St. Michael's Episcopal Church. *Author photo.*

but located in an unlovely spot (read: electrical wiring) against the back of the church.

Their younger brother, Thomas Pinckney, Continental Army officer, member of Congress and South Carolina governor, rests at St. Philip's, 142 Church Street, with their father, Charles Pinckney. Their mother, Eliza Lucas Pinckney, died in Philadelphia and was buried at St. Peter's Episcopal churchyard there.

RECOMMENDED READING

South Carolina in 1791: George Washington's Southern Tour by Terry W. Lipscomb (South Carolina Department of Archives and History, 1993) is stuffed with maps and historic pictures and is a perfect companion to exploring the president's travels in Georgetown and Charleston.

CHAPTER THREE

An Inauspicious Beginning

GEORGE WASHINGTON'S next big destination was Savannah, about two hours away by Honda Fit, five exhausting days by horse-drawn coach. There, he was subjected to a similarly bruising schedule of balls, dinners, toasts (some accounts claim 130 in all, complete with cannon fire, of course) and reunions with officers. There is also an unfounded rumor that Washington was over-served some of the local potion, Chatham Artillery Punch, and swore he would never return to Savannah. He didn't, but I doubt that was the reason.[73]

Aunt Susan and I arrived at mid-afternoon on a scorching day that seemed to be melting the asphalt in the welcome center parking lot where I handed her off to her husband, Bob, who had driven up from their home on

A dour John Wesley stands in Savannah's Reynolds Square. *Author photo.*

Jekyll Island. After good-bye hugs, my destination was Reynolds Square, which is home to a large monument to John Wesley, father of Methodism. Conveniently, the square faces the Olde Pink House, which stood at the time of Washington's visit, now beautifully restored as a restaurant. In 1791 it was the home of a wealthy planter named James Habersham Jr., who hosted many secret meetings of the patriots there during the revolutionary period.[74]

Lunch was no longer being served, but the lively Olde Pink House bar, decorated with tarnished trophies and hunting prints, had a tasty mid-afternoon menu, and the bartenders were hopping. I was waited on by a personable young man, Anthony "T.J." Gould, who urged me to try the restaurant's award-winning shrimp and grits—the grits came formed into triangular cakes with a savory crusty shell—and the refreshing Pink House Pink Lady, a mixture of cranberry lemonade and raspberry-flavored vodka.

Bartender Anthony Gould with a Pink House Pink Lady. *Author photo.*

OLDE PINK HOUSE PINK LADY

- 1.25 oz. Ghost Coast raspberry-flavored vodka (or substitute)[75]
- Fresh lemonade with a shot of cranberry juice for color

Pour into a tall, stemmed glass of ice and garnish with raspberries and a lemon slice.

Feeling cool and refreshed, I walked out to Reynolds Square. The statue of a gaunt and forbidding John Wesley, Bible gripped in one hand, the other outstretched, dominates the grimy square, which is apparently a favorite hang-out for Savannah's street people. My eyes widened when I saw Wesley's birth and death dates inscribed at the statue's base: He died in 1791, the same year George Washington came to town. By then Wesley had been preaching in his native England for more than fifty years, but for many of those years he had been sending missionaries to America to plant Methodist churches. He would soon have his "revenge" on Savannah and its hard-partying denizens, for the Methodists became the largest denomination in the country and led the nineteenth century temperance movement.

Wesley would certainly be surprised at what Savannah has become: a bustling city of 150,00 people with an annual influx of more than fourteen million tourists and a notoriously wet St. Patrick's Day celebration.[76] When he fled in the dark of night in 1738, rowed out of town clutching a loaf of gingerbread and a bottle of rum—no doubt to placate his rough companions—Savannah was a settlement of 180 or so simple wooden homes.[77] What would not have surprised him was the condition of the people in Reynolds Square, for they were the sort of souls he had hoped to save when he arrived less than two years before, an idealistic, if somewhat arrogant, thirty-three-year-old Church of England minister. He was recruited to see to the spiritual needs of the colony founded by philanthropist James Oglethorpe as a liquor-free, slave-free, egalitarian utopia where everyone was provided with the same amount of land and worked it themselves.

That didn't last.

Unlike Charleston, many of whose early English residents were well-heeled English adventurers by way of Barbados, Georgia was established as a Crown colony for the flotsam and jetsam of England's debtors' prisons. This group, which got free passage from the Crown, was augmented with European Protestants being persecuted by Catholics, including a group of German Moravians who sailed over with Wesley. By the time they landed in 1735, the settlers were easily availing themselves of rum and other strong

A statue of General Oglethorpe stands in Savannah's Chippewa Square. *Photo by Jennifer Morrow courtesy Wikimedia Commons.*

spirits smuggled over the border from the Carolina colony and envying the easy life of these neighbors who had bought imported African slaves to do their dirty work. The colony's liquor ban was lifted in 1742—though it had been ignored for years—and the one on slavery in 1749.[78] The Civil War ended slavery in 1865. When the state of Georgia next banned alcohol, in 1907, the law was ignored by its residents to the same degree as when it was a colony. Through rum running and bootlegging, Savannah became known as the "spigot of the South," a fact today celebrated by the American Prohibition Museum, located in a warehouse a few feet from where the proclamation of a dry colony was made.

The tale of Wesley's misadventures in Georgia is well told by Willie Snow Ethridge in her book *Strange Fires*. Wesley sailed from England with his minister brother, Charles, and two like-minded associates from Oxford College, where they had been jeeringly called Bible Bigots, Bible Moths, and finally Methodists, because of their methodical ways.[79] The four began stirring up trouble even before their ship left harbor. James Oglethorpe, who was aboard, was called upon to have a foul-mouthed cabin boy flogged, and to kick off a ladies' maid deemed "a known drunkard...suspected of theft and unchastity." The couple who employed the maid was so angry the husband danced around in his stateroom, which was atop the Wesley brothers', so they couldn't sleep at night.[80] During the voyage, the four pastors spent all their waking hours reading their Bibles, praying, preaching, and conducting religious classes for the passengers, most of whom had little interest in what they were selling. Wesley, who admitted to "the lust of the eyes" was especially troubled by Beata Hawkins, "a gay young woman," the wife of a doctor, with whom he spent many hours trying to turn her heart to Christ.[81]

When the ship landed near Tybee Island off Georgia's coast, Oglethorpe continued into Savannah and Wesley stayed on the island, where he took a long walk with Beata Hawkins, continuing her instruction. Upon their return, he found "all the members of the crew and practically all the passengers who had remained on board were riotously drunk." He destroyed what remained of the offending cask of rum.[82] Oglethorpe made a timely return with beer, which was not included in the liquor ban. Indeed, the colony's trustees hoped the Georgians would be able to grow grapes and make wine. Meanwhile, John Wesley and his companions decided to give up meat and drink only water. Later, they tried the bread-only diet.

JOHN WESLEY'S BREAD AND WATER REPAST

- One cup water
- One piece bread, the dryer the better, with no oil, butter, or other condiment added.

Chew the bread carefully, following each swallow with a sip of water. Try to make them come out even. Afterward, walk about town, feeling virtuous, and seek sinners to admonish in public. Be especially observant of those who might cross the street to avoid you. If necessary, seek admittance to parishioners' homes in order to admonish them in private.

The painting *Still Life with Bread, Bottle of Water, Pipe and Mirror* by nineteenth century Dutch artist Piet Meiners wouldn't quite please John Wesley, because it contains a pipe (a sinful indulgence) and a mirror (evidence of vanity, also a sin). *Wikimedia Commons*.

Although the previous minister had cautioned Wesley not to be heavy-handed with his congregants, he ignored the advice, announcing during his first sermon, "I must admonish every one of you, not only in public, but from house to house" and letting them know he would be enforcing Church of England practices just as if they were still living back home in jolly old England.[83] He also complained that their clothes were too fancy and they shouldn't wear jewelry to church. The grumbling soon began.

Meanwhile, Charles and another of the Bible Moths went to the new settlement in Fredericka on present-day St. Simon's Island, a sort of eighteenth-century *Survivor* setting, complete with palm frond huts and social gamesmanship. There they sparred with Beata Hawkins and another female troublemaker from the ship, Ann Welch. The young ministers first got into hot water by convincing Oglethorpe to ban hunting on Sundays—the only free day the colonists had to procure game for food—and then Charles got caught up in a catfight between Beata and Ann, who each claimed to have been seduced by Oglethorpe. John visited, trying to intervene, and Beata attacked him with a pistol and a pair of scissors, tearing off the arm of his cassock with her teeth.[84] The exasperated Oglethorpe spent so much of his precious time settling disputes that he suggested Charles would be happier in England.

Back in Savannah, John was soon having woman troubles too. He became fixated on young Sophy Hopkey, who lived in the household of her uncle, the chief magistrate. Over many months, as he gave Sophy religious instruction and tutored her in French, Wesley struggled with his determination to remain single and celibate. Sophy had been engaged to a ne'er-do-well fellow who was being held in prison in Charleston for counterfeiting, but she assured John she had no desire to marry him and would rather remain single and celibate herself. The young minister was much taken aback when he learned she had agreed to marry a boarder at her uncle's house, and that they were going to South Carolina for the ceremony without first "publishing the banns," a requirement of the church.[85] When the couple returned, John at first refused to accept their married state, then denied Sophy communion. It was a public humiliation her family could not let stand.

The long and short of it was that Sophy's uncle brought charges against the minister and, pending trial, made it a criminal offense to help Wesley leave the colony. With his protector Oglethorpe in England and everyone in Savannah pretty much sick of him, the only people willing to smuggle him out of town were three disreputable men in a boat. Wesley departed for Charleston, happy to shake the dust off his sandals, so to speak, and sailed home to England.[86]

Those he left behind were members of the final colony established by the British Crown, the last of the thirteen that would band together to revolt against the mother country. With the ban on liquor lifted in 1742—and certainly way before it was lifted—Georgians were drinking as much as the other colonists, which is to say a lot. Susan Cheever writes in *Drinking in America* that by 1776 the average colonist was drinking twice as much as the average adult today.[87] The Alexander Hamilton excise tax on liquor, which increased the price, ratcheted that back a bit, but Thomas Jefferson was opposed to the tax, and when he was elected president in 1800, he got

Congress to do away with it. The drinking escalated to the point that Americans were downing the equivalent of 7.1 gallons of pure alcohol per adult a year. That compares to less than 2.5 gallons today.[88]

So that brings us back to 1791. After George Washington left Savannah, he traveled back home via Augusta, Georgia, and into South Carolina, where he stayed in Columbia and Camden and met with some Catawba Indian chiefs near Yorkville. Traveling into North Carolina, he stopped in Charlotte—"a trifling place"—and continued to Salisbury and Salem. He stayed two days in Salem with the Moravians, the German-Czech Protestant sect[89] that had exerted a great influence on John Wesley, both in Savannah and after he returned to England. He then headed home toward Mount Vernon, arriving there on June 10, "in time for dinner."[90]

By the time of Washington's trip—despite all the toasting, drinking, and hard-core partying along the way—Methodism had a firm grip on the souls of people in both the South and the North and was well on its way to becoming the largest Christian denomination in America. So how had John Wesley gone from being a failed Anglican cleric in Savannah to the founder of this Protestant powerhouse? We might borrow the title of a Grateful Dead album and say, "What a long, strange trip it's been."

"Camp Meeting of the Methodists in N. America" is an 1819 engraving by Jacques Gerard. *Courtesy Library of Congress.*

According to Wesley biographer Sam Wellman, back in England after his humiliation in Georgia, Wesley was invited to guest-preach to several Church of England congregations, but his insistence on striving for Christian perfection was not well received, and he was not asked back.[91] He was almost at the point of losing his faith when he was called to the rough port city of Bristol, where the Church of England hadn't kept pace with the population, and was urged to preach to the unchurched, outdoors if necessary. Reluctant at first—he loved those "high church" trappings—he was astonished when he drew crowds of hundreds and even thousands.

Wesley's gatherings had little in common with the staid services of the Church of England. There was lots of joyous hymn-singing, for one thing, many of the words penned by his brother Charles. A prolific writer, he wrote thousands of hymns, including the ever popular "Hark, the Herald Angels Sing" and "Christ the Lord is Risen Today."[92] The meetings also became known for their emotionalism. Gripped in evangelical fervor, worshippers sometimes screamed and fainted. This unseemly behavior didn't sit well with some people, who paid surrogates to stir up trouble. Among other things, they threw rocks at Wesley, ran an ox into one of his gatherings, and poisoned his horse. Other rowdies just didn't like all the preaching about their sins and shortcomings. At one point, two competing mobs did their best to lynch him.

Nothing stopped him. Not only did he travel 250,000 miles and preach an estimated 40,000 sermons during his lifetime, Wesley recruited other ministers, including Charles, sending them on preaching circuits in England, Ireland, and, eventually, America. By the time of his death, there were 60,000 Methodists in America and 72,000 in the British Isles. Today, the United Methodist Church claims ten million members worldwide.[93]

His most successful American missionary was Francis Asbury, who arrived in 1771 and stayed on even during the Revolutionary War. By the war's end, he had more than doubled his Methodist followers, who shortly afterward established the Methodist Episcopal Church, with Asbury as its first bishop. The Historical Marker Database lists 166 places associated with the bishop, most of them in the South; according to the *North Carolina Encyclopedia* online, he made seventy-two visits.[94] In the last years of his life, he came to Savannah to preach at the first Methodist church established there, Wesley Chapel, one of many churches and institutions that bear Wesley's name.[95]

This stained-glass window in the Memorial Chapel of the Methodist retreat at Lake Junaluska, North Carolina, shows, from left, Charles Wesley, John Wesley, and Francis Asbury. *Wikimedia Commons.*

These Methodists were, by and large, sober folk. In establishing Methodism as a distinct sect within the Church of England and then as a separate church in America, John Wesley and his ministers came up with a list of "General Rules" of Methodism. The first rule dealt with avoiding evil, and the first three examples given were taking God's name in vain; buying, selling, or working on the Sabbath; and drunkenness, specifically, "buying or selling spiritous liquors, or drinking them (unless in cases of extreme necessity)."[96] It is interesting to ponder what those "extreme necessity" cases might be.

As an evangelical movement known as the second Great Awakening gathered steam in the early nineteenth century, Methodists, augmented by like-minded Baptists, Presbyterians, and Lutherans, began to exert a tremendous influence on the public's perception of alcohol and drunkenness. This led to the temperance movement, which spawned local, state, and national organizations, all with the aim of drying up America. The largest of these was the American Temperance Society, which by 1850 had 238,000 members.[97] Another was the George Washington Society, a forerunner of Alcoholics Anonymous, whose members tried to help each other stay sober.

In 1842, the Marine Washingtonian Total Abstinence Society was formed in Charleston in order to help sailors dry out.[98] I sometimes wonder what George Washington, the social drinker and distillery owner, would have made of the use of his name.

Some of the leaders of the temperance movement have familiar names. Susan B. Anthony and her BFF Elizabeth Cady Stanton saw temperance as a "gateway to women's rights," because women and children were at the mercy of drunken husbands and fathers.[99] They established a women's temperance organization in the state of New York before turning their attention to suffrage, but the temperance and suffrage movements were tightly intertwined from the beginning. It's no accident that the Eighteenth and Nineteenth amendments to the Constitution, banning alcohol and extending voting rights to women, respectively, were ratified within two years of each other. Abolition of slavery was another cause that Anthony, Stanton, and many women reformers embraced, at least in the North. In the South, the issue was so divisive that it led to a schism within the major denominations. The Methodists, with a quarter of a million members, split in 1845,[100] the same year that the Southern Baptist Convention was formed.[101] The southern Presbyterians broke away from the national church in 1861, and the Lutherans in 1863.[102]

Then along came the Civil War and President Lincoln's re-institution of the excise tax on liquor, wine, and beer to pay the costs of equipping an army. This was awkward for the northern Protestant denominations, which had begun recommending that grape juice replace wine in the sacrament of communion. Lincoln's liquor tax started out at 20 cents per gallon of liquor, then reached the sky-high rate of $2 per gallon by war's end.[103]

Seven Confederate states took the opposite approach, legislating bans on distilling both to conserve grain for food (for people and those all-important horses) and to cut down on drunkenness in the army.[104] Some years after the war, Jefferson Davis, the former president of the Confederate States, blasted attempts at prohibition, arguing that personal liberty was one of the cornerstones of the American government.

That was also the feeling of quite a few "freelance" Southern whiskey makers who, after the war, were confronted by federal revenue agents demanding an excise tax (which never went away, incidentally; today it is $13.50 per gallon of spirits). The resulting "moonshine wars" continued in the South for well over a hundred years, birthing such innovations and activities as stills made from car radiators, law enforcement still-busting, souped up Fords for running liquor and, eventually, stock car racing. I'll be focusing on that in the next chapter, so let's continue with the rebirth and growth of the temperance movement.

After the Civil War, with alcoholism still a major problem (though perhaps not as bad as in the 1830s) and women still denied the right to vote, there was a revival of the temperance and suffrage movements. The most prominent figure in temperance was Frances E. Willard, a devout Methodist from Evanston, Illinois. (She was born, appropriately enough, in Churchville, New York.) Her mother believed that parents should

Long-time WCTU President Frances Willard wears a tiny white ribbon on her dress, the emblem of the temperance movement. *Courtesy Library of Congress.*

"Let a girl grow as a tree grows, according to its own sweet will," an unconventional attitude at the time.[105] Willard's mind and outlook were further shaped by a first-class education and international travel. She spent two years exploring Europe and the Middle East. When she returned, she was determined to improve the lot of women, asking, "What can be done to make the world a wider place for women?" She became a popular lecturer, writer, and educator, and in 1874 became involved with a new organization that was sprouting chapters in the Midwest called the Women's Christian Temperance Union. There was a big emphasis on the "Christian," fairly strictly applied to mean Protestant Christian. Catholic clergy still drank wine with their communion—and other times, too. Yet Catholic leaders recognized the problems caused by alcoholism, and a Catholic Total Abstinence Union formed in 1872.[106]

As one of the WCTU's founders writes, the organization was "born, not in a manger, but on a floor of straw in an apartment into which the daylight shone through the holes and crevices."[107] The site of the "nativity" was the first gathering of the Chautauqua Lake Sunday School Assembly on the shore of a small lake in Upstate New York. Chautauqua was the brainchild of a Methodist leader and a wealthy Methodist industrialist who wished to

Until quite recently, alcohol was not served at the elegant Atheneum Hotel at Chautauqua Institution. *Author's collection.*

improve the education of Sunday school teachers.[108] Willard refers to the place as "that delightful sylvan University," which started out as a Methodist camp meeting and continues today as the Chautauqua Institution, a summer-long hive of activity for the liberal-leaning, who come to hear noted speakers, a world-class orchestra, and take classes on a myriad of subjects.[109] My husband describes it as staying in Pleasantville with TED Talks every thirty minutes.

Having attended two of these summer sessions, I heard quite a bit about the "old days" in the not-so-distant past when Chautauquans who wanted a nip sat on the wide porches of their rented homes or the hotel verandahs virtuously sipping something other than tea from china teacups. The sale of beer and wine on the grounds was not allowed until 2009, and restaurants could not sell liquor until 2017.[110] Judging by the current scene at the bar of the high-Victorian Athenaeum Hotel, it was a popular decision.

But in 1874, Chautauqua was in its infancy and the WCTU chose "the birthplace of grand ideas" as the spot to announce that a national convention would be held in Cleveland in November. At the Cleveland meeting, Willard was elected corresponding secretary. Within a few years, she became the president, a post she held until her death in 1898.

The WCTU laid out its cause and a list of methods for achieving it at the Cleveland convention: "Whereas, [m]uch of the evil by which this country is cursed comes from the fact that the men in power whose duty it is to make and administer the laws are either themselves intemperate men or controlled largely by the liquor power," followed by a long list of "therefores." These included asking political parties to stop nominating "intemperate" men, asking elected officials from the president down, along with their wives and daughters, to stop serving alcoholic beverages at public events and their "private tables," and urging "great manufacturing firms" to ask their workers to abstain and to begin paying them on Mondays instead of Saturdays so they wouldn't spend all their wages boozing it up over the weekend.[111]

They achieved notable success on one of these aims when President and Mrs. Rutherford B. Hayes declared the White House would no longer serve alcohol when they became its residents in March, 1877. Hayes was the winner of the contentious 1876 presidential election election that was decided by a back-room deal in Congress just fifty-six hours prior to the inauguration.[112] Both of the Hayes had graduated from Methodist colleges in Ohio and attended a Methodist church in Washington, though the president did not consider himself a Christian.[113] Mrs. Hayes became known as "Lemonade Lucy" for her temperance views, and the WCTU presented a flattering portrait of her in a sumptuous velvet dress to the White House art collection. Interestingly, the dress is the color of a nice glass of Merlot![114]

That this was a Christian crusade was not left to doubt. Resolution No. 11 stated that the WCTU would "pray and labor for a general revival of religion throughout our land..." Throughout the early WCTU literature, the outstanding women of the Bible, the "Deborahs and Miriams, the Hannahs and Elizabeths, and Marys" were held up as role models. [115] Another popular woman of the Bible was Rebekah, wife of

This Rebekah at the Well teapot is from the collection at the Lanier Library in Tryon, North Carolina. *Author photo.*

Jacob's son Isaac, who drew water from a well. The WCTU members sometimes wore cameo brooches depicting Rebekah at the well, and an Ohio company produced Rebekah at the Well teapots that were also embraced by the movement. Oddly, the Old Testament woman was usually shown in clothing more suited to Little Bo Peep in a village out of rural America![116]

Caroline E. Merrick from *Woman of Temperance* by Frances Willard.

While the WCTU got its start in the Midwest and Northeast, Miss Willard headed south in 1880, making two trips that she said, "were important steps in the only true policy of 'reconstruction.'" She recruited state leaders "to the manor born," most of them ladies who had done their part for the Confederacy but were now willing to let bygones be bygones and join their northern sisters in a new war on alcohol. By 1882, when the national WCTU meeting took place in that den of whiskey iniquity, Louisville, Kentucky, there were active chapters in every state in the former Confederacy.

Alabama leader Fannie Griffin said, "What could I do but follow [Alabama's] fortunes in victory or defeat? But let that pass. I can clasp hands warmly with you in this new warfare. Let us be friends."[117] Willard recruited Caroline Elizabeth Merrick, the wife of the chief justice of the Louisiana Supreme Court, to head the WCTU in that state, believing she could make the organization a success "even in the volatile city of the Mardi Gras."[118] Merrick, a Methodist, was an early and relentless advocate for women's suffrage, bolstered by the unequivocal support of her husband, whom she had married at the tender age of fifteen.[119] The state leader for South Carolina, who also became superintendent for the South, was Sallie F. Chapin of Charleston. She worked closely with African American churches to help former slaves break free from a bondage that she insisted was worse than what they had experienced prior to Emancipation: the bondage of alcoholism.[120]

In North Carolina, a state temperance meeting was held in Raleigh with the blessing of the state's Democratic governor, Thomas Jordan Jarvis. Willard wrote that the governor flew the stars and bars alongside the state flag, and that half the delegates were Black men. "The prejudices against color gave way at the eloquent utterances of some of the speakers and as former masters waved their hats, the temperance women thanked God that the color-line was broken at last by the Southerners themselves."[121]

This embrace of the formerly enslaved did not reflect the attitude of the Southern branches of the WCTU as a whole. Willard acquiesced to the leaders' insistence on separate chapters for Black and White women and contributed to the race problem by stating she pitied White Southern women who had to live where "the colored race multiplies like the locusts of Egypt" and joined them in evoking the specter of the drunken African American man raping White women. She got into a war of words with Ida B. Wells, the prominent African American journalist and activist who later co-founded the NAACP, over Willard's unwillingness to support anti-lynching and equal rights legislation.[122] North Carolina Governor Jarvis turned out to be a fair-weather friend to the formerly enslaved as well, becoming one of the leaders of White supremacists in a bloody coup d'etat against the elected bi-racial government of Wilmington in 1898. They destroyed Black-owned businesses, and many Black people were murdered. In the aftermath, thousands of African Americans fled for their lives and never returned to Wilmington.[123]

By this time, North Carolina and many other Southern states had thoroughly embraced the temperance agenda. The passage of local option laws had dried up individual cities and counties, though no Southern state had voted itself dry. That would come in Georgia in 1907 after another riot aimed at suppressing Blacks. North Carolina followed suit in 1908.

In the 1880s and 1890s, the WCTU developed other aims besides temperance under Willard's presidency, reflecting her personal motto of "Do everything." Empowerment of women in general became its aim, and departments were set up to address such social ills as prostitution, lack of day care for working mothers, and, of course, suffrage. Willard recognized the connectivity of all these causes under the overarching umbrella of "Protect the Home."[124]

THOMAS BRAMWELL WELCH AND HIS UNFERMENTED WINE

When the Methodists decided before the Civil War that it was sinful to drink wine at communion, even though the Bible expressly stated its use at the Last Supper—not to mention converting water into wine being the first miracle performed by Jesus—the question remained, what do we serve instead?[125]

Thomas Bramwell Welch. *Courtesy Vineland (N.J.) Historical Society.*

It took a few years, but finally a staunch Methodist and prohibitionist, Thomas Bramwell Welch, who lived in the "temperance town" of Vineland, New Jersey, came up with a solution. (Welch had unsuccessful earlier careers in ministry and medicine before he settled on dentistry, using the slogan "good chewers or no sale.") He developed a method of pasteurizing grape juice, thus halting fermentation, that resulted in a product he called Dr. Welch's Unfermented Wine. We know it today as Welch's Grape Juice. Dr. Welch and his son, Charles, also a dentist—as was his daughter, Emily—peddled the unfermented wine to area churches, but it was a sideline to their practices. The company finally took off in 1893 when Charles began devoting all his time to it and built a grape juice factory in Chautauqua County in New York. Today, grape juice is the standard communion fare at most Protestant churches, the outstanding exception being Episcopalians.

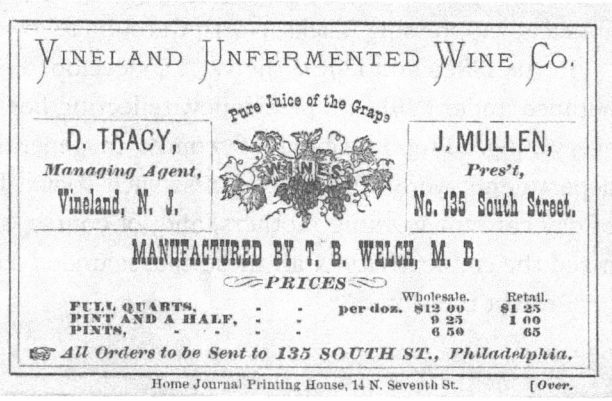

An early ad for unfermented wine. *Courtesy Vineland (N.J.) Historical Society.*

From its humble beginnings, Welch's, now based in Concord, Massachusetts, sells hundreds of grape products, from juice to jelly.[126] In 2015, Welch's began a collaboration with the Manischewitz kosher food company to produce kosher wine, later adding kosher grape juice to its products.

Covid-19 challenged all religious groups who observe communion by limited gathering at the communion rail and drinking from a common cup. A smart entrepreneur came up with the idea of pre-filled communion cups of grape juice, with a wafer under a plastic shield on top. This enabled Protestant churches to hand out communion while keeping worshipers spaced far apart and even to administer drive-through communion. An ad in *Christianity Today* offers them for "as low as 24 cents a cup."[127]

A Dainty, Unfermented Punch

An ad for Welch's Grape Juice ran in the July 24, 1912 issue of *The Presbyterian of the South*, an Atlanta newspaper, describing it as a "a popular Southland drink" (even though it was made in Westfield, New York). By then Georgia had been a "dry" state for five years. The ad included a recipe for "a dainty, unfermented punch."

- Juice of three lemons
- Juice of one orange
- One pint of Welch's Grape Juice
- One quart of water
- One cup of sugar

Add sliced oranges and pineapple and serve cold.

The last years of the nineteenth century also marked the ascendancy of another Methodist-led organization, the Anti-Saloon League. Its face was that of general counsel Wayne B. Wheeler, whose relentless lobbying and pressure tactics made the ASL one of the most successful single-issue policy organizations In American history. As Wheeler said, "I don't care how a man drinks, I care how he votes." And he meant it.

But that's enough about the Methodists for now. Let's check in with the moonshiners.

Prohibition Expedition: Savannah

The historic city of Savannah contains twenty-two squares, many with a fountain, statue, or other centerpiece. **Reynolds Square** is where John Wesley's brooding statue stands.

32 Abercorn Street • www.savannah.com/reynolds-square

Right beside it is **The Old Pink House**, a delightful place for a meal or a drink.

32 Abercorn Street • www.theoldepinkhouserestaurant.com

The James Oglethorpe statue is centered in **Chippewa Square**, but his fame has been eclipsed by that of Forrest Gump, who sat on a bench there and waited for the bus to take him to his beloved Jenny in the 1984 movie.

Bull Street at McDonough Street
www.visitsavannah.com/profile/chippewa-square/6117

The bench is now in the Savannah History Museum, which showcases Savannah's history from its founding in 1733.

303 MLK Jr. Boulevard • https://www.chsgeorgia.org/SHM/About

History museums are fine and good, but then there are truly amazing ones like the **American Prohibition Museum.** You can tour this fun, informative, and interactive museum, have a drink in the Congress Street Up speakeasy and even take a cocktail-making class. I covered the museum extensively in *Baptists and Bootleggers*, so I won't go into it any further here except to urge you to go.

209 W Saint Julian Street, Old City Market
www.americanprohibitionmuseum.com

Cemetery Side Trip

James Habersham Jr., former owner of the Olde Pink House, is buried beside his parents and his three brothers at Colonial Park Cemetery, 200 Abercorn Street, Savannah. Established in 1750 when Georgia was still a Crown colony, it ceased accepting burials about a hundred years later, so the six-acre park is the final resting place of many notable figures from the American Revolution. James and his brothers John and Joseph were active patriots in the fight for independence, while their father remained loyal to the Crown. The elder Habersham died in 1775, though, before the conflict began in earnest. Many of the older graves in this cemetery are unmarked, so it's probable that some of the people who tormented John and Charles Wesley are buried there. May they rest in peace!

Caroline E. Merrick, leader of the WCTU of Louisiana, is buried with her husband and other Merrick family members in the famous Metairie Cemetery, 5100 Pontchartrain Boulevard, New Orleans. It is stuffed with the "most famous, wealthiest, and notorious people of the past," according to the tourism website www.nola.com. The cemetery is known for its elaborate above-ground tombs and monuments. Curiously, her simple gravestone bears her maiden name, Caroline Elizabeth Thomas, and beneath it the words, "Wife of Edwin T. Merrick."[128]

A vintage postcard shows the monument to the Civil War dead of the Army of Tennessee through the gateway at Metairie Cemetery. *Author's collection.*

RECOMMENDED READING

Strange Fires: The True Story of John Wesley's Love Affair in Georgia by Willie Snow Ethridge (New York: Vanguard Press, 1971) is a detailed account of the founder of Methodism's ill-fated sojourn in Savannah. It is long out of print, but numerous second-hand copies can be found on the Internet.

John Wesley: The Great Methodist by Sam Wellman (Uhrichsville, Ohio: Barbour Books, 1997), is aimed at young adult readers, but I found it sufficient as a general briefing on Wesley's life and ministry. He has been the subject of numerous longer scholarly biographies for those who want a deeper dive.

CHAPTER FOUR

Mt. Airy
and Thereabouts

I WAS SITTING AT A TABLE at Snappy Lunch, a little sandwich shop in Mt. Airy, North Carolina, under a huge poster of Otis Campbell, the town drunk of Mayberry, waiting for my pork chop sandwich to arrive.[129] Mt. Airy is the hometown of one of North Carolina's most famous native sons, Andy Griffith, and the town is a pilgrimage for anyone who loved the television series he starred in throughout the 1960s. You can take a tour in a black and white patrol car, just like the one hapless deputy Barney Fife drove, and stay in the Aunt Bee Room at the Mayberry Motor Inn—furnished with items that belonged to actress Frances Bavier—or even the modest home where Andy grew up (now a B&B).[130] You can satisfy your sweet tooth at Opie's Candy Store or get your hair cut at Floyd's Barber Shop.[131]

Visitors can avail themselves of every Andy Griffith souvenir known to man, get their picture made with life-size bronze sculptures of Andy and his son Opie going fishing, or wander

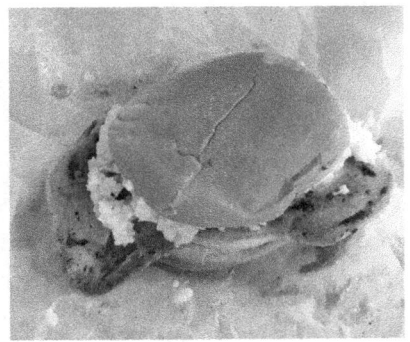

The pork chop sandwich at Snappy Lunch is a Mt. Airy institution. *Author photo.*

through the Andy Griffith Museum. For the full effect, there's a Mayberry Days festival each September, where special guests include people who appeared with Griffith in his various television shows, including the *Matlock* series where he played an Atlanta lawyer who never lost a case, sort of like Perry Mason in a seersucker suit.

Of course, the façade can wear pretty thin. The walls at Snappy Lunch are papered with pictures and memorabilia from the television series and the beloved actor's life, but my waitress had a ring in her nose. Hardly the picture that comes to mind of the never-seen Bluebird Diner waitress Juanita who Barney flirted with over the phone.

I had been advised to check out Snappy Lunch by a man working on the Stock Car Racing Wall of Fame, a collection of displays flanking an alleyway from the city parking lot, sponsored by the chamber of commerce. Indeed, moonshine runs a strong second to Andy Griffith as a tourist attraction in Mt. Airy. After perusing the wall, visitors can snack on a slice of moonshine pie at Miss Angel's Heavenly Pie or sample Roadkill Peach moonshine ice cream—"must be 21 years of age or older," a sign in the shop window admonished. There's a Mayberry Spirits Company and a festival in September, the Moonshine and Racer's Reunion, which in 2022 featured a band called Sons of Bootleg.[132]

It's all intertwined, the tribute to wholesome hometown life and the darker underside of the North Carolina and Virginia mountains, where the making and selling of blockade liquor led to feuds, violence, and murder in the years after the Civil War and continued well past the mid-twentieth century. Griffith's first big screen role was in the dark satire *A Face in the Crowd* in 1957, in which he played an alcoholic drifter discovered in a drunk tank who becomes a media star and political influencer before he lets his true feelings known over a hot mike. I watch it every time I can and never fail to be stunned by its relevancy—and Griffith's authenticity in the role.[133]

As I devoured my pork chop sandwich—a heart-stopping combination of deep-fried boneless chop, chili, tomato, and coleslaw served on a hamburger bun—I tried to remember which among the 249 *Andy Griffith Show* episodes dealt with illegal liquor. There are about a dozen, though Otis Campbell was a recurring character, frequently letting himself into "his" jail cell to sleep it off. One of the episodes was about a ceremony to present a plaque to the only resident of Mayberry who descended from a Revolutionary War hero, who was, of course, Otis. (From what we now know about the drinking habits of the patriots, this should not have surprised anyone.) Another dealt with Opie's discovery that the Revolution's revered "Battle of Mayberry" was actually a feud over a jug of corn liquor.[134]

That the fictional Otis's antecedent was a Campbell also is not surprising. North Carolina in the eighteenth century attracted more Highland Scots than any other place of origin compared to the rest of the thirteen colonies, and the largest contingent came from Argyllshire, dominated by the Campbell clan.[135] By 1790, a year before George Washington's visit, North Carolina, South Carolina, Georgia, and Virginia had the largest concentration of Scots in the young country.[136] Most came for economic opportunity, attracted to North Carolina, for example, by land grants. Others were criminals sentenced to "transportation" and indentured servitude for a period of years. There are numerous place names that refer to Scotland, including Scotland County and the towns of Highlands and Scotland Neck. The Scots brought with them their "clannishness": fierce family loyalty, an out-size culture of honor and revenge—with slights and disputes often settled by violence—and, of course, a strong heritage of whiskey making and imbibing.

It took a visit to the Mt. Airy Museum of Regional History, a short walk down Main Street, to uncover some of the truth about what was going on in the seemingly idyllic hills I had been driving through, the roadsides innocently dotted with orange daylilies and the bobbing parasols of Queen Anne's lace.

The Mt. Airy Stock Car Racing Wall of Fame connects the dots between moonshine hauling and race car driving. *Author photo.*

The museum is like many such local institutions—or the Smithsonian Institution, for that matter—showcasing a range of odd-ball relics, such as an appalling "tonsillectomy chair" from a mid-twentieth century medical office, along with larger historic displays. Among them were exhibits about the school days of Andy Griffith, the country music career of hometown girl Donna Fargo ("The Happiest Girl in the Whole USA") and the lives of the original Siamese Twins, Chang and Eng Bunker, who married sisters and settled near Mt. Airy prior to the Civil War.

Chang and Eng Bunker, the Original Siamese Twins

The wildly unlikely story about how the conjoined twins Chang and Eng Bunker wound up in North Carolina and fathered twenty-one children with a pair of sisters (happily, they were not also conjoined) raises all sorts of questions in my mind, including the very unseemly one about how did they, uh, do it? But it's also a cautionary tale about what happens when you are linked to your alcoholic conjoined twin through the liver, and you are a teetotaler.

The twins were born in 1811 in Siam—today's Thailand—joined at the sternum by a band of cartilage and a shared liver. They were discovered swimming in the Mekong River by a Scottish businessman, who convinced their parents to let him take the teen-age boys to America and put them on display. They signed a five-year contract, and their parents were given $500.

When they reached the age of twenty-one and adulthood, the brothers basically revolted against their owner-managers and oversaw their own tours for almost a decade, according to Yunte Huang, the latest of their many biographers. Their tours took them all over the United States and Europe,

Chang (left) and Eng Bunker, with their wives Adelaide and Sarah, and two of their sons posed for famed photographer Matthew Brady in 1865. *Wikimedia Commons*.

Mt. Airy and Thereabouts

and they came to enjoy the South. By the time they were twenty-eight, they had accumulated enough money to retire from show business. In his book *Inseparable*, Huang writes of their lives in rural North Carolina, where "almost like two Siamese Daniel Boones," they loved hunting and fishing.[137]

With their joint capital of $10,000, Chang and Eng were considered quite well-to-do by the local people. In 1839, they bought 150 acres of land in the Traphill community in Surry County. "Traphill would become a center for mass production and exportation of moonshine in the Prohibition era," writes Huang. "In the hills, hollows, caves and 'cutthroat ridges'—so named because they were inaccessible to intruders without the use of lethal force—flourished countless moonshine stills hidden well beyond the reach of the law."[138]

The brothers built a two-story house, established a general store, and began looking for wives, focusing on Adelaide and Sarah Yates, eighteen- and seventeen-year-old daughters of a large farm owner in nearby Mulberry Creek. "Not regarded as classic beauties, the two girls, nurtured by the mountain climate, were vivacious, imaginative, and, in nineteenth century parlance, exuberant like wildflowers," Huang writes.[139]

Chang and Eng made frequent visits to the Yates house, sometimes entertaining the family by playing duets on their flutes.[140] But courtship by conjoined Asian brothers in White North Carolina was not easy. While Adelaide seemed quite taken with Chang, her sister wasn't as "receptive" to Eng's advances, Huang writes."[141] The twins, hoping to win over Sarah, hosted an elaborate quilting bee, inviting the community, and providing an impressive feast in their home, which was rather more sumptuous than most in the community; many of the furnishings came from New York. "While the women began to stitch and chat, the twins circled around them, entertaining, wisecracking, and paying special attention to the Yates sisters—treating them like princesses and making them the envy of all the others," Huang writes.[142]

Sarah capitulated, but then the girls had to convince their parents, who were horrified and refused their consent. The persistent sisters were staunch members of a Baptist church, and the sympathetic minister, Colby Sparks, agreed to perform a wedding ceremony if they decided to elope.[143]

The girls' parents finally gave in, and despite considerable community opposition—the Yates's windows were smashed, and they were threatened with the burning of their crops—the wedding took place at the Yates home,

continues on next page

with Sparks presiding, on April 13, 1843. For the first time, the last name Bunker appeared on an official document. (The source of the name has many theories, but no one really knows. [144]) The Bunkers' father-in-law gave them their first slave as a wedding gift. [145]

Now comes the part I will have to leave to your imagination. The newlywed brothers took their brides home, writes Huang, "where an extra-wide bed—widest perhaps in all North Carolina or even North America—awaited the four of them."[146] There is no record of what happened there or how it was done, but within ten months, each wife had borne a daughter and babies would come routinely, with the last arriving just before the end of the Civil War.[147] All told, Chang had ten children and Eng had eleven. There are more than 1,500 Bunker descendants today, most of whom still live in North Carolina.[148]

As their families outgrew the space of their one home, the Bunkers bought a second piece of land and built a separate home for Eng, and henceforth they spent three days at one house with one wife, three with the other. In each home, the twin who lived there called all the shots, an agreement that worked most of the time for the brothers. Chang was a hard drinker with a short fuse, but Eng was a teetotaler who did not keep any liquor in his home. Interestingly, Eng seems not to have become intoxicated when his brother drank, even though they had conjoined livers.[149]

With farming of tobacco becoming their main source of income, the brothers began buying slaves, usually as children, then selling the males as they reached their twenties. How they treated the slaves is a matter of some debate. Huang in his book recounts some stories that claimed the Bunkers were considerate, others that they were hard taskmasters. The fact that they sold off the enslaved boys as they matured for fear they would rebel or run away seems to speak of the latter.[150]

When the twins got wanderlust, they went on tours, sometimes bringing along a few of their children as part of their attraction. However, the novelty of their act had worn off, and they found the tours less financially rewarding. Although they loathed the century's greatest showman, P.T. Barnum, in 1860 they agreed to a month-long commitment at his American Museum in New York. Barnum, in typical humbug fashion, later claimed to have coined the term Siamese Twins, though he did not. The Bunkers seem to have come up with that on their own.[151] They were in California on another tour when the Civil War broke out.

As loyal Confederates, each sent a son off to war and they invested heavily in Confederate bonds. The sons came home, wounded but alive, but at the end of the war the bonds were worthless, and the slaves were freed. The twins went back on tour to rebuild their finances.[152] In 1870, returning by ship from a humiliating tour in Europe where they had been laughed at rather than applauded, Chang had a stroke.

Back in North Carolina, Chang continued to drink, and Eng was stuck dragging around the partly paralyzed body of his failing brother. On January 17, 1874, Chang died of a stroke and Eng followed three hours later after suffering a heart attack. Some thought he died of fright.

The widowed sisters considered what to do, knowing that grave robbers were liable to dig up their husbands and sell them to medical schools for dissection, or worse, to side show promoters who would put the embalmed bodies on display. They finally allowed a distinguished team of doctors to come down from Philadelphia and take the bodies back for autopsy. They were returned to North Carolina for burial, minus their liver, intestines, and lungs.

The liver is still on display at the Mütter Museum of the College of Physicians in Philadelphia, along with a post-mortem cast of the twins' torso. Thousands of visitors come to the museum each year to see the twins' liver and such curiosities as the world's largest human colon on display (it once contained forty pounds of excrement), wax models of horrific skin conditions, and cross-sections of Albert Einstein's brain.[153]

There is a display of Chang and Eng Bunker's memorabilia in the basement of the Andy Griffith Museum in Mt. Airy, sort of a sideshow to the main event. A descendant has turned their former farm into the Mayberry Campground.

The Mt. Airy Museum of Regional History had a small display about moonshining and a large one that told of one of the most notorious crimes of the early twentieth century, a shoot-out in the Carroll County Courthouse, just over the state line in Hillsville, Virginia. In a gun battle that lasted just a couple of minutes, fifty-seven bullets were fired, seven people were wounded, and five others killed, including the presiding judge, the county sheriff, the prosecuting attorney, and the foreman of the jury. "This story is filled with intrigue involving blockaders, money, politics, power, romance and social injustice," a sign in the display said. The manhunt for the killers lasted for weeks, attracting the attention of reporters from the *New York Times* and the *Washington Post*, and resulting in the electric chair execution of an unrepentant father and son.

Such violence was the byproduct of a whiskey-making tradition that began with yeoman farmers turning corn into a highly portable product that could be sold for cash to pay taxes or bartered for any number of goods and services.[154] In his book *Tar Heel Lightning: How Secret Stills and Fast Cars Made North Carolina the Moonshine Capital of the World*, Daniel S. Pierce makes the case that moonshine was one of the state's largest industries during the century that began with the Civil War, along with tobacco, textiles, and furniture. He presents North Carolina's moonshine culture as "a convenient microcosm for the South as a whole" vis-à-vis the making of illegal liquor.[155] I think he makes a sound argument, so even as I focus on the mountains of North Carolina and Virginia here, what follows could apply to any of the Southern states.

The historic Carroll County Courthouse today, with a Confederate monument in front. It is now the home of the Carroll County Historical Society and Museum. *Author photo.*

Although whiskey had been made in the South since colonial days, it only became illegal when the makers refused to buy licenses and pay federal excise taxes. As we learned in earlier chapters, the tax was implemented under President Washington, repealed under President Jefferson, and reinstituted under President Lincoln, but when the South seceded, the tax wasn't collected there. When the Civil War ended and the South rejoined the union, commercial distilleries generally paid the tax, being able to absorb the cost due to economies of scale. But small-scale whiskey producers were highly averse to paying the federal excise tax. They proclaimed themselves "blockaders," a name linked to the daring boatmen who had dodged Union ships during the war to bring goods into blockaded Southern ports. Thus they earned the tacit approval of their fellow citizens who perceived the federal revenue agents as "Yankee" enemies. Firebrand North Carolina Governor Zeb Vance called them "red-legged grasshoppers."[156]

Foremost among the early blockaders was the notorious Lewis Redmond, who plied his trade in the mountains of North and South Carolina. In 1876 he killed a U.S. deputy marshal and then dodged the law for five years, trafficking moonshine and thumbing his nose at would-be captors. Finally nabbed in Swain County, North Carolina in 1881, he went to federal prison, but upon his return to South Carolina a few years later, he was met at the Columbia train station by both the current and former governors. They welcomed him with open arms and sent him on the last leg of his journey with their well wishes and a goody basket of victuals to make the trip more enjoyable. President Chester Arthur's pardon was the icing on the cake, and Redmond led a (mostly) law-abiding life going forward.[157]

This "normalization" of criminal activity was common throughout the South in the post-Civil War years. Focusing on North Carolina in particular, Pierce observes, "While most moonshiners in the state were reportedly otherwise upstanding citizens, involvement in one criminal activity led some to other types of criminality, including prostitution, gambling, and money laundering."[158] It also fostered an atmosphere of corruption, as illegal whiskey makers paid off sheriffs, prosecutors, judges, and other public officials to protect their underground industry.

Pierce's first poster boy for what he dubs his "N.C. Moonshine Hall of Fame (and Shame)" exemplified this.[159] Like Lewis Redmond, Amos Owens of Rutherford County defied federal revenue collectors after the Civil War. The difference was that he had been an accomplished liquor maker before

A twentieth century postcard purports to show a "typical" still in the North Carolina mountains. Note the rifles at the ready on the left. *Author's collection.*

the war, following the tradition of maximizing his farm's profits by turning much of his corn crop into corn whiskey. As a thoroughly unreconstructed Confederate, Owens saw no need to pay any tax to the Yankees, and was the frequent target of revenue agents, being repeatedly arrested beginning in 1868 and sentenced to the prison in Ossining, New York, known as Sing Sing, three times. But he kept coming back for more. His final arrest occurred in 1905 at age eighty-three.

In his last years, Owens attracted a biographer, M.L. White, who penned *A History of the Life of Amos Owens, the Noted Blockader of Cherry Mountain*, a flowery account of his colorful life. Of his aversion to paying excise taxes, White wrote, "He reverently believed that while bread was the staff of life, whiskey was life itself. That it was the chief end of man to raise enough corn to make whiskey and convert the remainder into bread."[160] Owens's postwar specialty was Cherry Bounce, unaged corn whiskey flavored with honey and cherries harvested on his own land. He became rich and infamous.

A diminutive man "with rosy cheeks and a constant twinkle in his eye," Owens strutted about in a black silk top hat and gold-rimmed glasses. "He had a reputation as a cheerful person who helped neighbors, a man who publicly professed Christianity at least twenty-eight times, and a person beloved by his community," Pierce writes.[161]

But behind this Santa Claus-like façade was a monstrous brawler, suspected Ku Klux Klan chieftain, and "the host of one of the most brutal bacchanalias imaginable at his home on Cherry Mountain," Pierce writes.[162] The annual Cherry Bounce Festival featured cherry picking and mountain music, but also unfettered drinking, bare-knuckle boxing, shooting matches (with the shooters as targets), cockfighting and dogfighting, with the sort of collateral damage that goes with such activities. White writes, "Amos was a host of remarkable versatility. If a man wanted to eat, a bountiful table was always prepared; if he wanted to fight, all he had to do was to go out a few steps and enter the ring. If anybody got 'past varigation' [insensibly drunk] he was piled into the cellar. One man was killed outright here and others have been probed, dismembered, maimed and their faces made to resemble an animated war-map."[163]

An illustrator imagined the death of an unlucky participant in the Cherry Bounce Festival. *Courtesy Library of Congress.*

While amusing to read about, between the lines we can intuit a sad story of hopeless drunkards, domestic violence, families impoverished by breadwinners who preferred their bread in liquid form, and the other assorted miseries that galvanized the temperance movement. The moral crusade against alcohol began its assault on North Carolina in the 1870s. Composed of Methodists, Baptists, a sprinkling of Presbyterians and the largely middle-class residents of towns and cities, the Women's Christian Temperance Union and the Anti-Saloon League started drying up North Carolina city-by-city and county-by-county before going whole-hog for the state. They got a boost from a visit to North Carolina by the country's most celebrated prohibitionist, hatchet-wielding grandma Carry A. Nation.

Carry A. Nation wore a large white bow at her neck, the symbol of the WCTU. *Courtesy Library of Congress.*

Nation came to Salisbury and Charlotte in June 1907, wearing her trademark long black dress and bonnet, the big white bow of the WCTU at her throat, but without the hatchet she had used to physically bust up bars all over the Midwest. She proclaimed Salisbury "a hell hole," adding, "I can see you have plenty of poverty, degradation and suffering in your midst." She also took a shot at North Carolina's even more sacred cash crop, tobacco, declaring, "Every time I see a tobacco leaf growing, I call upon God to blast it."[164] In North Carolina, that was a very tall order.

The following year, the results of a state referendum on liquor put all of North Carolina on the wagon. Not that local law enforcement was much more successful than the "red-legged grasshoppers" in stopping the flow of illegal whiskey. The fact that bordering states Virginia and South Carolina remained largely wet for several more years added to the many challenges facing the law in the Tar Heel state. And that brings us back to the case of the shoot-out in the Carroll County Courthouse in Hillsville, Virginia.

Floyd Allen was the head of a cantankerous clan of mountaineers that dominated Carroll County for decades. In his book *The Allen Chase: The*

Search and Capture of the Allen Outlaws as Reported by Period Newspapers, Ron Hall demonstrates that the Allens and their kinsmen, the Edwardses, were successful farmers, some-time illegal distillers, mill and store owners, and Democratic Party leaders.[165] But they were constantly at odds with the law, which they believed did not apply to them, and proud of a record of never going to jail for their misdeeds. A local attorney described Floyd Allen as a man of great personal honesty, yet someone who "would kill you in a second over some little matter most people wouldn't remember two minutes." In other words, classic Highland Scots temperament. He carried the evidence of his stance around with him. Even before the courtroom shootout in 1913, Allen's body "boasted thirteen bullet wounds, five inflicted in quarrels with his own brothers," the *New York Times* reported.[166] He collected a new bullet wound in the courtroom crossfire.

When the beetle-browed, ginger-whiskered Floyd heard his sentence of a year in prison for the crime of beating a deputy senseless and releasing a couple of cousins who were headed to jail, he declared, "Gentlemen, I ain't a goin'."[167] His words unleashed a hail of bullets in the courtroom. In seconds, the presiding judge, Thornton L. Massie, lay dead, as did the prosecuting attorney, William M. Foster, and the sheriff. The jury foreman and a nineteen-year-old woman who had been a subpoenaed witness later died of their wounds.

The Allens and their kin, minus Floyd, who was injured too badly to escape, headed for the hills where they were the subject of an intensive manhunt. The Virginia governor offered a handsome bounty and called out

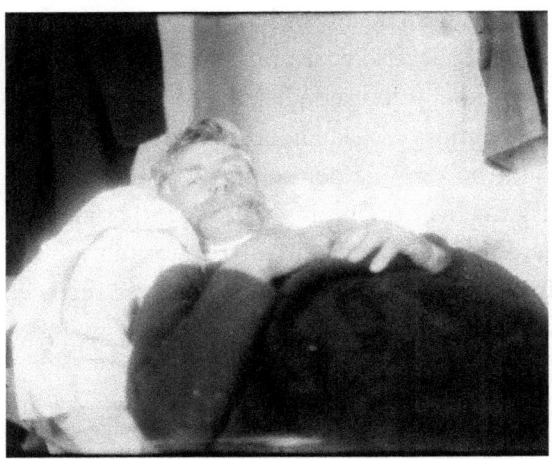

Shot in the stomach, Floyd Allen tried to slash his throat with his pocketknife to avoid being taken prisoner. This photo was taken at the Carroll County Jail. *Courtesy Library of Congress.*

a thousand-man posse, headed by members of the Baldwin-Felts Detective Agency (since the sheriff was no longer around).¹⁶⁸ The search extended into North Carolina, and within a few weeks most of the gang had been captured or had surrendered. The final two suspects, Floyd's brother Sidna and his nephew Wesley Edwards, were captured six months later, living under false identities in Des Moines, Iowa. Wesley's fiancée had traveled there from North Carolina to wed, (perhaps) unintentionally tipping off private detectives. The *Bluefield Daily Telegraph* uncharitably described Maude Delilah Iroler as "a decided blond [who] is not pretty."¹⁶⁹ Alas, the wedding did not take place, though Maude did eventually find a husband, and Wesley found a wife after many years in prison.

While contemporary news accounts quoted by author Hall portrayed the dead as martyrs to justice, circumstances called that into question. Judge Massie, fully aware of Floyd Allen's history, had appointed him a special deputy while he awaited trial. The Allens had gotten off with wrist slaps on criminal charges before, sometimes by intimidating witnesses, other times by seeking political protection as high as the governor's office. Attorney Foster had engaged in a bare-knuckle fight for his elected post with an Allen relative, leaving bad feelings and threats of political vendetta in its wake. Well, you get the idea.

And the shenanigans didn't end with the death sentence of Floyd Allen and his son Claude and the conviction of several other Allen clan members for murder. In a last-ditch effort to save them, advocates for the Allens met with the Virginia lieutenant governor while the governor was out of state and asked him to commute the sentences. Getting wind of this, Governor William Mann hurried back to Richmond and ordered the execution to proceed. Father and son died in the electric chair, nine minutes apart, on March 28, 1913. They were buried under a common headstone that was originally inscribed, "Sacred to the memory of Claude S. Allen and his father, who were judicially murdered in the Virginia penitentiary, by order of the government of the State of Virginia over the protest of 100,000 citizens of the state of Virginia. Placed here by a friend and citizen of Virginia."¹⁷⁰ The inscription rankled the Virginia government, and in 1926, it was replaced with the current one that was rather less in-your-face: "Asleep in Jesus, blessed sleep."¹⁷¹

Signa Allen's fine house outside Hillsville has recently been restored and is owned by the Carroll County Historical Society. *Author photo.*

Most of the other men convicted in the massacre were pardoned by subsequent governors in the 1920s. Several left the state for good. In his book *The Allen Chase*, Ron Hall writes, "None of the pardoned men were ever accused of violating a law in their later life."

The fall-out for the Allens ended their prosperity. Floyd and Sidna Allen's property was seized by the state, the proceeds of the sale to benefit the victims' families. This included the fine Queen Anne-style house that Sidna Allen had recently built outside Hillsville. Jack Allen, a brother who had not participated in the courthouse shoot-out, tried to intervene for Sidna's wife, to no avail. A few years later Jack was spending the night in a boarding house near Mt. Airy and got into an altercation with a known blockader named Will McGraw, who shot him dead. The *New York Times* reported the death, duly noting, "Allen was 50 years old and a typical specimen of the mountaineer type which knew no law but the freedom of the mountains."[172]

The Allen clan may have been vanquished, but the lawlessness of the Virginia and North Carolina mountains would continue for many years. Stay tuned!

Prohibition Expedition: North Carolina and Virginia Mountains

In Mt. Airy, you'll want to visit the **Andy Griffith Museum**, which is all things Andy and Mayberry.

218 Rockford Street • www.surryarts.org/agmuseum/index.html

Your museum ticket also admits you to the **Original Siamese Twins Exhibit**, including artifacts from the lives of Chang and Eng, among them their specially made bed. Lower level of the Andy Griffith Theatre.

https://www.surryarts.org/siamesetwins/index.html

For a fuller history of the region, including a display about the Carroll County shoot-out, visit the **Mt. Airy Museum of Regional History**.

301 N. Main Street • www.northcarolinamuseum.org.

There are plenty of places to eat, drink, and be merry in Mt. Airy, but a true Andy Griffith fan will make a pilgrimage to **Snappy Lunch**, which is open for breakfast and lunch. Don't dawdle. They close before 2 p.m.

125 N. Main Street • www.thesnappylunch.com

While you are downtown, check out the **Mt. Airy Stock Car Wall of Fame**. It connects Main Street with the municipal parking lot.

I don't expect it's quite as wild as in Amos Owen's day, but the **Cherry Bounce Festival** is still held each June in Forest City, North Carolina.

www.townofforestcity.com/parks-recreation/forest-city-pavilion-park-square/events-information/cherry-bounce-festival

The story of the Carroll County Courthouse shoot-out is on display in the **Carroll County Museum and Historical Society**, located in the very courthouse where the 1912 tragedy took place. The exhibits include a diorama of the courthouse scene. 515 North Main Street, Hillsville, Virginia.

www.carrollvamuseum.org/museum

The historical society also owns the **Sidna Allen House**, which is under restoration and can be seen from the road in Fancy Gap.

www.carrollvamuseum.org/jsidnaallenhome

CEMETERY SIDE TRIP

According to the Surry County Arts Council, which operates the **Andy Griffith** and **Chang and Eng Bunker** museums, the conjoined twins did not find a final resting place until Chang's wife Adelaide died in 1917 and they were buried together at White Plains Baptist Church. Even though the joint tombstone indicates Sarah is buried with them, her remains are nearby but not in the same grave. (Adelaide always seemed to be more into the whole twin thing than her sister.) 614 Old U.S. 601, Mt Airy.

The large Bunker headstone memorializes both brothers Chang and Eng and their wives. *Wikimedia Commons.*

The infamous Cherry Bounce moonshine maker **Amos Owens** also found a place of rest in a North Carolina Baptist churchyard. His simple stone gives his name and his company in the Confederate Army. Walls Baptist Church Cemetery, 749 Walls Church Road, Bostic.

RECOMMENDED READING

Inseparable: The Original Siamese Twins and Their Rendezvous with American History by Yunte Huang (Liverwright, 2018)

The Allen Chase: The Search and Capture of the Allen Outlaws, as Reported by Period Newspapers, edited by Ron Hall. (Hillsville, Virginia: Carroll County Historical Society, 2016)

Tar Heel Lightnin': How Secret Stills and Fast Cars Made North Carolina the Moonshine Capital of the World by Daniel S. Pierce. (Chapel Hill: University of North Carolina Press, 2019)

CRYSTAL STRAWBERRY

Do you like daiquiris? This strawberry and moonshine version was created by the legal moonshine distillery in Mayberry using its sorghum moonshine whiskey.

- 1½ oz. Crystal Moon Whiskey
- 6 strawberries
- 2 tsp sugar
- 1.5 oz. lime juice
- ½ cup crushed ice

Combine ingredients in a blender, pulse until mixed and the ice is slushy. Pour into a chilled margarita glass and garnish with a strawberry.

—Courtesy Mayberry Spirits Company, 461 N. South Street, Mayberry.
https://www.facebook.com/mayberryspirits

CHAPTER FIVE

The Anti-Saloon Juggernaut

IN THE FALL OF 2022, my husband and I took a trip to Europe, visiting Amsterdam for the first time since our honeymoon in 1978. At that time we were two bright-eyed kids just out of college, trying to make our money last as long as it could before we had to return home, face reality, and begin looking for our first career jobs. As recent graduates of the University of Georgia, naturally we drank a lot of beer. Highlights of our honeymoon included a tour of the Heineken brewery in Amsterdam and a couple of outings to Oktoberfest in Munich, and we spent evenings in small bars from England to Greece where we guzzled European lager while playing cards.

"Last night we ended up getting soundly snockered at the small café-bar next door," I wrote in my journal. "And with Dutch beer going for 50 cents a glass, who wouldn't?"

This was pretty much the attitude of Americans in the second half of the nineteenth century as cheap lager beer became widely available. Sometimes it even came with a free lunch! While Lewis Redmond and Amos Owens were peddling white lightning and Cherry Bounce in the Carolina mountains and Frances Willard's WCTU was leading the charge for temperance, German immigrants were setting up breweries all over the country, making

The Anti-Saloon League successfully demonized drinking places, as with this poster dating from 1917. *Courtesy Library of Congress*

the light, crisp, golden lager that was popular in Germany and environs. As beer historian Joe Hursey puts it, the refreshing lager made the ale and beer that had been more common in America taste "kind of like drinking hot cocoa in July."[173] Lacking a dependable source of hops, Americans had made beer flavored with everything imaginable, including spruce, molasses, and even persimmons. Yuck.

During a talk to the Piedmont Historical Preservation Society in Piedmont, South Carolina, Joe said that in the 1830s and 1840s, some 1.3 million Germans emigrated to America. They were generally a better educated class of people than earlier (and later) immigrants, with entrepreneurial skills and money to invest. Some of them saw a market for German-style lager, both to slake the thirst of their fellow immigrants and to tempt the tongues of other Americans.

Lager's ingredients include hops and lager yeast, and because these were hard to produce in America, they were often imported. Unfortunately, they didn't hold up well during the long journey from Europe by sailing ship.

That changed when the first clipper ships were introduced in 1833. It "was like a Ferrari vs. a tractor trailer," said Joe, who obviously has a flair with simile.[174] By 1866, German-style lager had replaced whiskey as the dominant alcoholic beverage in the United States.

The Germans didn't just introduce their beer to America; they introduced their culture of drinking beer. German-style beer gardens, where families could congregate and sip their suds outdoors, created some of the first urban green spaces in the country. The German brewers provided bands for entertainment and even sent trolleys and beer wagons to pick up people in the city and transport them to the beer gardens.

Adolphus Busch in 1890. *Courtesy Missouri Historical Society via Wikimedia Commons.*

The German brewers—including a very astute Union Army veteran named Adolphus Busch—began to develop beer empires, and the advent of pasteurization, refrigeration, and a nationwide rail system made it possible to ship beer all over the country. Indeed, Busch's St. Louis-based business was so vertically integrated that it included a glasswork for making bottles, ice plants, and even a refrigerated railroad car company.[175]

Not all the beer was being shipped. German brewers set up their own plants all over the South. In Augusta, Georgia, the Augusta Brewing Company was opened in 1888 by a couple of German-descended brewers from Kentucky named John Pank and Edward Herman. They produced a brand of lager called Belle of Georgia and also exported a Belle of Carolina beer across the border to South Carolina, which had started a state-run dispensary system in 1892, and North Carolina. They sold as far south as Florida—under the label Belle of Florida, of course—and even set up a branch in Cuba after the Spanish-American War in 1899.[176]

As the competition for customers heated up, brewers underwrote new saloons and struck exclusive sales deals with existing ones. They paid for licenses and rent, (and bribes when needed), and provided the fixtures and decorations, including large prints of a painting of *Custer's Last Stand*, a signature of Anheuser-Busch saloons. Customers were enticed to come in and stay awhile with live music and free snacks and lunches—also paid for by the brewers—which were loaded with salt, making it necessary to drink more beer to quench one's thirst before staggering back to work or home.

Naturally, the competing breweries wanted to have their own saloons across the street from each other, sort of like Walgreens and CVS today, so there was a tremendous proliferation of drinking places. According to Daniel Okrent's book *Last Call: The Rise and Fall of Prohibition*, "the number of saloons in the United States increased from 100,000 in 1870 to nearly 300,000 by 1900." [177] By 1909, 70 percent of them were owned or affiliated—"tied" was the jargon—with German brewing companies.[178] Sure, you could get a liquor drink in a saloon, but liquor was more commonly sold by the bottle in package stores, so the distilleries weren't as dependent on saloons as the brewers were. The hostility that arose between the liquor producers and the beer producers would contribute to the downfall of both.

This cartoon appeared in the *Hawaii Gazette* in 1902, showing the partnership between the WCTU and the ASL in fighting a brewer. *The University of Hawaii at Manoa via Wikimedia Commons.*

German brewers peddled their product as a health drink. Advertising posters often featured wholesome-looking women holding a frothy mug. Some brewers insisted you couldn't even get drunk from beer, all evidence to the contrary. According to Okrent, the United States Brewers' Association, the industry trade group, declared that spirits caused "domestic misery, pauperism, disease and crime." Beer was simply "liquid bread."[179] The fabulously successful and wealthy Adolphus Busch was probably still making that claim when he died in 1913 of cirrhosis of the liver.

The saloon-smashing Women's Christian Temperance Union leader Carry Nation would not have been surprised. "Beer is poison," she flatly states in her 1903 autobiography, *The Use and Need of the Life of Carry A. Nation*, relating how, to prove a point, she drank a bottle of Schlitz beer and had her friends take her to a local doctor who had been prescribing beer to patients. "I fell limp on the sofa and said: 'Doctor, what is the matter with me?'" The doctor took her vital signs and looked grave, whereupon she told him it was all due to drinking a beer—the same stuff he prescribed. "This Doctor was a kind man and meant well, but it must have been ignorance that made him say beer could ever be used as medicine," she concluded, adding that any doctor who prescribed beer or whiskey was either "a fool or a knave."[180]

No wonder many saloons bore signs that read, "All Nations Welcome Except Carry."

Saloon keepers, beholden to brewers, were under constant pressure to produce profits. Sometimes they did this by ignoring laws regarding business hours or by selling to minors or people who were visibly over their limit, but when sales lagged, they might turn to side hustles to bring in revenue. Unfortunately, these tended to be illegal and unsavory activities like gambling and prostitution, which made the saloons even more despicable places in the minds of the temperance crowd.

Temperance advocates were horrified that the German beer gardens were open on Sundays and that children were watching their parents drink beer. Even a brighter, cleaner, more cheerful saloon without prostitution and gambling was still a saloon where men had too much to drink, wasted their wages, and went home to beat up their wives and children. The growing unpopularity of the saloon led to the forming of an anti-alcohol group to take them on. Enter the Anti-Saloon League.

A Brief History of Brewing in Charleston

Charleston, South Carolina provides a microcosm of the American brewing industry, from the founding of its first brewery by an English immigrant, Edmund Egan, in the decade before the Revolutionary War, to the emergence of the craft beer industry in the last decade of the twentieth century.

According to Timmons Pettigrew's book *Charleston Beer*, Egan and a partner built a brewery on Charleston's Magazine Street around 1770. Originally, they had to depend on shipments of hops and malt from the northern colonies to make their beer. As British restrictions and resulting boycotts began hampering production, they turned to providing local farmers with free barley seeds and promising to buy their crops. By 1772, the products of Egan's brewery had gotten so popular that the company began using the motto, "Let the beer Justify itself."[181] Egan and his partner, John Calvert, were both supporters of the revolutionary cause, and their brewery, run largely by slaves, survived it. When George Washington came to town in 1791, it was still in business, though under another owner. The name of Edmund Egan is carried on today by Edmund's Oast, a brewery and restaurant which has locations on King Street and Morrison Drive in Charleston.[182]

Fast forward to 1857, when two brothers with the German surname of Döscher opened Palmetto Brewing Company in Charleston. Pettigrew writes that they brewed a German-style lager and sold it in glass bottles embossed

The bar at Palmetto Brewing Company gives a tip of the hat to the past with a mural depicting early Charleston beer makers. *Author photo.*

with a Palmetto tree, the state tree of South Carolina.[183] Their operation was a miniature version of Adolphus Busch's, with a brewery, ice factory, bottling operation, and stables for the horses that pulled their beer wagons. The brewery survived the Civil War and the devastating 1886 earthquake, celebrating with a special release Earthquake Beer. In the 1890s, the company hawked its German-style lager, Koppelman's, made with "the finest German hops." It even briefly changed its name to Germania Brewing Company, capitalizing on the popularity of German lager.[184] But trouble was coming. Even before South Carolina went dry in 1916, Germania Beer Company was having cash flow problems. It filed for bankruptcy in 1915 and closed the following year. (A similar fate met the Augusta Brewing Company, which was forced to change its name to Augusta Beverage and Ice Company. It struggled on for a few more years, then closed in 1921.[185])

Fast forward again to the late 1980s, when friends and beer enthusiasts Ed Falkenstein and Louis Bruce took a windsurfing vacation to Oregon and discovered a craft brewery they liked. They came home with the idea of starting a similar operation in Charleston and decided to honor the Döscher brothers by using the name Palmetto Brewing Company. It took some doing, as state laws governing alcohol production and sales were antiquated, but in 1993 the friends poured their first legal glass of Amber Ale. The brewery, at 289 Huger Street, was the first legal craft brewery in South Carolina.[186] When Pettit wrote his book in 2011, there were four breweries in Charleston. Today, there are close to forty in and around the city. ■

Begun in Ohio in 1893 by a visionary Methodist minister, the Rev. Howard Hyde Russell, the Anti-Saloon League became one of the most successful pressure groups in U.S. political history. Russell's chief acolyte and the ASL's leader in everything but name was its legal counsel, Wayne B. Wheeler, who so intimidated politicians that he came to be known as "Boss Dry." Working with the WCTU, the mainstream Protestant denominations, suffragists, and even hate groups such as the Ku Klux Klan, the ASL was able to dry up a large percent of the country state-by-state and finally convince an overwhelming number of Americans to put in place the first constitutional amendment that denied rights rather than expanding them.[187] Its methods were simple: a laser focus on the objective of getting rid of all alcohol, and retribution to anyone who stood in the way. (Carry A. Nation wasn't impressed with the ASL, by the way, declaring "those who control it are generally there for the salary."[188])

Of course, it wasn't just the persistence of the temperance lobby that made this happen. A confluence of factors led to the passage and ratification of the Eighteenth Amendment.

For one thing, there was the progressive movement, which began around 1890, with its over-arching goals of tightening the wide gap between the haves and the have-nots, fighting government corruption, and limiting the power of corporations.[189] Progressives came from both the Democratic and Republican folds, with different aims in mind: the vote and equal pay for women, civil rights for African Americans, improved working conditions for laborers, universal public education, and availability of birth control (it was then illegal to even share information about it). Not every progressive agreed with every aim, and some worked against them. Woodrow Wilson, elected president in 1912, had championed some progressive reforms as governor of New Jersey, but he was a native Southerner and segregationist who turned back the clock on civil rights for Blacks.

The linkage of the women's suffrage and temperance movements was another important factor. Republicans, who tended to oppose both, knew women voters were mostly dry and, when given the vote, would work for a dry country. Even here, there were divergences within parties. Theodore Roosevelt, a Republican, was a supporter of suffrage. Woodrow Wilson, who was very much a women-belong-in-the-kitchen kind of guy, proved immune to the pleas of the women picketing the White House until the eleventh hour. Incidentally, the two men loathed each other.

The stamp of the progressive period is evident when you look at the number of constitutional amendments passed in the second decade of the twentieth century: four, of which the first had a tremendous impact on the passage of the Eighteenth Amendment. This was the Sixteenth Amendment, ratified in 1913, which created the income tax and with it a new stream of revenue for the U.S. Treasury. The excise tax on alcohol, the collection of which had caused much consternation in the post-Civil War South, had been responsible for 30 percent of federal revenue in 1910.[190]

The Anti-Saloon League held its 1913 convention in Columbus, Ohio and announced plans to seek a constitutional amendment banning alcohol. *Courtesy Library of Congress.*

That year, the ASL had its annual convention in Columbus, Ohio and announced its intention to go after a national Prohibition amendment. It was introduced by Alabama congressman Richmond P. Hobson, who went down in history as "the father of Prohibition," even though the amendment barely got a majority of votes, far short of the two-thirds needed.[191] In fact, when the vote was held, Hobson had already lost his seat in Congress due to his slightly moderate stand on race. His constituents didn't share his view, nor did most of his fellow Southern lawmakers.

A button from the Virginia ASL used the same Latin phrase that John Wilkes Booth shouted when he shot Abraham Lincoln, meaning "thus always to tyrants." *Courtesy Virginia Historical Society.*

The Prohibition ball was really rolling now. Wayne B. Wheeler re-focused his efforts from Ohio to Washington, and a Methodist minister and future bishop in Virginia, James Cannon, Jr., began lobbying Southern lawmakers who were on the fence because of their concern for "states' rights." Daniel Okrent describes Cannon as "nasty, brutish, and short,"[192] but he was highly effective. The ASL harnessed its efforts to the prejudices that were escalating against minority groups, who were the objects of violent attacks by Whites throughout the first decades of the century.

The tidal wave of immigrants that had washed into the big cities aroused much suspicion and downright hatred from the temperance types, especially since so many of these newcomers were not Protestant and had lifestyle and religious practices that involved wine. The South and West had far fewer immigrants, but mob violence and lynchings were often set off by claims that a White woman had been raped by a Black man (or men). The temperance crowd used this as a scare tactic, raising the specter of the Black man enraged by liquor in order to move lawmakers into their column.

The immigrants who so aroused the distaste of the protestant Prohibitionists were from a different part of Europe than the founders of America, namely eastern Europe (Russia) and southern Europe (Italy and Greece). Many of them were Jewish and many were Catholic. But another immigrant group, one whose members were now second and third generation Americans, became the focus of hatred when the Great War broke out in Europe in July 1914.

Adam Hochschild writes of this time in his book *American Midnight: The Great War, a Violent Peace, and Democracy's Forgotten Crisis*. Although the United States was technically neutral until April 1917, the public was fed anti-German propaganda as soon as the war started in 1914. With the declaration of war, "patriots" attacked people who dared to speak German, no matter their American citizenry, and several states, including Louisiana, banned teaching the language in schools. "The American Defense Society, whose honorary president was ex-president Theodore Roosevelt, declared, 'The sound of the German language...reminds us of the murder of a million helpless old men, unarmed men, women and children...the ravishment and murder of young girls,'" Hochschild wrote.[193] He quotes a Methodist minister who declared, "It is the Christian duty of Americans to decorate convenient lamp posts with German spies and agents of the Kaiser, native or foreign-born."[194]

As America was sending its young men to France to die in the trenches and in fiery airplane crashes, almost laughable steps were taken. "Berlin, Iowa, became Lincoln," Hochschild writes. "Chicago's Bismarck Hotel became the Hotel Randolf. The hamburger was now the liberty sandwich, and German shepherds, Alsatian shepherds. Some transformations are still with us, such as from the frankfurter to the hot dog."[195]

If this all seems silly, remember that in 2003 when we were ticked off at the French for their unwillingness to support the first Gulf War, the owner of a restaurant in North Carolina changed his menu to list "Freedom Fries" rather than "French Fries." The notion was taken up by his member of Congress, who got the capitol cafeterias to use it too. Thankfully, the fad was short lived. By 2006, the cafeterias' menu listing was quietly changed back to French Fries with no fanfare.[196]

But the violence and discrimination leveled at Germans in the United States was anything but silly. People with German accents lost their jobs. Some were tarred and feathered. In Illinois in the spring of 1918, a German-born miner was lynched, and the eleven men indicted for his murder were acquitted after less than an hour of jury deliberation. Their attorney had argued that "patriotic murder" was not a crime, and the culprits were photographed outside the courthouse, waving American flags. This was the only lynching of a German during the war years, but thousands were interned.[197]

The German brewers did their best to resist, in ways both obvious and nefarious. They bribed friendly publishers, for example, and underwrote the campaigns of wet candidates for office. They also redoubled their efforts to present beer as a healthy beverage. A Detroit brewer published advertising cards that showed a rosy-cheeked toddler in a highchair hoisting a large stein, with the words, "The youngster, ruddy with good cheer/Serenely sips his Lager Beer."[198]

A Gies Beer advertising card suggested even babies enjoyed a good brew. *Courtesy Detroit Historical Society.*

All of this was red meat to the temperance crowd, who had managed to get the two-thirds of the votes they needed to pass what became the Eighteenth Amendment in December 1917. By the time the Armistice was declared at 11 a.m. on November 11, 1918—the time was significant, because fighting continued up to the last second, costing thousands of lives—most of the ratification votes were in hand. Mississippi had been the first to cast a favorable vote, followed by Virginia, in January 1918. Most of the other Southern states cast their "yes" vote by the end of that year. North Carolina was the last, casting its "yes" vote on January 16, 1919, the same day Nebraska's ratification put a bow on the package. Only two states, Connecticut and Rhode Island, opposed ratification. The country had a full year to figure out what to do with all the booze it had on hand and how to enforce the new law.

One member of Congress who was delighted to be in the thick of shaping a dry America was a freshman from Georgia named William David Upshaw. The editor of a Christian newspaper, an evangelist and speaker, he had been vice president of Georgia's Anti-Saloon League and was instrumental in passing the state's "bone-dry" law in 1907. His nicknames included "Earnest Willie" and "the Georgia Cyclone."[199]

Born near Newnan, Georgia the year after the Civil War ended, Upshaw suffered a serious spine injury as a boy when he fell off a farm wagon and spent seven years in bed. He was using a wheelchair by the time he began classes at Mercer University in Macon, but eventually was able to get about on crutches. He never tried to hide his condition, flaunting his crutches in every photograph taken of him, even when sitting down.

W.D. Upshaw proclaimed himself "the driest of the dry." Here, he and other members of Congress hold giant bones as they take the "bone-dry" pledge. *Courtesy Library of Congress.*

When he ran for Congress in 1918, he designated "the American flag and the American home" as the main planks of his platform but was firmly in favor of a national solution to the liquor problem, which he deemed even more important than an infringement on the South's beloved "states' rights." He told the *Atlanta Constitution* that "a national evil requires a national remedy."[200] He also parted ways with many of his fellow lawmakers—including the entire Georgia delegation[201]—in supporting women's suffrage. "The war demands upon woman and her wonderful patriotic response to these demands have inevitably thrust forward the cause for which many of America's 'uncrowned queens' have contented [sic] for many years," he said. And, of course, most of those women would vote dry.

But in other ways, Upshaw hewed to the dark forces that were in place in the war and post-war years. During a speech in Savannah in December 1919, he suggested the rest of the nation could learn something from the South with its "Anglo-Saxon manhood...negro labor...and orthodox ideals in building God-fearing character." In other words, he was a White supremacist. The resurgence of the Ku Klux Klan had begun in 1915 in Atlanta, which was the district he represented, and he was a staunch defender. He also "urged the expulsion of alien enemies, radicals and Bolshevists," a newspaper report said.[202] J. Edgar Hoover, an avowed hater of radicals and Bolshevists, must have been rubbing his hands together in glee.

Upshaw was returned to office in 1920 and came to Washington in 1921, eager to get to work. So did the Republican majority, its "vote dry-drink wet" president, Warren G. Harding, and a slew of unsavory characters who joined his administration.

ELLIOTT WHITE SPRINGS AND THE 'LOST GENERATION'

Now, imagine you are a young service man coming home from the war. Somehow you have survived the hellish trench warfare, German U-boat assaults on your navy vessel, or the aerial dogfights of the fledgling army air force. In Europe, you have gotten accustomed to drinking alcohol; indeed, it was part of military life. Rum and whiskey were used medicinally to treat shock and shell shock. Soldiers were given tots of rum or gin before they went over the

continues on next page

Elliott White Springs cut a dashing figure as a pilot during the Great War. *Courtesy Springs-Close Family Archive.*

top of the trenches, and the aviators were famous for drinking while on duty and, especially, while on leave. (Sailors had to labor under the alcohol ban of Navy Secretary Josephus Daniels, a strict teetotaler, who banned anything stronger than coffee. That's why we still call it a "Cup of Joe.")

So the doughboys came home, many of them horribly mutilated and mentally unbalanced, some already desperately alcoholic, to a country where even 2.5 percent beer and light wine would be banned on January 16, 1920. Is it any wonder that so many of them high-tailed it back to Europe to join the expatriates of the "Lost Generation"?

One of the top American flying aces of World War I was a South Carolina cotton mill owner's son named Elliott White Springs. His biographer, Burke Davis, described him as "one of the most fearless of combat pilots—and the most accomplished bartender in uniform."[203] Born in Lancaster, South Carolina in 1896, Springs was a daredevil and a rake from an early age, once luring a neighbor girl under his house with a churn of strawberry ice cream. By the time he got to Princeton in 1913, he had more sophisticated tools to entice young ladies. He purchased his first car, a Stutz Bearcat convertible, by putting it on his bill at New York's Vanderbilt Hotel and paying with a check from his tyrannical and often-exasperated father. [204]

Springs was accepted into flight training for the U.S. Army Signal Corps in 1917, becoming fast friends with two other young pilots from the South, John McGavock Grider of Arkansas, and Laurence Callahan, a native of Louisville, Kentucky. They called themselves the Three Musketeers. After completing their training, they took a ship to England, planning to join a squadron in Italy. (On the ship over, one of their fellow passengers was Captain Fiorello La Guardia, who became one of Prohibition's greatest foes as a member of Congress.) They took additional flight training in Great Britain and, instead of going to Italy, were attached to a British squadron headed to the front in France.

It's a wonder they made it out of England. In between daredevil flying at the training camp—Springs cracked up two planes in two days—they gave a dinner party in London in which their scanty food rations were accompanied by "a large tub of eggnog with pitchers of robust mint juleps and cocktails in addition," biographer Davis wrote. "There was a bottle of port and one of champagne at each place at the dinner table."[205]

The heavy drinking continued when the Three Musketeers flew to France. Elliott christened his plane the *Mint Julep* and winged over the English Channel with a full flask and an extra-large cocktail shaker in the cockpit.[206]

Like many of the American pilots who came to the front in the last year of the war, Springs arrived with youthful exuberance and departed in near despair. The men were flying Sopwith Camels, finicky contraptions made of canvas airplane cloth on a plywood and metal frame, and the casualties were horrible.[207] The Three Musketeers lost one of their squadron leaders and many of their fellow pilots in fiery crashes, and the daily patrols, bombing raids, trench strafing, and dogfights were nerve shredding and soul destroying. The hardest loss for Springs was that of Mac Grider, who disappeared during a raid in June and was reported dead a few weeks later.

Springs continued to fly all summer, avenging his comrade's death by shooting down enemy planes, but in one devastating raid he was the only member of the flight he was leading to come back alive. In September 1918 he was sent to Paris to recover from the influenza that was ravaging the troops and, by the time he was well enough to fly again, the war was over. Suffering from what we would today call PTSD, he was troubled by depression for the rest of his life and continued to be a heavy drinker, Davis writes.

He shared his thoughts about Prohibition in a letter to his stepmother. In typical sardonic style, he wrote, "Makes me think of that film 'Intolerance.'[208] One half of the world has already been trying to 'high tone' the other half... Of course it will make the U.S.A. a cleaner, more wholesome, efficient and decent place to live in. Imagine a fanatic of the 15th Century saying to another—'If you can only kill off a few of their leaders and force the others to join our church or kill them, too. Europe will be saved and the kingdom of God exalted.'"[209]

He concluded, quite accurately, "Not that it makes any difference to me."

continues on next page

He returned home in February 1919 and spent the next years alternately slaving for his taskmaster father and escaping to a life of excess in the speakeasies of New York. As a member of the wealthy class, Springs always had a ready supply of bootleg liquor on hand and had entrée to the best nightspots—although when home in South Carolina, he often had to make do with "corn." He chronicled his World War I experience and his enjoyment of drinking and fast women in nine novels and many short stories which were published in the best-selling magazines of the 1920s, earning the equivalent of $4 million.

In his novel *Leave Me with a Smile*, he described his main character, a shell-shocked aviator, meeting his girlfriend in New York:

"She had arranged parties for every day and every night. The pace was faster than ever—the pace they loved. There were many old friends. Prohibition was the new national joke and he was initiated into flask-carrying, shown the new speakeasies and introduced to bootleggers."[210]

To the surprise of almost everyone, when Elliott White Springs inherited his father's business in 1931, he expanded it into one of the most successful textile empires in the South. He died of pancreatic cancer in 1959, having watched his only son perish at age twenty-one in the fate he had been spared at the same age: a fiery airplane crash. ■

The signature drink of *Leave Me with a Smile*, one of Elliott White Springs's most successful novels, was the brandy smash. This recipe came from a cocktail book—which was complete with recipes for bathtub gin—self-published in New York in 1928 by Charles S. Warnock. *Giggle Water* has one of the longest subtitles of any book I've come across: *Including Eleven Famous Cocktails of the Most Exclusive Club of New York As Served Before the War When Mixing Drinks Was an Art*. I'm sure Elliott knocked back a few during his many visits there.

Giggle Water, published in 1928, coined a phrase still used to describe a drink.[211]

AVIATORS' EGGNOG

According to Ann Y. Evans, archivist of the Springs Close Family Foundation, eggnog was a Christmas tradition in the Springs family going back to the early 1800s. In Elliott Springs's 1926 book *War Birds: Diary of an Unknown Aviator*, the narrator writes from a training camp in Scotland:

"Everybody has gone crazy over eggnog: Springs and Oliver found a dairy where they got some cream and they made eggnog. Everybody demanded more. The next day they made five gallons and it lasted ten minutes. Then we got a big dairy vat and put all the Waacs [Women's Army Auxiliary Corps] to work beating eggs...Springs's father sent him ten pounds of sugar and we had three cases of brandy. It must have made fifteen or twenty gallons. Everybody from the Colonel down came over to drink it. By lunch time every officer in Ayr was full of eggnog."[212]

This recipe uses the same ingredients and will satisfy a squadron, making eight and a half gallons of eggnog.

- 10 dozen eggs
- 22 quarts cream
- 8¾ quarts spirits
- 2½ pounds sugar

Separate the eggs. Beat the yolks hard and long. Slowly pour and stir in the cream. Stir in the sugar. Add the spirits in a thin stream, stirring at the same time. Beat the egg whites and divide into equal portions. Pour and stir in half, and then pour the other half on top without stirring.

To quench the thirst of a smaller crowd, make two gallons of eggnog with 2 dozen eggs, 4 quarts of cream, 3 pints of spirits and a pound of sugar.

—Recipe adapted from Franklin Farms Eggnog in
Eat, Drink and Be Merry in Maryland by Frederick Philip Stieff[213]

BRANDY SMASH

(Use small bar-glass)

- Take 1 teaspoonful of white sugar
- 2 tablespoonfuls of water
- 3 or 4 sprigs of tender mint
- 1 wine-glass full of brandy [I guess the size of the glass is up to you!]

Press the mint in the sugar and water to extract the flavor, add the brandy, and fill the glass two-thirds full of shaved ice. Stir thoroughly and ornament with half a slice of orange, and a few sprigs of mint. Serve with a straw.

Prohibition Expedition: Ale Trails

Craft breweries have sprung up everywhere in the past two decades. You probably have one in your town, or in a nearby city where the staff will be glad to tell you about their methods and specialties and let you sample a single beer or a flight. Google "ale trail," "brew trail," "beer trail," or any variation of these plus a location and you're sure to find a listing of places that will quench your thirst for beer. One of the recent phenomena is the creation of family-friendly breweries, with playgrounds and games for the kids. Maybe the Germans had the right idea with their nineteenth century beer gardens! Here are a few in the Charleston, South Carolina area.

An oak tree with low-hanging branches attracts children visiting the Holy City Brewery in North Charleston. The brewery also has putt-putt greens, a corn hole game, and concerts. *Author photo.*

Charles Towne Fermentory—The Garden
809 Savannah Highway, West Ashley's Avondale neighborhood
www.chsfermentory.com/thegarden

Holy City Brewing • 1021 Aragon Avenue, North Charleston
https://holycitybrewing.com

Edmund's Oast Brewing Co. and Taproom • 1505 King Street #115, Charleston
www.edmundsoast.com

Ghost Monkey • 522 Wando Lane, Mt. Pleasant
www.ghostmonkeybrewery.com

CEMETERY SIDE TRIP

Elliott White Springs, his wife, and son are buried under a common tombstone in the churchyard of United Presbyterian Church, 303 Tom Hall Street, on the edge of downtown Fort Mill, South Carolina. Springs Industries, like most of the Southern textile empires of the 20th century, has a much-diminished presence in South Carolina. The company merged its home furnishings business with the Brazilian textile firm Coteminas in 2005 and announced in 2007 that it would be closing the last of its South Carolina manufacturing plants that year, ending 120 years of textile making in the United States. At its peak, the company employed 15,000 people in South Carolina.[214] Now operating under the name Springs Global, it continues to use some of the brand names developed under Elliott White Springs, including Springmaid, but all production is done in South America.

The graves of the once prominent Springs family are surrounded by a rusting fence in a Fort Mill cemetery. *Author photo.*

RECOMMENDED READING

Last Call: The Rise and Fall of Prohibition by Daniel Okrent (New York, Scribner, 2010), is my go-to book for the history of drinking in America and the travesty of Prohibition. It was the basis for the outstanding Ken Burns series *Prohibition*, which first ran on public television in 2011.

American Midnight: The Great War, a Violent Peace, and Democracy's Forgotten Crisis by Adam Hochschild (New York: Mariner Books, 2022). Woodrow Wilson, J. Edgar Hoover, Attorney General A. Mitchell Palmer and other zealots used the war as an excuse to find "radicals" under every rock and mete out punishment that would never be tolerated today. One hopes.

War Bird: The Life and Times of Elliott White Springs by Burke Davis (Chapel Hill: University of North Carolina Press, 1987) is a warts-and-all portrait, well-illustrated with photographs.

Charleston Beer: A High Gravity History of Low Country Brewing by Timmons Pettigrew (Charleston: History Press, 2011) tells the story of beer making in the Holy City from colonial days to the birth of the craft beer industry in post-Prohibition days.

Chapter Six

The Department of Easy Virtue

AS A SMALL CHILD in Concord, North Carolina, Gaston Bullock Means stole the coins his mother had been collecting for the Episcopal church's mission committee, pinning the crime on the maid. Mrs. Means believed her dimpled darling. The innocent maid was dismissed and left in tears, while Gaston, gazing at her through a window and fingering the coins in his pocket, remembered them making "the sweetest music I've ever heard."[215]

It was the beginning of a life of duplicity that didn't end until he was buried in the family plot under a marker bearing nothing but his name and the dates of his birth and death. The space between those dates has quite a story to tell.

FBI director J. Edgar Hoover called Means "the most amazing figure in contemporary criminal history"—and he knew some doozies. Edwin P. Hoyt titled his biography of Means *Spectacular Rogue* and called him the "symbol of American criminality and corruption in the gaudiest and most lawless era in the nation's history."[216] Means's own granddaughter, writing more than eighty years after his death, described him as an "arch-swindler and master liar."[217]

According to biographer Hoyt, Gaston Means was the eldest son of the mayor of Concord, himself an attorney. He attended the University of

The Means house is on a tree-lined street near downtown Concord, N.C. *Leo Smith photo.*

North Carolina for a few years, distinguishing himself neither academically nor on the football field, then got a sales job with Cannon Mills, owned by his down-the-street neighbor James W. Cannon. Working for Cannon—originator of the Cannon terry cloth towel—he lived a high life in New York and Chicago for about a decade. When he was thirty-four, he met a convent-educated young woman named Julie Patterson and used his silver tongue—well coated with a honeyed Southern accent—to woo her. Originally uninterested in the obese, balding "old man," Julie admitted that she became "wild about him." [218] They were married in 1913. After a roller coaster of a life with Means, Julie recalled telling her mother: "Mamma, I'd hate to marry a man who just went to the office every day. I want more out of life than that." She concluded, somewhat ruefully, "I got it."[219]

According to Hoyt, Means lost his job with the Cannon company the following year. He had a lifelong fascination with intrigue and bluffed himself into a job at the Burns Detective Agency, run by the then-well-respected William J. Burns. A former chief of the U.S. Secret Service, Burns has been called the "American Sherlock Holmes" for his ability to solve a crime on the slimmest of clues.[220] At his agency, Burns's methods were effective, if not always quite legal, which suited Means just fine. While in his employ he also served as a German agent and propagandist during the first World War and was approached to safeguard the interests of a dim-witted wealthy widow. As her business manager, Hoyt wrote, he embezzled more than half a million dollars of her money and, when she was about to discover she was broke, took her rabbit hunting late in the evening outside Concord and brought her back with a hole in the back of her head. He claimed she had accidentally discharged the new handgun he had given her.[221] He was tried for the murder of Maude King in December 1917 at the Cabarrus County Courthouse, with eight of North Carolina's most prominent attorneys on his defense panel. After deliberating overnight, the jury declared him innocent, and he went home to celebrate Christmas with his family.[222]

Means would not find future juries quite so sympathetic.

In 1921 he got a job with his old friend Burns, now heading up the Bureau of Investigation (later renamed the Federal Bureau of Investigation) at the Department of Justice, which Means used as a perch for milking bootleggers for hundreds of thousands of dollars in bribes, damaging the reputations of two cabinet secretaries, and convincing half the country that Florence Harding had murdered her husband.[223]

William J. Burns was called the "American Sherlock Holmes. *Courtesy Library of Congress.*

Means was perfectly at home working at what became known as "the Department of Easy Virtue," led by Harry M. Daugherty, whose only qualification for attorney general, other than being a lawyer, was that he had managed Warren G. Harding's successful presidential campaign. Harding, an Ohio newspaper publisher who readily admitted he was not up to the job of chief executive, headed the most corrupt presidential administration of the 20th century—the 19th and 21st have their own contenders—partly because he was a hypocritical fool with untrustworthy friends and partly because Prohibition created unheard-of opportunities for accumulating illegal wealth. By the time Harding took the oath of office in March 1921, Prohibition had been in effect for more than a year, and the machinery that would keep the country lubricated with illegal booze was up and running. It would get more efficient—and more deadly—as the decade wore on.

The South, of course, had a head start on much of the nation when it came to making, obtaining, and moving illegal booze. By 1919, when the Eighteenth Amendment was ratified, every Southern state except Louisiana had already enacted alcohol bans. In response, moonshiners ramped up production and rum runners sailed to the Caribbean islands to buy alcohol and smuggle it back to the states—some of it locally produced rum and some fancier stuff exported from England and Europe. The small producers and rum-running entrepreneurs, like the legendary Bill McCoy of Jacksonville, Florida, were soon put out of business by criminal gangs. In addition, booze was being smuggled over the Canadian and Mexican borders by the millions of gallons and produced in smaller quantities everywhere from slum kitchens in Chicago to abandoned mines in the West.

Andrew Volstead sponsored the legislation that created the enforcement mechanism for Prohibition. *Courtesy Library of Congress.*

While banning the production, transportation, and sale of "intoxicating liquors," the Eighteenth Amendment contained no other specifics except that the federal government and the individual states would have "concurrent power" to enforce it. The old saying "the devil is in the details" proved true when the regulatory machinery for Prohibition was enacted late in 1919, over the veto of President Woodrow Wilson. The Volstead Act, named for its Republican sponsor, Representative Andrew John Volstead of Minnesota, was heavily influenced by Wayne B. Wheeler, legal counsel and political boss of the Anti-Saloon League. Enforcement of the law was placed under the Bureau of Internal Revenue, presided over with little enthusiasm by Treasury Secretary Andrew W. Mellon, with prosecution handled by the Bureau of Prohibition at the Justice Department.

The Volstead Act, nineteen pages in small print, may have been an eye opener to people who had supported the Eighteenth Amendment simply because they didn't like saloons. Much to the surprise of many Americans, the act didn't simply apply to "intoxicating liquors" as the amendment specified, but to *any* beverage that contained more than half a percent of alcohol, including beer and wine. An exception was made for beverages produced from fruits (other than grapes), a sop to the nation's farmers who didn't want to be denied a refreshing draught of hard cider. Senator Alben W. Barkley of Kentucky asked, perhaps facetiously, why the juice of corn couldn't be exempted as well. [224]

Another important exception, aimed at placating the upper classes, was alcohol that an individual had on hand when Prohibition went into effect. Many wealthy people simply stocked up before January 17 and hoped to ride things out. The Eighteenth Amendment didn't make drinking alcohol illegal, remember, just the manufacture, sale, and transportation of it. So the Volstead Act allowed people to keep alcohol for personal use and to serve to "bona fide" guests in their homes. This enabled President Harding to bring his liquor stash into the White House, where First Lady Florence Harding served it to his cronies while they played poker and to occasional visiting cabinet members, such as Daugherty and Mellon. (Incidentally, Woodrow Wilson also took his liquor along when he moved out of the White House, but he had vetoed the Volsead Act, so at least he wasn't being a hypocrite about it.)

Two more exceptions helped keep the country very damp. The law allowed wine to be used in religious sacraments and ceremonies, which resulted in an astonishing increase in the number of purported rabbis in the country—including two with the surnames Maguire and Houlihan—and liquor to be used as medicine.[225] Under the act, a licensed physician could prescribe one pint of liquor every ten days, to be dispensed by a licensed pharmacist. (You may remember that Jay Gatsby, the bootlegger in F. Scott Fitzgerald's novel *The Great Gatsby*, was said to own a chain of drug stores. In fact, the Walgreens drugstore chain grew from twenty stores to 525 during Prohibition.[226]) The American Medical Association, which had

This prescription for medicinal whiskey was written for a man living in Covington, Kentucky in 1929. It was offered in an auction on eBay.

determined just a few years before that liquor had no medicinal applications, made an about-face when its members realized they could charge three dollars or so for each scrip they wrote. In 1922 the AMA suddenly discovered twenty-seven ailments, ranging from snakebite to old age, that could benefit from a shot or two.[227]

Twenty-nine million gallons of alcohol that distillers had on hand when Prohibition began had to be placed in government bonded warehouses under twenty-four-hour guard and could only be withdrawn with government-issued permits. In Louisville, the makers of Old Grand-Dad bourbon created a legal company called American Medicinal Spirits Company and sold one-pint bottles to drugstores. This was perfectly above board and kept several of Kentucky's largest distilleries in operation.

Illegal practices included buying shuttered distilleries and slowly "milking" the barrels in storage for sale on the bootleg market, replacing the booze with water and industrial alcohol. This is what happened to the Jack Daniel's distillery, which had vacated Lynchburg, Tennessee for St. Louis, Missouri when Tennessee went dry in 1908, and had 893 barrels of whiskey on hand slowly evaporating in its warehouse. Daniel himself had died by then, and his nephew, Len Motlow, was trading mules and waiting for the country to come to its senses. In 1923, he agreed to sell the stock for $125,000, not knowing the buyer was a front man for the notorious Cincinnati bootlegger George Remus.[228]

The crimes outlined in the Volstead Act were classified as misdemeanors but carried penalties of up to $2,000 (almost $30,000 in current dollars) and five years in prison. Enforcement was funded with a paltry $2.1 million (about $36 million in current funds), and states took up their "concurrent" duties with a widely varying degree of vigor.[229] At the insistence of the drys, Prohibition agents were not hired through the civil service, thus creating a police force of political appointees who were often unqualified, ill-trained, inept, and/or corrupt. The straight-arrow assistant attorney general in charge of prosecution, Mabel Walker Willebrandt, bewailed the impossibility of finding 4,000 agents who could not be

Mabel Walker Willebrandt did her best to enforce the Volstead Act. *Courtesy Library of Congress.*

bribed. During her eight years in office, she dismissed over 750 for misconduct and delinquency.[230]

Sadly, many Prohibition agents and other law enforcement officers lost their lives trying to keep the country dry. By early 1923, thirty agents had met violent ends, twenty of them in the South, according to Roy A. Haynes, the first head of the Prohibition Bureau. Others perished due to accidents while on raids, including a South Carolina agent who fell into a hole where the boiling contents of a still had just been poured. Fellow officers carried him to a nearby creek to relieve his agony, but he died of his burns.[231] The toll would continue throughout the Prohibition years, including a deputy U.S. marshal and a Wilmington, North Carolina police detective who were shot and killed while raiding a still in a swamp in 1924. Their bodies were found punctured with buckshot and bullet wounds; the moonshiners also killed their police dog.[232] A father and son were quickly arrested, convicted, executed, and buried under a joint headstone with the epitaph "At Rest."[233] It was reported that, while the verdict was being read, the siren on the police car in which the two agents had traveled to their deaths spontaneously went off and the wiring had to be severed to make it stop.[234]

As one of a handful of honest people in top leadership positions in the Harding administration, Willebrandt, known as the "Portia of Prohibition" scored some impressive victories over a ring of bootleggers in Savannah, an allegedly "bone-dry" Kentucky congressman, and some of the most prominent citizens of soaking wet Mobile, Alabama. Before long, county jails and federal prisons were teeming with violators. Most of them were small fry, though, as the still busting that made such good newspaper pictures hardly made a dent in the alcohol supply. In the South, the preponderance of people put in jail were poor Whites and poorer African Americans. Henderson Lanham, the police court judge in Rome, Georgia in 1926, occasionally mentioned a Prohibition violation in his diary. Typical was his entry for March 8, when a "bunch of Negroes" were brought in after a chitterling party. "Whisky and chitterlings were much in evidence," he wrote.[235] Meanwhile the most flagrant violators were often protected by influence, bribes, and clever legal counsel. This is where Gaston Means found his next opportunity to get rich.

As Means's biographer Hoyt tells it, he began working at the Justice Department in November 1921 and almost immediately got the word out that he could "fix" Prohibition cases. Soon though, even with the staunch

Gaston Means prepares for one of his trials. *Courtesy Library of Congress.*

backing of Bureau of Investigation Chief Burns, he aroused enough suspicion that Attorney General Daugherty put him on suspension. Curiously, he was allowed to keep his office there, and, even more curiously, landed a job with the Prohibition Bureau at the Department of Treasury, which dispatched him to New York. He uncovered some activity, alright, but quickly turned it to his own advantage, taking bribes from the big bootleggers to protect them.

Means's method, as he described it to writer May Dixon Thacker, a Virginia-born evangelist and writer for *True Confessions* magazine, was to engage two rooms at the Vanderbilt Hotel in New York. He placed a large glass goldfish bowl on a table in one room where the bootleggers were instructed to put their bribe money while he watched them through a peep hole from the connecting room.[236] He scored some points with Prohibition Bureau Chief Haynes and Willebrandt when he turned in bootleggers who would not pay him off.

Among those who did pay was Willie Haar of Savannah, Georgia, who Willebrandt would later send to prison. Means convinced Haar he could fix his income tax problems—the gambit Willebrandt had originated to convict big-time Prohibition violators who couldn't be put out of business any other way.[237] (It was what eventually sent Al Capone to prison.) One who turned him down was George Remus, a canny lawyer from Cincinnati, who had become one of the biggest bootleggers—and bribe-payers—in the country.[238] He became another Willebrandt victory, winding up in the cell beside Willie Haar's at the Atlanta Federal Penitentiary.

By October 1922, Julie Means said her husband was "hand in glove with the big bootleggers of the era," and "our futures skyrocketed." She seemed untroubled about the source of their income, recounting how they rented a mansion at 903 16th Street in Washington's tony Dupont Circle neighborhood equipped with four servants, bought a Cadillac limousine, and entertained endless streams of politicians. "Lord how the money rolled in—and out!" she wrote. [239] Not only did Means promise protection to people in the underworld, he also gave them forged withdrawal permits to remove liquor from bonded warehouses. "Anyone who approached Means suspiciously, and many of these wary bootleggers did just that, was likely to be won over by Gaston's dimpled and sincere smile, and by his businesslike manner," wrote biographer Hoyt. "Means smoked cigars and blew clouds of blue smoke in the air as he expounded on the services he could perform for his clients."[240]

Inevitably, Means's activities were so flagrant that he was caught. In October 1923, he was charged with more than a hundred violations of the Volstead Act.

President Harding had died in August while on a cross-country tour, and Daugherty's hold on the Justice Department was loosening, even though Calvin Coolidge kept him on as attorney general when he assumed the presidency. During the spring, a congressional committee called an investigation of Daugherty, and Means testified, trying to smear the reputation of Andrew Mellon as well. Daugherty was asked to resign by President Coolidge.

That summer Means was convicted and sent to prison in Atlanta. The prosecutor mockingly suggested that he spend

A political cartoon depicted the beleaguered attorney general Harry Daugherty trying to keep the skeletons in his office closet. *Cartoon by Charles Henry Sykes courtesy Wikimedia Commons.*

his time there writing a memoir to be titled *Adventures of Gaston B. Means Among the Bootleggers*. This may have planted an idea in Means's head, for upon his release in 1928, he collaborated with May Dixon Thacker to produce *The Strange Case of President Harding*. Among other things in the book, he alleged that Florence Harding, incensed by her husband's sexual affair with the young Nan Britton, had poisoned him.[241] He also threw more mud at Harry Daugherty, who had been acquitted of corruption in 1926. The book became a best-seller, six years after Mrs. Harding had died and could no longer defend herself. Though Means later admitted the whole thing was a hoax, some people to this day believe the president died at the hands of his jealous wife.

Upon his release from prison, Gaston Means took the train to Concord and entertained questions on the front porch of his Union Street North home from a reporter with the local newspaper. Among them was if he believed in Prohibition. His answer was a telling one: "I don't know, I've never seen it tried."[242] More and more people around the country were feeling the same way, but the "noble experiment" still had a few more years to run.

Gaston Means's Final Hoax

Gaston Means's final and arguably most reprehensible act was involving himself in the kidnapping case of Charles and Anne Lindbergh's infant son in 1932. He had nothing to do with the crime itself but used it to con a gullible Washington socialite out of $104,000 and land himself in prison again. The money was never found, and he never left prison.[243]

Evalyn Walsh McLean was the heiress of a silver mine fortune, the owner of the Hope Diamond, estranged wife of the publisher of the *Washington Post*, and BFF of former first lady Florence Harding. She was also a vastly silly woman with far more money than sense, once "losing" the huge diamond while staying at her vacation home in Aiken, South Carolina and finding she had hidden it in the horn of her gramophone.[244]

As Julie Means recalled it, her husband was outraged and furious when reading of the kidnapping, which occurred on March 1, 1932; the twenty-month-old Charles Jr. was snatched from his crib in the Lindbergh home in

New Jersey. "Whoever did it should be shot!" he declared. But then his mind turned to making money on the case. He knew Mrs. McLean was a friend of the Lindberghs and convinced her he could act as a go-between with the kidnappers to get the baby turned over to her. The kidnappers wanted $100,000, he said, and Mrs. McLean eagerly paid him. For the next six weeks, he led her on a merry chase, telling her the hand-over would be made first in Aiken, South Carolina and then in El Paso, Texas. He asked for and was given an additional $4,000 "for expenses." Mrs. McLean didn't have that much liquid cash and was at the point of pawning one of her diamonds when her lawyers got involved and demanded the return of the ransom money. This was where J. Edgar Hoover stepped in.

Evalyn Walsh McLean wears the Hope Diamond in this 1932 photograph. *Courtesy Library of Congress.*

Although Hoover had begun his career as a no-holds-barred communist chaser during and after World War I, he was also on the short list of honest people in the Harding Justice Department and had succeeded William J. Burns as head of the FBI. He had spent eight years cleaning up the mess left behind by Daugherty and his cohorts and was determined to create a professional

J. Edgar Hoover, shown in 1932, succeeded William J. Burns as the head of the Bureau of Investigation and emphasized "scientific policing." *Courtesy Library of Congress.*

national police force that used modern methods, such as fingerprinting, to solve crimes and catch more communists. The Lindbergh case was the catalyst that eventually gave the agency authority over kidnappings, but at this point Hoover's men were working on the case in an advisory capacity only.

continues on next page

However, they did have jurisdiction over crimes committed in the District of Columbia, where Mrs. McLean lived.

As biographer Hoyt explains, Hoover had been following Means's involvement in the Lindbergh case with interest. On May 5, Means got into his chauffeur-driven limousine and traveled from his Chevy Chase, Maryland mansion into the district. There federal agents stopped the car, and he was arrested by a U.S. marshal, charged with larceny after trust.[245] Swiftly convicted, Means was sentenced to federal prison for fifteen years, but didn't live long enough to complete his sentence.

At the end of his life, desperate for attention, Means began claiming he had masterminded the Lindbergh kidnapping and that Bruno Hauptmann was an innocent man. Hauptmann was arrested in 1934 and executed in 1936. Means died in 1938. Hoover served as FBI chief until 1972, abusing his power by harassing and blackmailing lawmakers, political dissidents, and civil rights activists. ■

For more than eighty years, people running afoul of the law in Cabarrus County, North Carolina spent time in a jail located on a lonely road outside the little town of Mt. Pleasant. Many of them had been caught for violations of liquor laws. The jail, opened in 1929, closed in 2011 when a new law enforcement and detention center was completed in downtown Concord. Today, the former jail is one of the more interesting homes of a craft distillery. Southern Grace Distilleries, which began making liquor there in 2016, produces bourbon under the label Conviction.

The place still looks like a jail. The original brick barracks, which once housed up to 200 men in dormitory-style bunkbeds, now houses 700 barrels of aging bourbon, according to Emily Burkhart, director of operations and tourism. (Her father once worked as a guard there.) Bars remain in place, as do stenciled signs reading "Cell Block West" and "Cell Block East." At the edge of the basketball court, the forbidding "hot box," where prisoners were confined for infractions, holds more barrels. Pointing out its chimney, Emily said the only time a fire was built there was in the summer. One of the four original guard towers is intact, and rows of concrete picnic tables speak of a time when prisoners met with their families outside, rain or shine. At the new detention center, meetings take place by video.

Even a Christmas wreath doesn't do much to change the grim facade of the Southern Grace barrel house, formerly a county jail. *Author photo.*

A second barracks building, built in 1987, is where the distilling in copper-lined stills, bottling, and shipping take place. The former mess hall is now the gift shop, decorated with police mug shots of celebrities such as Frank Sinatra, Mick Jagger, and Elvis Presley. There, visitors can arrange a tour and tasting for $14, order cocktails to enjoy indoors or out, and buy bottles of liquor to take home along with locally produced candles, pottery, and liquor-related items. During a shop-and-sip craft market there in December, bartender/tour guide Virginia Harper said she made almost 400 drinks.

The 1929 prison once housed 200 men. Now it houses 700 barrels of aging whiskey. *Author photo.*

If Conviction means anything, it means high proof. Burkhardt said founder Thomas Thacker doesn't like watering down his product. As a result, his Conviction Founder's Reserve is 125 proof, "aged in the sweltering heat of a prison grain bin," according to the website.[246] The cask-finished straight bourbons, like the Conviction Naranja, get flavoring from casks previously used to age wine, sherry, or cognac, and are all about 100 proof. "Naranja" is a Spanish wine flavored with Seville oranges and one of the distillery's most popular products, Emily said.

All of the whiskey, including the 130-proof Sun Dog moonshine, is made of the same mash bill of 88 percent corn and 12 percent barley.

Emily said about half the distillery's products are sold on-site to visitors who mostly hear about Southern Grace by word of mouth. That was bolstered by the television series *Ghost Hunters*, which filmed an episode there titled "Poltergeist Prison" in 2021. Emily said a man named Rufus, possibly a relation of Gaston Means, is said to be haunting the gift shop, but he doesn't show up much in the daytime when tours are given.

Conviction's Naranja bourbon whiskey is aged in casks that originally held a Spanish wine. *Photo courtesy Southern Grace Distillery.*

While my husband Leo and I shared an old fashioned made with the Conviction Naranja bourbon, Virginia Harper told us some stories about the prison she heard from relatives who had worked there. "Red" Rowland was a known moonshiner who had a pet monkey he had trained to do tricks and accept money. One day his home was raided and the monkey, terrified, ran under the house and returned with a big wad of cash. Aha! said the deputies. Evidence! But in court, Red argued that it was the monkey's money, not his. He got off that time, but later was convicted and spent a year and a day at the jail.

NARANJA OLD FASHIONED

Using a rocks glass, add

- ½ tsp of raw sugar
- 2–3 dashes of your favorite bitters
- 1 tsp water

Stir to create a slurry in the bottom of the glass. Add 2 oz. Conviction Naranja Cask Finished Bourbon. Slide in one large ice cube and stir around the cube. Rim glass with orange zest and add the peel to the drink.

Prohibition Expedition: Cabarrus County, North Carolina

The Gaston Means House, a handsome Queen Anne-style residence, is located at 138 Union Street North. The home of Cannon Mills founder J.W. Cannon is two doors down at No. 122.

In Means's youth, the commercial section of Union Street housed grocery and dry goods stores. Today you can find restaurants, coffee shops, bars, specialty boutiques and a few interesting combinations of the latter two, such as **Streakers Cold Beer and Running Gear**, 110 Union Street South, and **The Mullet Thrift n' Sip**, 27 Union Street South, where you can sip on a beer while you browse second-hand items.

Old Cabarrus County Courthouse is at 65 Union Street South. The circa 1876 courthouse, where Gaston Means was acquitted of the murder of Maude King, is now the home of the Concord Museum, www.historiccabarrus.com and the **Cabarrus Arts Council**, which operates the Davis Theatre in the former courtroom. www.cabarrusartscouncil.org

For a really good Southern-style meal to line your gut before heading to the nearby **Southern Grace Distilleries**, 130 Dutch Road, www.southerngracedistilleries.com. Stop for lunch at **Buddy's Place**, 1470 S. Main Street, Mt. Pleasant. The multi-page vinyl-coated menu offers everything from meat-and-three combinations to sandwiches, pizzas, steaks, and seafood. The Buddy Big Boy Burger boasts a meat patty weighing a full pound. While you wait, take in the décor of old farm implements and taxidermy, including a timber wolf caught in mid-howl. Still deciding? Look at the menu online at www.ourrestaurantmenu.com/buddysplace

The historic Cabarrus County Courthouse is where Gaston Means was acquitted in 1917. *Author photo.*

CEMETERY SIDE TRIP

Although he lived a life of vulgar excess (when he wasn't in prison), **Gaston Bullock Means** has a very modest grave. He is buried with his parents, two sisters, and a brother in the Oakwood Cemetery, 471 Church Street, Concord. It took some looking and the help of a cemetery maintenance man to find the graves, which don't have headstones but simple ground markers. When you go into the second entrance to the cemetery from downtown, hang a right. If you can see a Hardee's outside the fence on the right, you are getting close. The marker of Means's father, the one-time mayor of Concord, is slowly being uprooted by an oak tree, so that it looks like it is trying to climb the trunk.

Dale Earnhardt Boulevard and **Dale Earnhardt Tribute Plaza**. We'll be delving into NASCAR and its ties to bootlegging in a future chapter, but while you are in the neighborhood, journey over to Kannapolis, former home of Cannon Mills, which is connected to Concord by a highway named for Dale Earnhardt Sr., one of North Carolina's most famous NASCAR drivers. In the heart of his hometown is a meticulously maintained park featuring a nine-foot-tall bronze statue of the driver known as "The Intimidator," wearing his off-the-course uniform of short-sleeved shirt, Wrangler jeans, and cowboy boots, aviator shades peeping out of his shirt pocket. Earnhardt, the son and father of winning drivers, died in an accident during the Daytona 500 in 2001, age forty-nine. His father, Ralph, died at age forty-five of a heart attack while repairing a race car in his shop.[247]

NASCAR legend Dale Earnhardt's bronze statue stands in the heart of his hometown, Kannapolis. *Author photo.*

RECOMMENDED READING

Spectacular Rogue Gaston B. Means by Edwin P. Hoyt (Indianapolis: Bobbs-Merrill, 1963) is, unfortunately, out of print and hard to find. But if the case intrigues you, your search will repay you with a blow-by-blow account that is well worth reading.

My Life with Gaston B. Means as Told by His Wife, Julie P. Means, is based on a series of newspaper articles Mrs. Means wrote to support herself after her husband's death. Her granddaughter, Julie Means Kane, compiled and edited the columns, with annotations and illustrations, in a self-published book in 2021.

CHAPTER SEVEN

The Worm Turns

ON A BALMY JUNE AFTERNOON, I was standing on the verandah of a house built in Newnan, Georgia in the 1920s, drinking a mint julep ladled out of a tremendous silver punchbowl and listening to a bluegrass group. Newnan, about half an hour south of Atlanta, has long been called the "City of Homes," and three of the loveliest were being showcased at the annual Bourbon on the Porch fundraiser for the Newnan Carnegie Library Foundation.

It was also Southern LitFest weekend, with activities ranging from a hilarious children's play, "The Trial of the Big Bad Wolf," to a Lewis Grizzard impersonator (during his lifetime, the proudly redneck native son was one of the most popular newspaper columnists in the country), to a sobering talk about a miscarriage of justice in Jim Crow Georgia, to a display of historic Bibles at the First United Methodist Church. The Bible display kind of added balance to the weekend, which had begun with a dinner featuring a panel of local authors in a spirited toasting contest.

Late Saturday afternoon, Bourbon on the Porch commenced. Ticket holders were presented commemorative whiskey glasses, paid for by the mayor's real estate firm, that they carried on the verandah circuit. They wound up on the lawn of the McRitchie-Hollis Museum for barbecue, music, and a special dessert cocktail, Patty's Boll Weevil.

Guests enjoy barbecue and dessert cocktails at the Bourbon on the Porch event in Newnan. *Author photo.*

PATTY'S BOLL WEEVIL

The recipe for this dessert beverage came from Bourbon on the Porch organizers Michael and Larisa Scott's next-door neighbor, Patty Gironda, who runs a B&B, the Casa Bella, with her husband, Ron. Michael writes, "She is a gourmet chef. I asked her six months ago to come up with a memorable and signature cocktail for Southern Lit-Fest. Every other week she would call, and Larisa and I would walk next door to sample her concoctions. Week after week we would stagger home thinking, 'This is not quite what we need.' Well, on the fifth try she came up with the recipe you tasted on Saturday."

FA coconut popsicle dipped in brown liquor makes a refreshing dessert. *Author photo.*

He explained that the brown of the Creme de Cacao represents the boll weevil, an insect that devastated the South's cotton economy in W.D. Upshaw's day, while the coconut popsicle represents the cotton, and "the rich caramel of the bourbon captures the warm hospitality of the town that embraces inspirational authors and artists from all over the world."

In a small, wide, footed glass pour:

- **One shot bourbon (They used Fiddler Bourbon from Atlanta)**
- **One shot Creme de Cacao**

Stir contents and hand to guest along with a coconut popsicle, to be dunked into the glass. Yum!

As I looked around at the tables of people happily imbibing right out there in public, I thought to myself, "W.D. Upshaw must be spinning in his grave." At the time, I didn't realize how hard it would be to *find* the grave of the late congressman from Newnan who had styled himself "the driest of the dry," but read on.

By the time 1926 rolled around, the country was deeply divided about Prohibition. The noted American bandleader John Phillip Sousa weighed in during a visit to Birmingham, Alabama. What the people need, he said, is temperance, not Prohibition. "The two are vastly different, and Prohibition is an insult to every law-abiding American. All men who have been great laugh-provokers have taken a drink now and then, but they have been temperate. The man who really likes liquor will get it, even if it is bootleg. That is the futility of Prohibition."[248]

Sousa's words were echoed by a large faction, especially people who had from the beginning opposed the national ban on producing, transporting, and selling alcohol. Others, like Congressman Upshaw, argued that the Volstead Act just needed better enforcement and even stronger penalties to succeed. Still others took a middle ground, wanting the act modified to more closely reflect the language of the Eighteenth Amendment and allow sales of low-alcohol beer and wine.

That winter, newspapers all over the country conducted reader polls on the issue. Readers were invited to fill out a ballot and vote for or against the "sale of light wines and beer under strict government license and regulation," with an option in some polls supporting outright repeal. (The *Atlanta Constitution*, whose ballot is show here, did not allow its readers the repeal option. It had to bring in extra clerks to handle the deluge of ballots.) In early April, *The Literary Digest*, one of the country's most influential magazines, totaled up the mostly completed polling data and concluded that there had been nearly 2.8 million votes for modification or repeal and 546,000 against, or a vote of five to one.[249]

The ballot, part of a national newspaper poll, ran on the front page of the *Atlanta Constitution* for several weeks in early 1926.

Breaking down the data further, the Newspaper Enterprise Association reported that only two states' respondents voted for continued Prohibition as it was: Kansas—hatchetation grounds of Carry A. Nation—and South Carolina. Drys had pluralities in six others, including Arkansas, Kentucky, and North Carolina. The wet majority was two to one or less in six other states, including Florida, Georgia, and Tennessee. "The figures indicate that there has been, during the last four years, a definite trend in sentiment toward modification of the Prohibition law," the NEA concluded.

Both Wayne B. Wheeler of the Anti-Saloon League and the Justice Department's "Portia of Prohibition" Mabel Walker Willebrandt scoffed at the validity of such "straw polls." Willebrandt claimed that people with a "grievance are the ones who vote, and those who are satisfied don't bother to send in a ballot."[250] Wheeler sniffed that "the supporters of Prohibition are too busy in constructively supporting the enforcement of Prohibition to engage in futile balloting on the subject."[251]

In April, Congress began taking the national pulse when a subcommittee of the Senate Judiciary Committee, whose members included an unpleasant wet showboat from Missouri named James A. Reed, began holding hearings on the Volstead Act. According to Prohibition historian Daniel Okrent, Reed "treated his political enemies as if they were fish he had landed" and inflicted "as much pain as he could as he yanked out the hook." There was no "fish" he hated more than Wayne B. Wheeler.[252]

In a typical publicity stunt, W.D. Upshaw posed holding an umbrella over the Capitol to keep it "dry." *Courtesy Library of Congress*

For three weeks, the senators heard witnesses, both wet and dry. Naturally, Reed, the only wet on the committee, gave dry witnesses the fishhook treatment, while to the wets he "displayed the manners of a maître d', presented with the charm of your favorite uncle."[253] Among the most persuasive arguments on the wet side came from Senator William Cabell Bruce of Maryland, who pointed out that the liquor tax revenues—more than $443 million in 1919—were now being denied the U.S. Treasury, and proceeds from illegal alcohol sales were enriching criminals.

This would have been evident to anybody reading a newspaper. America was in the grip of a terrible crime wave, and Prohibition violators seemed to be behind many of the most violent incidents. Lurid headlines in the daily newspapers in the South reported on the gang warfare of the big cities of the North as well as violent Prohibition-related crimes in every Southern city and small town. The problem had even gotten the uncharacteristic attention of President Coolidge, who favored a hands-off federal government. It was joked that he was so passive that he was "distinguishable from the furniture only when he moved."[254]

On February 13, a front page story in the *Atlanta Constitution* trumpeted the news that Coolidge "today placed the full weight of his administration and the vast power of the federal government behind the move to rid Chicago of the gangs of alien gunmen who are terrorizing that community."[255] This was, of course, an oblique reference to the gang of Al Capone, who had been handed control of the Chicago Outfit by its founder Johnny Torrio after Torrio was almost killed in an attack by a rival gangster, American-born George "Bugs" Moran, in 1925.[256] Although Capone was born in America, Torrio, his associate Frankie Yale, and many of the gang members in Chicago were born in Italy. But rather than focusing on the root cause of the crimes, Coolidge blamed the Department of Immigration for allowing Italian criminals to enter the country.

Serious crime had been declining in America for decades after the Civil War, but the temperance movement reversed that trend, according to a Cato Institute study by Mark Thornton. In major cities, the homicide rate rose 78 percent in the 1920s compared to the pre-Prohibition years, from 5.6 murders per 100,000 to 10 murders per 100,000 population.[257] The rate in Chicago rose from 10.5 murders per 100,000 in 1920 to 14.6 murders in 1930. [258] And it wasn't just Italian, or French, or German, or even Irish immigrants and their offspring who were causing problems. Native-born

Americans with Anglo-Saxon names whose families had settled in the country before it was a country were in on the liquor racket too. Untold riches were available despite lack of education or social connections, and because so many legitimate jobs in the alcohol and related industries disappeared with Prohibition, there were many unemployed people looking for something to do. Anyone who wanted to make a lot of money and didn't mind the risk of going to jail or getting murdered got into the action.

DRINKING WITH THE OUTLAWS

A few years ago, the little wine bar my husband Leo and I frequent began serving 19 Crimes wine. You've probably seen it at your grocery store. The labels are, ahem, arresting. Each features a miserable looking person in the rough clothing of a convict. They were real people who had committed one of the crimes that was punished in nineteenth century England by "transportation" to the penal colony of Australia. In an especially clever piece of marketing, each cork bore the name of one of the crimes, which ranged from petty larceny (less than a shilling) to stealing a shroud from a grave (ew!). For a while, the bar offered a special: If you could guess which crime was on the cork of the bottle you had ordered, you got it for half price.

19 Crimes lures customers with photos of desperate looking convicts on its labels. And Martha Stewart. *Author photo.*

Jane Castings, a Female Fagin. The 19 Crimes website makes no bones about its aggrandizement of these criminals. "Cheers to the Infamous!" its website shouts, inviting customers to become an "infamous insider" and read the stories of "The Crew."[259] They include one woman, Jane Castings, whose official record shows she was transported to Tasmania in 1846 for receiving stolen goods consisting of cheese and bacon. Though Mrs. Castings, the mother of four, pled ignorance of the source of the goods and threw down the mother card, evidence showed her to be the leader of a gang of street urchins, rather like a female Fagin in the Charles Dickens novel *Oliver Twist*. She never returned to England, dying of "senility" in 1895. Appropriately enough, she is the brand cover girl for the "Hard Chard," a Chardonnay that contains a whopping 16 percent alcohol.[260] Recently 19 Crimes has expanded its repertoire to include labels featuring two contemporary "outlaws": the rapper Snoop Dogg and design maven Martha Stewart, both of whom have spent time in jail.

Bill McCoy, Gentleman Rum-Runner. Several new premium liquor brands have traded on the history of famous crooks who are long dead and thus blissfully unaware of how their infamy is being exploited. Take for example Bill McCoy, an early Prohibition rumrunner, who said he got into the game for the money in 1920 and stayed for the fun. Originally an honest Florida boat-builder, McCoy was the man who coined the term "Rum Row" to describe the gatherings of liquor ships just outside the legal limits of the U.S. coast, where bootleggers and individual customers journeyed to buy booze. McCoy stood out as an honest broker—his stuff was "the real McCoy," not adulterated or watered down. Eventually his luck ran out; he was arrested and served nine months in prison.

The Real McCoy Rum was the idea of a documentary film maker, Bailey Pryor, after producing an Emmy-award winning film for PBS about McCoy. Pryor worked with a Barbados-based rum maker to produce the line of rums, which have gone on to win all sorts of prizes. A 750 ml. bottle of the basic rum costs about $5 more than a mainstream rum like Bacardi. By most accounts (don't believe his portrayal on the HBO series *Boardwalk Empire*), Bill McCoy was a decent guy who knowingly broke laws that would eventually be repealed, served time, and then went straight. (He lived to be seventy-one years old, and his ashes were scattered at sea.) Not so for some of the other outlaws whose names and faces grace bottles of booze. They left a trail of blood and sometimes bodies in their wake.[261]

continues on next page

Lewis Redmond, Robin Hood or Robber? Lewis Redmond was the nineteenth century "blockader" we read about a few chapters back, the post-Civil War moonshine maker who refused to pay the hated federal excise tax. Redmond was both a notorious criminal and a folk hero. A native of the North Carolina mountains, he plied his trade in what is called the "Dark Corner" of the Appalachian Mountains of Greenville and Pickens counties. He first got the attention of the authorities when he shot dead a U.S. deputy marshal, who had been a childhood friend. Redmond's crimes included shooting two revenue agents who were trying to take him to jail, surrounding the home of one of the wounded men with a band of ruffians, kidnapping his wife and forcing her to cash a check for him, and then stealing the revenue man's best horse. It got progressively worse. Redmond was captured (taking six bullets in the process) in 1881. After serving a sentence in federal prison, he lived out the rest of his days quietly and is buried in a small church yard in Oconee County, South Carolina, under a marker that reads "He was the sunshine of our home."

A boutique distillery in Greenville County, South Carolina, Dark Corner Distillery, produced a Lewis Redmond bourbon. Dark Corner went under during the covid-19 pandemic, but the whiskey is still sold by its "sister" distillery, Hilton Head Distillery. It appears to be sort of the red-headed stepchild in the company product line, which is heavy on flavored rums.[262]

George Remus, the Bootlegging Lawyer. The final outlaw on my list is George Remus, a criminal attorney who became a criminal when he saw how much his clients were making by bootlegging. Remus set up his operation in Cincinnati in 1921 with his wife, Imogene, as his partner in crime, and soon controlled more than a third of the illegal liquor in the country. (He, too, was a character on *Boardwalk Empire*, portrayed somewhat accurately.)

They lived large. Take, for example, the New Year's Eve party the Remuses threw to ring in 1922. Remus lighted his guests' cigars with hundred-dollar bills, put a thousand-dollar bill under each dinner plate, and presented diamond stickpins to the male guests and brand-new Pontiacs to the women. When the center of the festivities shifted to the Imogene Baths (the newly finished pool), Remus dove into the water in his tuxedo, but then bid his guests good night and retired, Gatsby-like, to his handsomely appointed library, to enjoy a bowl of ice cream as he read a biography of Abraham Lincoln. Unlike his guests, Remus never drank.

The website for George Remus Bourbon confides, "Some rules are made to be broken. Prohibition for example." It has toned down some of its earlier verbiage—there's no more "All Hail King George" or "Saying George Remus was just a bootlegger is like saying Hemingway was just a writer," though it does still enthuse, "In the 1920s, if baseball had Ruth, bourbon had Remus."

Like Bill McCoy, Lewis Redmond, and countless other violators of liquor laws, Remus was eventually caught, tried, and sent to prison. During her husband's imprisonment in Atlanta, Imogene Remus began an affair with, of all people, the Prohibition agent who had helped put him away. By the time George was released, Imogene and her love had absconded with all his money and stripped his fancy mansion of all its furnishings. On the way to their divorce hearing, he spotted her car, ran it off the road, chased her into a public park, and shot her dead. In an even more incredible twist, he was found not guilty by the jury by reason of insanity—and he served as his own lawyer! Remus, too, went straight after he was released from a short stay in a mental institution and lived in obscurity until his death in 1952 at age seventy-four.[263]

So what does this say about us?

The companies that brand and market wine, beer, and liquor do their homework. They know there is not much of market for Stalin Vodka or Hitler Bavarian Beer or Benito Mussolini Italian Wine. Why are we attracted to a brand that bears the name and visage of a convicted criminal? It's something to ponder as you sip a glass of beer, wine, or other adult beverage. ■

The Virginia mountains, settled by immigrants from the British Isles in the sixteenth and seventeenth centuries and largely populated by their descendants, would draw the attention in 1929 of a commission appointed by President Hoover. It claimed that 99 out of every 100 residents of Franklin County were connected to the moonshine industry.[264] "The networks of police, judges, politicians and community members scattered throughout the region's isolated hollows and rough roads successfully resisted efforts to resist their web of production and supplies," writes Lisa McGirr in *The War on Alcohol*. Mountainous Dickenson County was the site of a notorious shoot-out in the summer of 1926 that illustrates the point. Sheriff C. Pridemore Fleming shot James Sherman Mullins in front of the county courthouse in Clintwood. Mullins shot back. Both died. The sheriff was a drinking man. Mullins was a Prohibition agent. They were also cousins with bad blood between them.[265]

The story was written off for decades as just another hillbilly feud, until Jenny Cooper, Mullins's granddaughter, did some investigating and discovered correspondence that proved he had died in the line of duty. He was trying to serve warrants on the drunken sheriff for protecting bootleggers. The sheriff drew his revolver and emptied it, hitting Mullins three times. As he walked away, Mullins, who had lost an arm in an automobile accident the year before, managed to draw his revolver and shoot the sheriff in the back. The men were buried the same day in adjoining cemeteries. Sheriff Fleming's gravestone has the inscription, "A TRUER NOBLER HEART NEVER BEAT WITHIN A HUMAN BREAST." Agent Mullins's reads simply, "The most noble of men."[266]

As this case illustrates, the problem was that the "full weight" and "vast power" of the federal government when it came to enforcing Prohibition was still a joke. Even though Coolidge had appointed an honest attorney general, and J. Edgar Hoover was now heading the Bureau of Investigation rather than William J. Burns and his sidekick Gaston Means, enforcement of the Volstead Act was still left to the Prohibition Bureau in dubious cooperation with local law enforcement. Mabel Walker Willebrandt continued to insist Prohibition could be enforced, but she was becoming increasingly disillusioned, especially after General Lincoln Andrews was appointed head of the bureau in August 1925. A military man who had served in both the Spanish-American War and World War I, Andrews made a promising start by requiring Prohibition agents to be hired through the civil service rather than as political appointees, which cut out many of the unqualified hacks who wanted a sinecure with access to booze. He added a new qualification that only "bone-dry" officers would keep their jobs, with one notable exception: tasting confiscated liquor to make sure it contained alcohol for the purposes of testifying in court. "It is sad to contemplate that anyone must be compelled to drink whisky in view of the fact that the product now available is of the most atrocious quality," he said, describing agents who did this difficult duty as "poor devils."[267]

But Andrews also reorganized the enforcement districts, placing M.O. Dunning, who was based in Savannah, over not only Georgia and the Carolinas, but also Florida, Virginia, West Virginia, Maryland, Delaware, and the District of Columbia. He said this improved efficiency would have a marked positive effect on enforcement.[268] The reorganization resulted in the layoff of hundreds of agents, including the pair who had the most successful record in the country: Izzy Einstein and Moe Smith of New York. (Andrews was said to be jealous of the favorable press the flamboyant agents had been given.) Several of the people he hired seem to have taken the job out of self-interest rather than any interest in keeping the nation dry. Writing several years later from her vantage point as an ex-federal employee, Willebrandt snorted that "It will take many a day...for law enforcement to recover from the setback it suffered from General Lincoln C. Andrews."[269] Andrews refused to comment.[270]

"[P]olitics," she stated flatly in her 1929 book *The Inside of Prohibition*, "from the county courthouse and the city hall to the national Capitol and White House in Washington, has been most responsible for the failures of Prohibition enforcement."[271]

Even Sam W. Small, an evangelist and early Prohibitionist who had been handsomely paid for speaking by the Anti-Saloon League, poked some fun

A cartoon in the March 16, 1926, *Atlanta Constitution* showed how liquor violations were destroying American's moral code.

at the testimony in the Senate in a newspaper column. He compared the anti-saloon and anti-Prohibitionist factions flocking to Washington for the hearings to "bunches of locoed coyotes, filling the air with noise and going nowhere fast." [272] If you believed the dry crowd, he continued—mentioning specifically Georgia congressman W.D. Upshaw—all that was needed was more and better law enforcement, "for President Coolidge to unlock the national treasury to General Andrews, declare rum-runners to be pirates, bootleggers to be traitors, recruit the army to a million men, quintuple the navy, and deploy the whole armed outfit over the continent and the high seas."

Some Americans, horrified at the crime on their doorsteps, would have been fine with that. In mid-July, Georgia newspapers carried front-page headlines about a young Macon couple found murdered in a rented automobile on a rural road. The headline labeled the death scene of Hilda Smith and her boyfriend E.W. Wilson as a "bootleg farm." A local chapter of the Ku Klux Klan offered a $100 reward to anyone who could supply sufficient evidence to convict Miss Smith's killer.[273]

The lurid story played out for days, with several related arrests made for Prohibition violations, and a Baptist preacher thundering that anyone who bought from bootleggers was not welcome in his church. A Black man named Ed Glover eventually confessed to the murder, claiming he was promised $25 and a gallon of corn whiskey for killing young Wilson by a

Photos of E.W. Wilson and Hilda Smith appeared in the *Macon Daily Telegraph*, July 16, 1926.

White bootlegger who said Wilson owed him money. If that was indeed true, Miss Smith was just a victim of circumstance; if not, the young couple died because they picked the wrong lovers' lane.

Justice moved quickly in those days. The murders were committed July 14, Glover was convicted on July 28, and died in the electric chair at the state prison in Milledgeville on September 10.[274] On September 3, Bars Davis, the man Glover claimed had bribed him—and the one who had "discovered" the bodies—was convicted of second-degree murder by a jury, which recommended mercy, and was sentenced to life in prison.[275] Jim Crow ruled in Georgia. The jury deliberated for ten minutes in Glover's case, eighteen hours in Davis's.

THE KKK, THE ASL, AND W.D. UPSHAW

The white-robed and hooded members of the Ku Klux Klan had emerged as a vigilante group during Reconstruction, inspired by the Scottish clans who were subdued by the British after the failed Bonnie Prince Charlie Rebellion in 1746.[276] The original Klan terrorized freed slaves, but once Jim Crow laws were passed throughout the South, there wasn't much need for a vigilante force; the state and local governments had, unfortunately, taken over the job.

The KKK resurgence was the work of a former Methodist circuit pastor from Atlanta, William J. Simmons, who was inspired by the 1915 silent film *Birth of a Nation*, directed by D.W. Griffith. The film revived the "Lost Cause" sentiments of Southerners and cast the Klan as heroes. Simmons and some colleagues gathered in November of that year at Stone Mountain, where a stupendous monument to the Lost Cause was being planned and burned a cross to signal the revival of the Klan. (The burning cross had been used by Scottish clans as a call to arms.) This time the KKK added to its original persecution of Blacks the terrorizing of Catholics, Jews, immigrants, or Blacks.

continues on next page

The KKK worked hand-in-hand with the Anti-Saloon League, the Women's Christian Temperance Union, and other groups to get Prohibition passed.

It was a relatively small organization until 1920, when membership snowballed and Klan groups sprouted nation-wide. "Post-war social conflict, including a new militancy among organized labor and African Americans, and more permissive sexual norms, fueled White Protestant nationalist anxieties and created a fecund climate for Klan mobilization," author Lisa McGirr writes in *The War on Alcohol*, adding that the banning of alcohol provided the leverage needed to win the Klan two to five million members by 1925.[277] The most dominant areas were Ohio, Illinois, and Indiana, where 40 percent of Klan members lived.[278]

In this 1923 cartoon, the Anti-Saloon League, aka "Mr. Dry," shakes hands with one of its Prohibition allies, a Klansman with a lynching rope in his hand. *Courtesy Library of Congress.*

The hoods and robes that hid the identities of members meant your local police chief could well be a Klan member. Indeed, some law enforcement leaders welcomed the addition of Klan volunteers as they raided the bases of suspected liquor operations, especially those in minority communities. The police chief of Birmingham, Alabama, a Klan member named J.J. Shirley, advised a law enforcement colleague in Nashville "to organize his own klavern [chapter]" to help with raids.[279] Women had a role too. Though Klan membership was only open to men, women could join the Klan auxiliary; some of the women who did so had cut their teeth with the WCTU on the Prohibition cause.[280]

A warning about the danger of the Klan was sounded by the much-respected *New York World* newspaper in a 1921 exposé that claimed the "invisible empire" had half a million members, many of whom had been elected to office or held other powerful positions. Alarmed, the House Rules Committee of Congress called hearings to investigate. One of the chief witnesses questioned was the Klan's imperial wizard, William J. Simmons himself, whose dear friend turned out to be his congressman, W.D. Upshaw.

Upshaw introduced Simmons at the hearing as "an honest and patriotic man" and said he was willing to "underwrite his every utterance."[281] When Simmons, who claimed to be ill, collapsed and fell from his chair during his first day of testimony, Upshaw hobbled up on his crutches to come to his assistance. The proceedings halted for the day and resumed the following week, but after a day of questioning Simmons, the committee chairman called a short recess and returned to announce the hearings were ending. Unless the investigation being conducted by William J. Burns at the Justice Department made some substantial discovery, the Klan could go about its business as usual.[282]

While Rep. Upshaw denied that he had championed the Klan's cause, what he *had* done was introduce a resolution saying that the committee should investigate not only the Klan but "each and every secret organization in the United States." In a statement, Upshaw said he thought it unfair to focus on the Klan when there are "many oath-bound secret organizations led by high officials with weird, high-sounding titles" that should be investigated as well.[283] Apparently, this made some members of Congress who belonged to such organizations nervous enough that the hearings were called off.

By then the Klan was already in trouble, not because of the newspaper exposé or congressional hearings, but because of a series of murderous scandals in the Midwest that caused a deep decline in its membership.[284] Even Wayne B. Wheeler was trying to distance the ASL from the Klan. Upshaw continued to insist he had never been a member, but in the last decade of his life he emerged in California as the close friend of Roy E. Davis, who held various high positions in the Klan until his death in 1966. Davis and Upshaw worked the evangelism circuit together in California—Davis combining preaching with recruiting for the Klan—where Upshaw claimed in 1951 to have been spontaneously healed of his lameness by Davis's protégé, evangelist and faith healer William Branham, and discarded his crutches.[285]

Georgians got another dose of death two weeks after the double-homicide in Macon, when front-page banner headlines in the *Atlanta Constitution* screamed about the cold-blooded murder of "Nemesis of Underworld" Bert Donaldson, fifty-four, the chief investigator of the Fulton County Solicitor General's Office.[286] In graphic detail more suited to a true crime pulp magazine than a family newspaper, the story described how Donaldson was found "[s]prawled stiff in death, a great gaping hole in the back of his head; another in the small of his back" at the fashionable Georgian Terrace Hotel on Peachtree Street. The room in which he was murdered had been registered to a W.B. Sands of Macon, which turned out to be a phony name.

"Scarred-Faced Gunman Sought as Leader of Band of Four Men Who Perpetrated Most Carefully Planned Crime in Annals of Atlanta," the sub-headline said. The reporter wrote, "Gambling houses, bootlegging establishments and vice interests all feared and hated Donaldson, who kept on their trail with unflagging energy and made life miserable for them." Although the solicitor general initially declared the killers were "imported" from outside the city, the following spring eight Atlantans were indicted for the murder.[287]

According to follow-up articles in the *Constitution* in 1927, one of the men, roadhouse owner Jack Lance, was tried, convicted, and sentenced to

Bert Donaldson was shown on the job prior to his murder in two photos printed in the *Atlanta Constitution* on July 31, 1926.

death, but on appeal, the Georgia Supreme Court overturned the conviction, declaring key evidence used by the prosecution was inadmissible, and ordered a new trial. The solicitor decided he could not win a conviction of Lance, and charges against the others were dismissed as well. Donaldson's killers were never brought to justice. Lance promised to go straight but was soon arrested on drunken driving and gambling charges.[288]

Donaldson's death led to a call for beefing up the police department in Atlanta, which was exactly how Wayne B. Wheeler had concluded his testimony before the Senate subcommittee in April.[289] "The very fact that the law is difficult to enforce is the clearest proof of the need of its existence," he said.[290]

It was pretty much the same argument Enoch "Nucky" Johnson, crime boss of Atlantic City, New Jersey, gave for the need for contraband goods and services: "If the majority of people didn't want them, they wouldn't be profitable and they wouldn't exist."[291]

In other words, neither side was willing to give an inch.

But a crack had been made in the armor of the ASL. A 1926 Senate probe of campaign finance got from the ASL an accounting of what it had paid various temperance speakers over the previous decade to fight for the dry cause. The total came to an astonishing $44.9 million, or more than $665 million in current funds. Among the best paid was former congressman Richmond P. Hobson of Alabama, the so-called "Father of Prohibition," and "Honest John" F. Kramer, who became the first head of the Prohibition Bureau under Woodrow Wilson. Both were paid tens of thousands of dollars.[292]

Apparently, Congressman W.D. Upshaw wasn't shy about asking for honorariums either, although his compensation paled next to Hobson's and Kramer's. He asked for taxi fare and $25 to speak at a league event just outside Washington in 1924, claiming that he did not even have enough money to go home to Georgia for Christmas.[293]

By the 1926 election cycle, Upshaw had competition for his congressional seat from two Democratic challengers, both drys, but neither buffoonish nor as closely associated with the Anti-Saloon League. He lost the primary on September 6 to Leslie J. Steele, a lawyer and state legislator, and blamed it on "liquor interests" that he claimed had spent $100,000 in his district to defeat him.[294] In South Carolina, the *Columbia Record*, a wet newspaper, skewered "the chief cock of the Volstead walk" in an editorial, challenging

Upshaw to name names. The liquor interests, the editorial continued, "was somewhat hard to page. It now includes countless homebrewers and scores of bootleggers, and certainly we doubt if they opposed Rev. Upshaw, for hundreds of them have blossomed out in Cadillac cars and brownstone homes, who used to live on chance hotdogs before Rev. Upshaw and others like him gave them a big business."[295]

Upshaw's defeat in the primary was followed in the November general election with a beating at the polls for the Republican Party which, outside the South, was the major proponent of Prohibition. The front-page wire story carried by the *Atlanta Constitution* on November 3 proclaimed it a "revolt against Volsteadism," as the Republican majority in the Senate "has melted away, almost, but not quite, to the vanishing point."[296]

FLAPPER FICTION

South Carolina Senator Coleman Blease could have been one of those politicians Wayne B. Wheeler loved: he drank wet and voted dry. Blease was, at least, unapologetic about his personal habits, claiming he was just voting as his constituents wanted. On the other side of the coin, he opined, "The man who thinks we have prohibition in this country is an ignorant fool. The only man who has prohibition is the poor devil who has not got the money with which to buy liquor; and everybody knows it."[297]

What he really hated were foreigners. One January morning in 1926, he gave a speech on the floor in which he complained about the embassies in Washington serving alcohol. Because embassies are considered foreign soil, alcohol ran freely at these Washington sanctuaries during Prohibition. Blease "read a newspaper account of the young woman arrested in Washington after she had driven her automobile into a lamp post and appeared in night court clad in a bathing suit, silk pajamas and silver slippers. The senator declared the girl's sister was reported to have told police that they had been 'celebrating on embassy refreshments.'"[298] Blease's beef was with diplomatic immunity rather than the drunk driving practices of young women, but the picture of the tipsy flapper in night court does linger in the mind.

Ah, those silver slippers.

F. Scott Fitzgerald was the literary chronicler of the Jazz Age in his short stories and novels, but he had company in writing about these young women who threw convention to the winds and happily drank and danced through the 1920s. One such storyteller was Fulton Oursler, an incredibly productive writer from the 1920s to 1940s, who turned out novels, plays, and innumerable articles as editor of *Liberty* magazine. However, his fictional characters were much seamier than the gentleman gangster Jay Gatsby and his feckless love Daisy Buchanan. Writing under the pseudonym Bobbie Meredith, he published the novel *Speakeasy Girl* in 1931.[299]

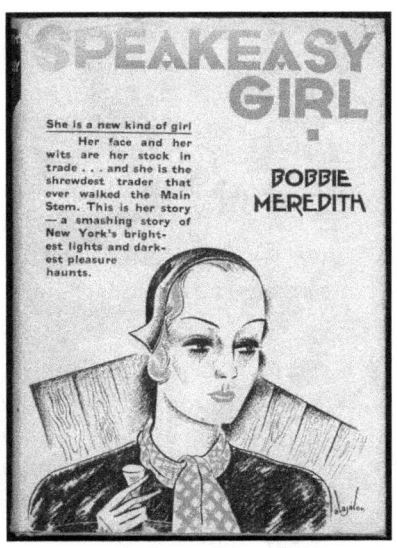

The woman gracing the cover of *Speakeasy Girl* held the tiniest cocktail glass I've ever seen. *Author's collection.*

"There is a new kind of girl in America," read the jacket notes. "She arrived on the scene with Prohibition and she has come of age. She is as immoral as she is wise, as pretty as she is young. The speakeasy is her office, just as the saloon was once her father's club."

The book, loosely based on the story of Vivian Gordon, whose wide contacts in the underworld led to her murder in 1931, follows the rise and fall of prostitute and blackmailer Corinne Martin. She was "a small-timer in the nightlife of New York" but had finally targeted a mark she could extort to finance her wildest dreams: "We'll own a big bootlegging system and the greatest dope-ring on earth and a dozen or so gambling monopolies."[300] Not to mention a brothel or two. Having seduced this wealthy St. Louis businessman and then showed her true nature when he brought her home intending to install her in a cozy "love nest" as his mistress, she thought, "The poor sap! He needed just such a lesson as he would get from her. She would be doing him a kindness. She could tumble down his whole marble palace over his head and the heads of every member of his smug Methodist family!"[301]

Like Gatsby, Corrine flew too close to the sun and wound up dead. He was shot in his swimming pool; she was garroted in a taxicab. The same thing happened to Vivian Gordon.

Ah, those silver slippers!

THE SILVER SLIPPER

Anne Peck-Davis, co-author with Diane Lapis of *Cocktails Across America: A Postcard View of Cocktail Culture in the 1930s, 40s, and 50s*, took the Prohibition-era recipe for a drink called Silver and dressed it up as the Silver Slipper especially for this book.

- 1¾ oz. of gin
- ¾ oz. Luxardo Maraschino Liqueur
- ¼ oz. Parfait Amour Liqueur (Crème de Violette can be substituted)
- 1 oz. fresh lemon juice
- 1 egg white
- Dash of orange bitters

Anne Peck-Davis not only makes great cocktails, she also takes beautiful photographs of them.

Dry shake egg white in cocktail shaker until frothy, add all other ingredients with ice and shake again. Strain into a cocktail glass over specially prepared ice cube. Garnish with maraschino cherry.

Specialty ice cube: Add ¼ oz Parfait Amour Liqueur, 1 dash of orange bitters, and filtered water to a square or spherical ice mold (approximately 2 oz. size), freeze overnight. The ice cube adds a subtle floral note to the drink as it begins to melt, but it is not necessary.

What do you do with the rest of that egg? You could always make a **Golden Slipper** using this standard recipe:

- ¾ oz. yellow chartreuse
- 2 oz. apricot brandy

Stir well and strain into a cocktail glass. Float an unbroken egg yolk on top.

Alternatively, if it's been one of those nights, save the yolk for a Prairie Oyster. In another terrific flapper novel, *Single Lady* by John Monk Saunders, a young American woman named Nikki is squired around 1920s Paris by a squadron of hard-drinking flyers recovering from the Great War. Heavily hungover one morning, she joins them in the bar at the Carlton Hotel. They are drinking prairie oysters. When Nikki asks if she might have one, Charles the bartender begins to prepare it.

"What's that?" Nikki asked as he dashed a few drops of something in a glass.

"Worcestershire sauce."

"And that?"

"Brandy."

"And that?"

"Paprika. The genoowine Hungarian."

"Voici," said Charles, setting the glass before her.

Nikki picked it up a little hesitantly.

"Happy landing," Shep said as Nikki tilted back her head and poured the drink into her mouth. Almost instantly, a startled look came into her eyes; she stiffened, her throat contracted, and the egg, bursting like a star shell, exploded in all directions. She fell into a violent paroxysm of coughing. The onlookers ducked, but it was too late.[302]

Saunders was an accomplished pilot and flight instructor during World War I, but never flew in combat, which he keenly regretted. After the war he became a successful screenwriter in the late silent and early talking movie years. *Wings*, the first movie that won an Academy Award for best picture, was based on his novel of the same name. Its star was Clara Bow, the "It Girl" of the late 1920s. Considered one of the handsomest men in Hollywood, Saunders was married to the beautiful actress Fay Wray (best known for her role as the love obsession of *King Kong*), but they divorced due to his heavy drinking and womanizing. Broke and desperate, he hung himself with the sash of his bathrobe in the closet of a Fort Myers, Florida beach cottage in 1940.

Clara Bow starred in the 1927 silent movie *Wings*, based on the novel written by John Monk Saunders. *This photo is a still from the movie trailer, accessed through Wikimedia Commons.*

Prohibition Expedition: Atlanta

The **Georgian Terrace Hotel**, where Bert Donaldson was murdered in a third-floor room in 1926, is an outstanding example of a fine twentieth century hotel that survived the wrecking ball and is thriving in the twenty-first. Opened in 1911, the Beaux Arts hotel was built of brick and marble to emulate a Parisian hotel. It was for years considered the most luxurious hotel in the city, hosting such luminaries as Calvin Coolidge, opera singer Enrico Caruso, Walt Disney, and, during the 1939 premiere of *Gone with the Wind*, Clark Gable and his wife Carole Lombard, among other cast members.[303] In 1920, a Georgia Tech student named Arthur Murray began teaching ballroom dancing lessons there to pay his tuition and made so much money he dropped out of school. His Arthur Murray Dance Studios became world famous.[304] The current hotel has a speakeasy-style bar in its basement called **Edgar's Proof and Provision** that specializes in small bites and bourbon flights, but also offers wine, beer, and other cocktails.

Atlantans were shocked by the murder of a police detective in one of the city's best hotels, shown in this vintage postcard. *Author's collection.*

695 Peachtree Street (across from the Fox Theatre)
www.thegeorgianterrace.com

Atlanta has a number of speakeasy-style bars, including one you enter through a British red box phone booth. Search out the latest at www.atlantaeats.com/blog/atlantas-secret-speakeasies/

Stone Mountain, where the Ku Klux Klan held its 1915 coming-out party, is now a state park with features such as a scenic railroad, two golf courses, natural areas for hiking and fishing, and a paddle wheel boat. It draws four million visitors a year and hosts annual events such as Scottish highland games. Dominating the park is the 90x190-foot relief of Confederate leaders on horseback. It has been described as "the Mount Rushmore of the Confederacy," though in fact the carving is larger than the one in South Dakota. Since the Black Lives Matter movement came into prominence, there has been discussion about what to do about the monument, but partly because of practical challenges related to its size and depth—it's the size of a football field—there have been no conclusions.[305]

1000 Robert E. Lee Road, Stone Mountain, Georgia
www.stonemountainpark.com

CEMETERY SIDE TRIP

Murdered law man **Bert Donaldson** was buried under a joint tombstone with his widow's first husband, J.B. Martin, in Casey's Hill Cemetery in the Hills Park section of Atlanta. The handsome art deco-style headstone assigned a Bible verse to each man. Martin's was John 16:3, "And these things will they do unto you, because they have not known the Father, nor me," while Donaldson's was John 17:3, "Now this is eternal life: that they know you, the only true God, and Jesus Christ, whom you have sent." Their mutual widow, Narcissa Emily Casey Donaldson, joined them at the cemetery in 1933 when she died at age 82. According to her obituary, Mrs. Donaldson met her second husband at the Atlanta Federal Penitentiary where he was serving a sentence for robbing a post office. She converted Donaldson, who had been a career criminal, to Methodism and helped him use his vast knowledge of the underworld to put away his former associates.[306]

RECOMMENDED READING

The War on Alcohol: Prohibition and the Rise of the American State by Lisa McGirr (New York: W.W. Norton, 2016) is a penetrating analysis of Prohibition that redefines it as the "seedbed for a pivotal expansion of the American government, the genesis of our contemporary penal state." McGirr is a professor of history at Harvard, but don't let that put you off. She knows how to tell a story!

Where All Good Flappers Go: Essential Stories of the Jazz Age (Pushkin Press, 2023) is a collection of flapper fiction edited by David M. Earle, a professor of English at West Florida University. The collection includes writings of authors from the celebrated to the obscure.

CHAPTER EIGHT

The Crème de la Crime

IN JANUARY 1926, New York Governor Al Smith announced he would leave politics when his term ended the following year. He said it was time to go into private business where he wouldn't have to answer to political bosses.

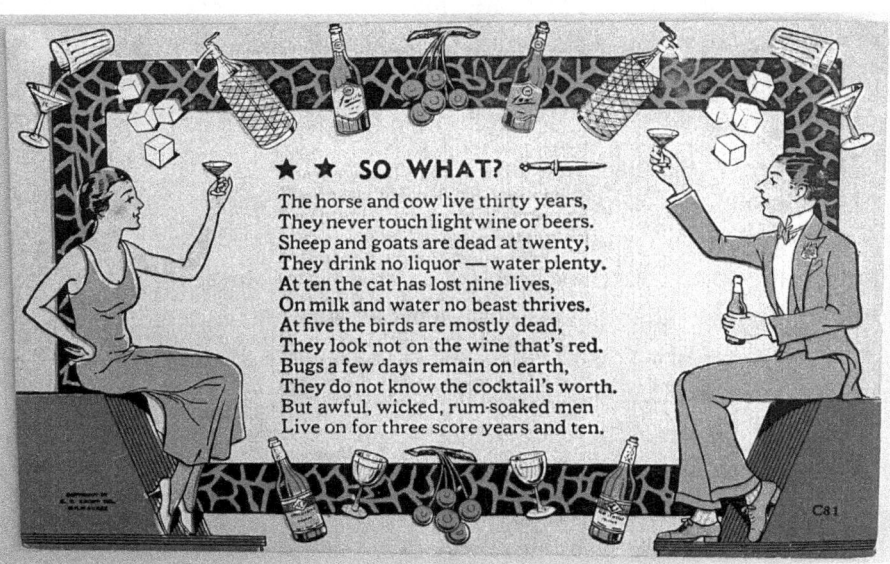

This amusing postcard from the late Prohibition period argues for the return to drinking for all. *Collection of A.P. Davis.*

(Smith neatly sidestepped the point that he was a pretty big political boss himself.) [307] The popular Democratic Party leader would eventually get his wish—but not for some time. In 1928, at which time he said he wanted to be out of politics, he was not only still the governor of New York, he was also the party's nominee for president, facing Herbert Hoover. Smith's opposition used his Catholicism, background in big city politics, and stance on Prohibition against him, snidely branding him "the Cocktail President."

Five weeks before election day, Smith and his supporters placed beseeching calls to Warm Springs, Georgia, where Franklin Delano Roosevelt, who had made Smith's nominating speech at the Democratic National Convention, was happily ensconced. He was running a rehabilitation center for polio survivors and trying to learn to walk again, firmly stating that if a man was going to run for office, he had to be able to walk first. Smith, worried about the election outcome, begged Roosevelt to run to succeed him as governor of New York, hoping Roosevelt had long enough coattails to carry what was then the country's most populous state for him. Roosevelt finally acquiesced and squeaked out a victory. Smith lost in a landslide to Hoover, who had served with distinction as secretary of commerce in both the corrupt Harding administration and somnolent Coolidge administration. Smith swept Georgia by a large margin, but Hoover carried four other states in the formerly "Solid South": Virginia, Florida, North Carolina, and Texas.[308] The only state Smith won outside the South was Massachusetts; even the Roosevelt coattails were too short in the state he had dominated for his entire political life.

In Georgia, W.D. Upshaw tried to win his old congressional seat back in a rematch with Leslie Steele, the man who had defeated him in 1926. Democratic Party leaders attempted to disqualify him from entering the primary because of his outspoken support for Hoover, but he got on the ballot anyway, losing by 5,000 votes and carrying only his home county.[309] A sore loser as usual, Upshaw accused Steele of taking "Tammany money"—Tammany Hall was the base of Democratic machine politics in New York—but was conveniently out of the state when he was called to testify before a grand jury investigating his claim.[310]

Upshaw had spent the months prior to the primary and general elections as a vocal member of the "Anti-Smith Democrats," speaking and holding rallies to convince Democrats to vote for Hoover, right up until the night

Governor-elect Franklin Delano Roosevelt takes a picture of his personal secretary, Marguerite LeHand, in this undated newspaper clipping. Roosevelt artfully propped himself up on a car to hide the fact that he could not stand on his own.

before the election, when he was the keynote speaker at a rally in rural Cave Springs.[311] The "driest of the dry" former congressman then tried to start a new Democratic Party divorced from liquor interests, but it didn't get any traction. He was not through with politics, however—or Prohibition.

To anyone but W.D. Upshaw and his Sahara-dry friends, the handwriting was clearly on the wall for the Eighteenth Amendment.

Between 1926 and 1928, blow after blow had been struck in efforts to enforce Prohibition, usually with unintended and even disastrous consequences. Denatured alcohol—the industrial type used in countless products like antifreeze—was legal, but the federal government decreed in 1906 that it had to contain "noxious" ingredients, some of which were poisonous, so people wouldn't drink it.[312] A capable chemist could remove the poison, but sometimes people got hold of the bad stuff anyway, resulting in paralysis, blindness, and even death. In a famous statement in 1927, after a wave of such deaths in New York during the Christmas holidays, the ASL's Wayne B. Wheeler said, "The person who drinks this alcohol is a deliberate suicide."[313] For once, his canny political instincts had deserted him, and there was furious public backlash. Wheeler, exhausted and ill, went to the famous health sanitarium in Battle Creek, Michigan for a time, then joined his family on vacation in a bucolic "Christian" retreat. In a string of tragedies, his wife caught fire in their vacation cottage, her father died of a heart attack after witnessing her conflagration, and she succumbed to her injuries the following day. In a matter of weeks, Wheeler was dead himself at age fifty-seven,[314] his aged mother declaring, "Wayne always was a good boy."[315] The ASL continued its quest to dry up America, but it had lost its political mastermind.

Meanwhile, Prohibition-related crime increased and became decidedly more gruesome in nature. Just three weeks before Herbert Hoover took office in March 1929, the simmering warfare in Chicago between Al Capone's Outfit and the gang of Bugs Moran erupted in a shoot-out in a garage that killed seven members of Moran's gang. The press immediately tagged it the St. Valentine's Day Massacre. Capone was in Miami Beach, where he owned a home, and had a handy excuse: he was being questioned in the county prosecutor's office at the time. The case became one of hundreds of unsolved homicides in Chicago.[316]

According to one study, between 1919 and 1933, there were 729 "gangland" style killings in Cook County, which encompasses the greater Chicago area.[317] The murders were reported in newspapers all over the country, perhaps giving the public an impression of more violence and lawlessness than there actually was. The front page of the *Atlanta Constitution* was

Georgians opened their *Atlanta Constitution* on February 15, 1929, to find this gruesome photo.

dominated on February 15 by a photograph of the freshly massacred gangsters, which the cutline bragged was rushed to the newspaper by the Chicago office of the Associated Press and was "one of the clearest ever sent by wire."[318]

But the violence wasn't limited to Chicago and other big cities. In Richmond, Virginia, hometown of Methodist Bishop James Cannon, Jr. of the ASL, the murder rate tripled between 1920 and 1925. Richmond had eight murders in 1920. In 1935, it had thirty-seven.[319]

The Republican-dominated Congress, emboldened by the election results, passed the Increased Penalties Law, an amendment to the Volstead Act, two days prior to Hoover's inauguration. What had once been mere misdemeanors were transformed into felonies, with greatly lengthened prison sentences and much stiffer fines for even a first violation.[320] The law was passed in both houses with huge margins and was the final piece of legislation signed into law by President Coolidge before departing Washington. It took effect immediately.[321]

In his rain-drenched inaugural address, Hoover faced head-on the problem of growing public disregard of the law in general and the Volstead Act in particular. He blamed Prohibition's failure in part on the states that had been lax in partnering with the federal government in enforcement—likely in part a dig at Al Smith, who in 1923 had signed legislation ending New York's efforts to police the Volstead Act.[322] But Hoover also scolded John Q. Public: "There would be little traffic in illegal liquor if only criminals patronized it," he said. "We must awake to the fact that this patronage from large numbers of law-abiding citizens is supplying the rewards and stimulating crime."[323]

Hoover was right. Studies show that in the first years of Prohibition, drinking had fallen to about thirty percent of its pre-1920 level. But it was climbing steadily, particularly among very heavy drinkers, and would reach an estimated 60 to 70 percent of the pre-Prohibition level by 1933.

The new president offered "a searching investigation of the whole structure of our Federal system of jurisprudence, to include the method of enforcement of the eighteenth amendment and the causes of abuse under it." That was enough for a woman who had been one of his staunchest supporters and fundraisers, Long Island socialite Pauline Morton Sabin. She was so disappointed that his National Commission on Law Observance and Enforcement wouldn't solely focus on Prohibition that she resigned

President Hoover, third from right, sits on the White House lawn with his newly appointed crime commission. It became known as the Wickersham Commission because of its chairman, George W. Wickersham, sitting to Hoover's right. The lone woman on the commission was Ada Comstock, president of Radcliffe College. *Courtesy Library of Congress.*

from the Republican National Committee—she had been the first woman appointed—and immediately founded the Women's Organization for National Prohibition Reform. She and her "Sabine women" would soon be at war with the WCTU and the ASL.[324]

Hoover's remarks—which drew cheers from the shivering, umbrella-shrouded inaugural crowd—made it clear that he planned to continue to enforce Prohibition, but his main objective was to restore law and order in the country. He set his sights on Al Capone as a symbol of all the gangsters who were terrorizing America's cities. Because efforts to prosecute Capone on serious criminal charges had come up empty, Hoover focused on the novel gambit devised by Mabel Walker Willebrandt: tax evasion.[325] He charged Treasury Secretary Andrew Mellon with bringing Capone to justice. He also turned to J. Edgar Hoover (no relation) at the Justice Department's Bureau of Investigation to take a bigger role in law enforcement. The kidnapping and murder of Charles and Anne Lindbergh's infant son in 1932 resulted in the rebranded Federal Bureau of Investigation getting purview over kidnappings. Until 1934, though, Hoover's agents couldn't make arrests or even carry guns.

Pauline Morton Sabin, fourth from right, was a savvy organizer and spokesperson for the Women's Organization for National Prohibition Reform. This picture of Sabin and the WONPR officers was taken in the spring of 1932. Their goal was repeal, plain and simple. *Courtesy Library of Congress.*

In her book *The War on Alcohol,* Lisa McGirr argues the expanded federal role in law enforcement under President Hoover set the stage for the federal government's intrusion into every aspect of American life under Franklin Roosevelt. For one thing, the crime wave related to Volstead violations had resulted in a prison overcrowding crisis. Far from the prediction the temperance crowd had made that the prisons would all be empty if America went dry, federal, state, and local jails were overflowing. "In Virginia," McGirr writes, "liquor-law felonies outstripped all other forms of felony." A fourth of the prisoners in Virginia jails in 1928 were Volstead violators.[326] "Virginia's penal population doubled between 1923 and 1931," McGirrr writes. North Carolina's tripled.[327] Georgia sent its overflow of prisoners into chain gangs and prison camps, where an escaped inmate complained on capture that they were given nothing to eat but peas with weevils in them, cornbread, and rancid meat. "It's enough to make any fellow want to get away," he said.[328] The same was true of federal prisons, which had been minor centers of incarceration before Prohibition. Fort Leavenworth, Kansas, where Gaston Means would spend his last years, in 1929 held almost twice as many prisoners as it was designed for. Riots broke out that year and in 1931 over the crowded conditions, harsh discipline, and poor food.[329] Hoover asked for and Congress funded a tremendous construction program of federal prisons, including the first prison for women.[330] While construction got underway, the former military prison on Alcatraz Island off the coast of San Francisco was turned into a maximum security facility where Al Capone and a Memphis, Tennessee bootlegger nicknamed "Machine Gun" Kelly would reside. But Capone's first stop after exhausting his appeals of his income tax conviction in 1932 was the Atlanta Federal Penitentiary, where he spent two years. He was prisoner No. 40866 among 3,000 inmates and was subjected to humiliating command performances before visitors President Hoover wished to impress.[331]

President Hoover had a full plate with just the crime wave and Prohibition to deal with. Then, in October 1929, the stock market crashed, and the Great Depression followed. Many volumes have been written about Hoover's response to this unprecedented economic crisis. By 1932, when he was nominated for his second term at a Republican National Convention noteworthy for its lack of enthusiasm, one in four workers in America was out of a job and Chicago, where both parties held their conventions,

This bird's-eye-view postcard of the Atlanta federal prison was mailed in July 1934, about the time Al Capone was ending his residency there and heading to Alcatraz. Curiously, the note on the back of the card reads, "Got here OK 9 o'clock. Had to wait until one o'clock for train to Montgomery." We assume the writer just chose the card off a rack at the Atlanta train station and wasn't visiting the penitentiary! *Author's collection.*

was dotted with shanty communities disparagingly dubbed "Hoovervilles." Hoover later bitterly remarked, "I'm the only person of distinction who has ever had a depression named after him."

Nevertheless, the issue that obsessed delegates at both conventions was Prohibition. The Republicans, to please Hoover, accepted a plank that tried to placate both sides, while the Democrats wholeheartedly embraced the repeal of the Eighteenth Amendment. Pauline Morton Sabin and WONPR gladly endorsed Franklin Delano Roosevelt.

Considering the Republicans' namby-pamby stand on Prohibition and the drenched position of the Democrats, W.D. Upshaw saw an opportunity. Chosen as nominee by the Prohibition Party, he campaigned energetically around the country, stating during a campaign stop in Richmond that Hoover was as likely to win re-election "as I am to be elected King of England."[332] While admitting he was a longshot for the office, Upshaw promised that his first action as chief executive would be to "smash every bottle and every jug in official Washington and call for the resignation of every official who drinks liquor."[333]

Upshaw was realistic about his chances for victory but must have been dismayed by the overall election results. On November 8, 1932, he came in fifth, behind Roosevelt, Hoover, and the nominees for both the Socialist and Communist parties. However, he garnered over 81,000 votes and continued thundering about the evils of liquor across the country at every church and temperance gathering that would host him.

Roosevelt had not only won in a historic landslide, but the Democrats had captured both the House and the Senate. During the long interregnum between FDR's election and inauguration, the lame duck Congress voted to repeal the Eighteenth Amendment by passing the Twenty-first, then sent it to the states to be ratified. Fifteen days into office, having gotten Congress to pass legislation saving the banking system and cutting the federal budget, Roosevelt decided it was a good time to give Americans a beer. Accordingly, he sent up to Congress a modification of the Volstead Act much like the option that had drawn overwhelming support in the newspaper poll of 1926. Cleverly titled the Beer and Wine Revenue Act to give cover to those still toeing the dry line, it made beer and wine containing 3.2 percent or less alcohol legal again. The bill passed Congress in an hour and the president signed it into law on March 22.[334]

Machine Gun Kelly, Bootlegger-turned-Bank Robber

The outlaw who became known as "Machine Gun" Kelly had a fearsome reputation as a man "who can write his name in bullets discharged from such a gun." In actuality, he was "probably the most inept of Depression-era criminals," according to Bryan Burrough in his book *Public Enemies: America's Great Crime Wave and the Birth of the FBI, 1933–34*.[335]

Kelly was born George F. Barnes in Chicago in 1900 but raised in Memphis, Tennessee in an upper-class home, the son of a prosperous insurance executive. Handsome and charming,

George "Machine Gun" Kelly. *FBI Photo*

his life began to go awry when his mother died while he was still in his teens. He dropped out of school and became a bootlegger. His frustrated father sent him to college for a semester, and when the boy quit, the elder Barnes disowned him.[336]

George got a second chance at respectability when he convinced a Memphis millionaire's daughter to elope with him. His father-in-law gave him a job, and he and his wife had two sons. But the call of the lawless life was too strong. He went back to bootlegging and was arrested in 1924 and sentenced to six months in federal prison, which was enough to send his wife packing with the children. Upon his release, he worked for a grocery store in Kansas City, embezzled money to purchase a truck, and went right back to bootlegging. He was arrested again, this time for selling liquor on an Indian reservation, and went to Leavenworth prison for five years.

Kathryn Kelly. *Courtesy DeGolyer Library, Southern Methodist University*

That's where he got his education, Burrough writes. He hooked up with a bunch of bank robbers from St. Paul, Minnesota—called "yeggs" in gangster parlance—and joined them there after his release. He really got into trouble when he met a twice-married party girl named Kathryn Thorne who J. Edgar Hoover wrote "was one of the most coldly deliberate criminals of my experience." Hoover portrayed her as an evil female Svengali who pulled Kelly's puppet strings, even building his reputation as a Thompson machine gun artiste to help him get bank jobs.[337]

Unfortunately, Burrough writes, "Kelly was a lousy bank robber, so nervous he sometimes vomited before bank jobs."[338] He decided in 1932 to try his hand at kidnapping, nabbing a man who Kathryn had randomly picked out of a phone book. He had to let the man go when his family couldn't come up with ransom money.

He had better luck when he and an accomplice kidnapped Charles F. Urschel, an Oklahoma City oil man, in July 1933. Waving his Thompson machine gun, Kelly nabbed Urschel at home one evening while he and his wife were playing bridge with another couple. Mrs. Urschel paid the $200,000 ransom and her husband was released unharmed after nine days. The Kellys fled to St. Paul, where, in true gun moll fashion, Kathryn was soon decked out in a new fur coat and diamond jewelry, and the couple bought a Cadillac. But the fun didn't last. J. Edgar Hoover had gotten personally involved in the case from the moment Mrs. Urschel reported it, and his FBI agents began dogging the Kellys' heels. A combination of good luck and the ineptitude of the pursuing law officers enabled them to evade capture for almost two months.

This small house at 1408 Rayner Street in Memphis was where Machine Gun Kelly and his wife Kathryn were apprehended. *Photo by Thomas R Machnitzki, accessed through Wikimedia Commons.*

Their final hideout was a small house in Memphis, where an FBI agent working with local police trapped them in the early hours of September 23, 1933.[339] Kathryn was asleep in green silk pajamas in the house, which was strewn with empty gin and Old Brown Cabin bourbon bottles. Kelly emerged

continues on next page

from another bedroom wearing only his underwear and holding a .45, which he dropped when confronted with a double-barreled shotgun. The couple was quickly tried and convicted. Kathryn attempted to shorten her sentence by informing on other inmates at her prison, and finally finagled a new trial in 1958. By then most of the witnesses were dead or couldn't be found, and she was released to live out her life, avoiding further notoriety. Her husband served time at Alcatraz and Leavenworth, where he died in 1954.[340]

"Machine Gun" Kelly's capture was the first major victory for the FBI, which was simultaneously hunting down the gangsters "Baby Face" Nelson, John Dillinger, the Barker Gang, and Alvin Karpis in what FDR's attorney general Homer S. Cummings had proclaimed as a "War on Crime." J. Edgar Hoover claimed that Kelly's words when he dropped his gun were, "Don't shoot, G-Men!" but this was a fabrication. Actually, Burrough writes, it was Kathryn Kelly who used the name G-man—short for government man—after her arrest, and the name was soon popularized in pulp magazines and in the 1935 film *G-Men* starring James Cagney, who had earned his acting chops by playing gangsters in films such as *Public Enemy*. [341]

Hoover and Cummings reveled in the publicity achieved for the nascent agency, and at the suggestion of their friend Fulton Oursler—yes, the author of *Speakeasy Girl*—built up the reputation of the FBI and its G-men with publicity stunts.[342] In one of them, Hoover took an airplane to New Orleans on May 1, 1936 to personally arrest Alvin Karpis, the last of the big-time gangsters.[343] In *The War on Alcohol*, Lisa McGirr writes, "The favorable publicity legitimized anticrime legislation and erased the public association of federal agents with criminality and the abuse of rights that had flourished during national Prohibition."[344] Fulton Oursler continued to promote the FBI and lionize Hoover when he became senior editor of *Reader's Digest* magazine in 1944. By then, of course, Hoover had begun to secretly orchestrate the worst of his agency's overreach, leading witch hunts for communists and keeping secret files on everyone from Albert Einstein and John Wayne to Fulton Oursler himself.[345]

Americans had barely whetted their whistles on low-alcohol beer when the ratification of the Twenty-first Amendment was accomplished. On December 5, 1933, it was again legal to transport and import alcohol in every state and territory in the United States.³⁴⁶ And here came the rub. Each state was then free to decide if it wanted to allow manufacture, sales, and possession of alcohol and develop its own system of alcoholic beverage control. Eighteen states stayed dry for a time as quite a few were still populated by Methodists, Baptists, and other Protestant adherents to Prohibition, especially in the South.³⁴⁷ Enforcement of alcohol laws was again primarily a state and local matter, though there were still federal liquor laws and regulations, such as the excise tax, to consider. Enforcement of these shifted back to the Treasury Department's Internal Revenue Service, which created a new arm that eventually became known as the Bureau of Alcohol, Tobacco, and Firearms and Explosives or ATF. Through the late 1970s, it worked with state alcoholic beverage control boards and local police to bust up stills, arrest moonshiners, and send violators to federal prison.³⁴⁸

The Model A Brewing Company in Tega Cay, North Carolina proclaims the end of Prohibition in a sign painted over its bar. Tega Cay is in York County, home of World War I flying ace Elliott White Springs. The peppier Model A, introduced by adamant teetotaler Henry Ford in 1927, was the preferred vehicle for bootleggers. Ford cars continued to be favored by bootleg runners throughout the 1940s and 1950s. *Author photo.*

When the South Turned on the Spout

Six Southern states ratified the Twenty-first Amendment, two rejected it, and three did not consider it. Deciding what to do next took a while. Here is what the individual states did.

- **Alabama.** Ratified July 18, 1933. Allowed statewide alcohol sales with local option limits, 1937.[349]
- **Arkansas.** Ratified August 1, 1933. Conditions for local option established 1935.[350]
- **Florida.** Ratified November 14, 1933. State local option law passed 1934.[351]
- **Georgia.** No vote.[352] Law nullifying state-wide prohibition passed in 1938.[353]
- **Kentucky.** Ratified November 27, 1933.[354] State prohibition repealed 1934.[355]
- **Louisiana.** No vote.[356] State repealed its prohibition law, the Hood Act, in April 1933.[357]
- **Mississippi.** No vote. Ratified and ended statewide prohibition in 1966.[358]
- **North Carolina.** Rejected amendment.[359] State local option liquor laws passed in 1935.[360]
- **South Carolina.** Rejected amendment.[361] State liquor laws passed in 1935.[362]
- **Tennessee.** Ratified August 11, 1933.[363] Repealed state prohibition in 1937, local option passed in 1939.[364]
- **Virginia.** Ratified October 3, 1933. Department of Alcoholic Beverage Control created in 1934.[365] ■

A picture that appeared December 6, 1933, in the Shreveport, Louisiana *Times* shows bartenders serving drinks in a local bar five minutes after the Twenty-first Amendment was ratified.

The task of the treasury agents wasn't to dry up the country, as it had been under Prohibition, but to claim the revenue that was going unpaid by moonshine producers and sellers. In no place was it a bigger problem than Franklin County, Virginia, which had been especially cited for its liquor lawlessness by the Wickersham Commission's report in 1931. When treasury agent Thomas Bailey arrived there to do undercover work in 1934, he decided to try a novel approach. Instead of going after small producers, he recruited them as witnesses to catch the men he believed were the ringleaders of the county's liquor conspiracy: none other than the district attorney, Charles Carter Lee, plus the sheriff and his entire department of deputies.[366] Lee, then twenty-eight years old, had succeeded his father when the elder Lee died in office. Likewise, when the sheriff died, his son took his place both in office and in running the cartel.

In his book *Spirits of Just Men: Mountaineers, Liquor Bosses and Lawmen in the Moonshine Capitol of the World*, Charles D. Thompson Jr. writes of the sensational 1935 case in which Lee and thirty-three co-conspirators were indicted.[367] Agent Bailey made a case that the sheriff had created a system dividing the county into sections policed by deputies. They had a monopoly on whiskey still components, sold out of the courthouse in Rocky Mount—allegedly with Lee's full cooperation—and then charged the moonshiners protection money for each "haul" they made. The trial opened April 22 at the federal building in Roanoke and lasted for forty-nine days, the second-longest in Virginia's history.[368] The untimely murder of the deputy who had turned state's evidence, witness tampering, and a judge who showed a marked preference for the defense probably saved Lee

The Great Moonshine Conspiracy Trial was held in the federal building in Roanoke in 1935. *Author's collection.*

from conviction, not to mention his kinship to Robert E. Lee and the fact that Bailey was from Pennsylvania, site of the Battle of Gettysburg. Writes Thompson, "Colonel Thomas Bailey might as well have been a Northern spy infiltrating General Lee's territory during the Civil War."[369]

Although Lee and two minor players got off, the rest were given relatively light prison sentences.[370] It was estimated the liquor ring defrauded the government out of $5.5 million in tax revenue between 1928 and 1934.[371] Lee was re-elected three times and was in private law practice when he died of a heart attack at age fifty-two. His obituary, buried on an inside page of the *Roanoke Times*, mentioned he was the great-nephew of Robert E. Lee but ignored his role in the Great Moonshine Conspiracy Trial of 1935.[372]

So which was the true "moonshine capital of the world"? Daniel S. Pierce has his own candidate in *Tarheel Lightning: How Secret Stills and Fast Cars Made North Carolina the Moonshine Capital of the World*.[373] North Carolina rejected the Twenty-first Amendment and by 1945 all but twenty-five of its one hundred counties were still dry. But how dry was North Carolina, really?

Legendary Florida stock car driver Fireball Roberts poses with his trophies at the Daytona Speedway in 1958. Roberts' car caught fire during a race in Charlotte, North Carolina in 1964 and he died of his burns. *Courtesy State Library and Archives of Florida.*

The title of Pierce's book makes it obvious: not very. Because North Carolina lawmakers still catered to the dry crowd—Pierce points out that it was an unwritten requirement for every gubernatorial candidate into the 1950s to promise to bring back state prohibition—they turned a mostly blind eye to the tremendous underground market in moonshine production. It was, indeed, one of the state's largest industries, though North Carolina collected no license fees or taxes on the millions of gallons of booze gushing out of thousands of stills. Ironically, the dry and moonshine interests sometimes teamed up to keep a locality or county from opening a legitimate state-run liquor store. "Dry forces could always count on significant 'moral' and financial support from the county's moonshiners and bootleggers any time a referendum to allow ABC stores came up," writes Pierce.[374]

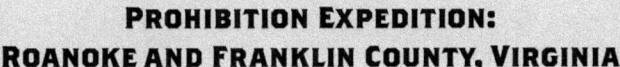

PROHIBITION EXPEDITION: ROANOKE AND FRANKLIN COUNTY, VIRGINIA

When my Aunt Susan and I were traveling toward Mount Vernon to begin our George Washington Tour, we spent the night in a former bank building in Roanoke that has been transformed into a lovely fifty-four-room boutique hotel. It was built in 1910, operated as the First National Bank, and is listed on the National Register of Historic Places.

The Liberty Trust • 101 S. Jefferson Street • www.libertytrusthotel.com

For dinner, we walked around the corner to **202 Social House**, 202 Market Street SE, which looks like an ordinary sports bar. But you go down a hall and open a door and you are in a cozy little speakeasy. www.202socialhouse.com

You are also in easy walking distance to the former **federal courthouse** where the Great Moonshine Conspiracy Trial was held. It now houses the U.S. Bankruptcy Court and a number of other agencies. 210 Church Avenue.

The Blue Ridge Institute and Museum in Ferrun, Virginia is packed with exhibits tied to Franklin County's moonshine-making history, as well as the life of the people of Appalachia.

20 Museum Drive • www.blueridgeinstitute.org

Twin Creeks Distillery, the maker of the first legal moonshine in Franklin County since Prohibition ended, is owned and operated by the grandson of James Walter "Peg" Hatcher. He was one of the liquor kingpins convicted in the 1935 moonshine conspiracy trial as well as of a subsequent charge of witness tampering in the first case. The distillery makes moonshine, apple brandy, and Peg Hatcher's Straight Whiskey.

510 Franklin Street, Rocky Mount, Virginia • www.twincreeksdistillery.com

The moonshine industry entered what Pierce calls its heyday in 1941. Mountain boys driving souped-up Fords full of corn liquor hurtled down the highways to the big cities, chased by law enforcement. The drivers' need for speed led to informal races on farmers' fallow fields and pastures, which led to stock car racing, which eventually led to NASCAR. The same thing happened in Alabama, Arkansas, Georgia, Kentucky, Tennessee, South Carolina, and Virginia, each with its moonshine haulers-turned-racing heroes.

Florida didn't have mountains, but it claims the title as the birthplace of NASCAR because of its founder Bill France Sr. and his role in building the Daytona International Speedway.

THE HIGHBALL: QUINTESSENTIAL POST-PROHIBITION COCKTAIL

With Prohibition over, liquor companies could again openly advertise their wares. An ad in the Shreveport, Louisiana *Times* gave the recipe for the perfect highball using a bourbon brand that had, during Prohibition, been owned by George Remus.[375]

The 1943 ad promised a $2,000,000 "dream of a drink," using Fleischmann's 100 proof Straight Kentucky Bourbon. You can substitute your own favorite bourbon for the Fleischmann's, but I am quoting the recipe exactly as it was written in the ad:

$2,000,000 Dream of a Drink

...because that's what Fleischmann invested in grain, skill, and research before we released one golden bottle of this rich, luxurious straight bourbon whiskey.

1. Place ice cubes in an empty 6 oz. or 8 oz. glass. Connoisseurs say the ice *must go in first!*

2. Then, add 1½ ounce of delicious Fleischmann's Bond. A good highball needs Fleischmann's smooth creaminess!

3. Fill with club soda or ginger ale. For a perfectly mixed drink, place ingredients in the order given!

Know how to make a correct highball? Lots of people don't, so we're giving you the recipe below! We call it a $2,000,000 "dream of a drink"—because that's what Fleischmann invested in grains, skill and research before we released one golden bottle of this rich, luxurious, straight bourbon whiskey. We make it in limited amounts. We have to— it's so good!

World War II provided a new opportunity for moonshine makers because legitimate distilleries were largely converted into making industrial alcohol needed in the war effort. Writes Reid Mitenbuler in his book *Bourbon Empire: The Past and Future of American Whiskey*, "The spirits industry called its wartime production of alcohol 'cocktails for Hitler.'"[376] Nevertheless, shortages of manpower and raw materials, particularly sugar, impacted the moonshine industry like many others. Under the headline "Bootleggers Vanish," an Associated Press news item in March 1943 noted that "for the first time since the Eighteenth Amendment went into effect there were no liquor cases on the docket" at U.S. District Court in Elizabeth City, North Carolina. "Officials expressed the view that sugar rationing and high wages in defense jobs have just about wiped all the illicit manufacture and sale of liquor."[377] But it was just a blip. Pierce writes that North Carolina was dotted with military bases and defense industries, and the men who worked there were happy to drink the local booze. Or at least willing. When the war ended, and with it sugar rationing and high-paying defense jobs, making and selling moonshine became more lucrative than ever.[378]

As during Prohibition, efforts at enforcement were as futile as the legendary Dutch boy putting his finger in the leaking dike. North Carolina led the way in federal records of stills seized, whiskey confiscated, and moonshine arrests, Pierce writes. One of the most audacious cases occurred in Cabarrus County, birthplace of Gaston Means, in 1968 when a huge, sophisticated underground distillery was found on a farm, complete with a dozen 1,000-gallon capacity mash tanks and a conveyor belt. Pierce writes, "Officials believed operators had been running the still for several years and probably netted up to $1 million in tax-free revenue per year."[379]

Thomas R. Allison's career as a treasury agent or "revenuer" for the ATF began in Anniston, Alabama in September 1955. Reporting to the state office in Birmingham, he was issued "a .38 caliber revolver, a pocket commission (identification with photograph), a box of ammunition, and a pair of handcuffs" and told he was responsible for buying his "own holster, green work clothes, and a pair of lightweight boots for running." Allison found no one in the Anniston office when he reported—indeed, the blind man who ran the concession stand downstairs unlocked the office door for him. Instead, he found a note reading, "New man, have on green clothes and running boots and someone will pick you up in front of the Post Office at 3:00 a.m."[380]

So began a twenty-five-year adventure of tracking down illegal distilleries at all hours of the day and night, busting thousands of stills, arresting moonshiners and bootleggers, and trying to bring them to justice. Recounting his many interesting cases in his book *Moonshine Memories,* Allison wrote, "I did not mind the long hours since looking for stills and running down moonshiners was so exciting. I sometimes wondered why they paid me since the job was so fun."[381]

The last still he busted was a "sorry-looking outfit" in a barn beside a smelly hog pen. "The whole area was covered with flies, and the condenser was an old car radiator that had been soldered with lead several times," he wrote. It was 1978. Marijuana and cocaine had replaced moonshine as the drugs of choice and the ATF shifted its focus to policing illegal guns and explosives.[382]

Allison pointed with pride to the campaign begun in South Carolina, Georgia, and Alabama in 1962 called Operation Dry-Up. By then, more sophisticated means for detecting stills had been found, such as aircraft reconnaissance. The ATF would flood a heavy producing region with its own agents, working with state and local law enforcement, to smash large networks. They also went after bulk buyers of sugar, one of the key ingredients of moonshine. At the same time, a public service campaign educated potential customers about the dangers of drinking moonshine produced by stills made of old auto parts. The message was literally driven home with a bumper sticker that said simply, "Moonshine Kills." Paper fans—the type distributed in unairconditioned churches by funeral homes—were another effective messaging item.[383]

This collection of public service messaging items was part of the Operation Dry-up campaign conducted in the 1960s and 1970s. *FBI Law Enforcement Bulletin*, March 1971, Vol. 40, Number 3.

By the time he left ATF, Allison had earned a law degree and spent the next ten years working as an Alabama assistant attorney general. "I never had any regrets," he said of his ATF career. "Where else would I ever have encountered so many amusing characters like the old Clay County farmer who 'ain't never turned in nobody' but reported the location of his neighbor's still because he was 'damned tired of my dog staggering home drunk.'"[384]

Six months after the Bourbon on the Porch event in Newnan, Georgia, I was back, attending the annual Scottish Heritage and Robert Burns Birthday weekend with many of the same history-, culture-, literature-, and fun-loving people I had partied with during the summer. This time the schedule included a Scotch-tasting at the Newnan-Coweta Historical Society museum, with dashing men in kilts educating us about the niceties of tasting and appreciating Scotch.

THE BOBBY BURNS

At a dinner celebrating the January 25 birthday of the Scottish poet Robert Burns as part of Newnan Scottish Heritage Weekend, we were served haggis—a dish made of sheep entrails that is peculiar to Scotland—and a signature cocktail made with Scotch. It's a simple one and tasty served on ice, as shown, or straight up in a cocktail glass.

- 2 oz. Scotch
- 1 oz. sweet vermouth
- 1 tsp Benedictine
- **Lemon peel for garnish**

Mix ingredients with ice and strain into a cocktail glass or serve on ice.

Scottish rocker Rod Stewart would approve of the Bobby Burns cocktail. *Author photo.*

On the way into the tasting rooms, I passed the museum gift shop and spied a copy of Dot Moore's book *No Remorse: The Rise and Fall of John Wallace*, which introduced me to a weird convergence of moonshine, Andy Griffith, Johnny Cash, and Newnan, the seat of the county where one of the most notorious murder trials of twentieth century Georgia took place—and also the birthplace of W.D. Upshaw.

John Wallace was an influential landowner in Meriwether County, where Warm Springs and the Little White House are located. According to Moore, he wielded enormous power but was secretly in debt to his eyeballs, and like many farmers, he made moonshine on the side to supplement the income from his legitimate enterprises. Both Meriwether and adjoining Coweta County remained dry for years after Prohibition ended.

Wallace served two prison sentences related to his illegal liquor enterprises, one under the Volstead Act and one after Prohibition ended for non-payment of excise taxes. He took up dairy farming after his second release and was proud of his herd of Guernsey milk cows, claiming he had paid $3,000 for a single cow. But when his cash flow was tight, he started making liquor again on the q.t. After all, he was on probation.[385]

He was known as a cruel man with a violent temper. Unprovoked, he had shot an African American man in broad daylight on the street in Chipley, where he was a member of the Methodist church. As the man lay dying, Wallace put his own pocketknife into his hand and shouted, "Self-defense! Self-defense!" He was never charged. He had killed at least two of his black employees as well, without consequence.[386]

In 1945 Wallace hired a young White man named William Turner to work for him. He later provided a house for Turner, his wife and child, and allowed him to share-crop on his land. Turner also helped out at Wallace's still. Wallace claimed that he discovered Turner was operating his own still and turned him in to the authorities. In revenge, Turner stole a number of Wallace's cows, including one of his prize heifers. The prize cow was recovered in Meriwether County, where the sheriff was in Wallace's pocket. He and Wallace arranged to have Turner released the next day and Wallace was waiting for him outside the jail with some of his cronies.[387]

This is where it got complicated. Turner was driving a brand-new truck—something else that rankled Wallace—and led his pursuers on a seventeen-mile chase, running out of gas in front of a tourist court in Moreland. That's the birthplace of Lewis Grizzard, by the way, just over the line in Coweta County. Witnesses later testified in court that they saw Wallace pull Turner from the cab of the truck, whack him on the head with the butt of his shotgun, and load him into the car he was riding in. Turner was never seen again.[388]

In Moore's telling, Lamar Potts, the Coweta County sheriff, was not a friend of Wallace's. Sheriff Potts arrested Wallace and the man driving the car on the charge of kidnapping and began searching for the corpse. At the time, Georgia law stated that murder could not be charged unless there was a body. When it almost looked like the case was lost, Potts got a search warrant for Wallace's house and found his blood-stained clothes in a laundry hamper. An anonymous tipster told him Turner's body had been burned to ashes in a former whiskey still. Two Black field hands told Potts that Wallace forced them to burn the body, which had first been secreted in a well, and then throw the cremains into a nearby creek. Bone shards that filled a tiny matchbox were found in the water, and that was enough to satisfy the law.

The trial, which opened at the Coweta County Courthouse in Newnan on June 14, 1948, created a sensation. One of Wallace's defense lawyers, A.L. Henson of Atlanta, couldn't even find a parking space near the courthouse square and recalled, "Little concession stands were on every corner, serving the crowd with soft drinks and hot dogs." Henson cited a number of irregularities in the trial, including the casual way in which the all-White, all-male jury was called, and the surprise witnesses Sheriff Potts kept under wraps—the two Black field hands who had helped Wallace burn up the body. They gave damning testimony.[389]

On the last day of the trial, Wallace took the stand, against Henson's advice, and spoke for seven hours. He gave a long accounting of his life,

Sheriff Lamar Potts, left, sits beside John Wallace and attorney Fred New during Wallace's 1948 murder trial. *Courtesy Newnan-Coweta Historical Society.*

right up until the day he alleged he had accidentally shot Turner in Meriwether County. At that moment, he said, his mind "just went blank" and he couldn't recall anything that had happened.[390] The courtroom visibly turned against him at this point, not because he murdered someone—that happened all the time—but because he had shown such disrespect for the body. A verdict of guilty was reached before defense attorney Henson had walked half a block to his hotel. Wallace was sentenced to die in the electric chair—the first white man in Georgia ever convicted on the testimony of a "colored man."[391]

With appeals and whatnot, the sentence was not carried out until November 3, 1950, when Wallace was strapped into "Old Sparky," the electric chair at Tattnall Prison in Reidsville. He continued to maintain his innocence until the end. His last words were, "Good-bye, men. I love everybody. I know I'm on my way to Heaven."[392] Wallace's funeral took place at the Methodist church in Chipley followed by his burial at the nearby cemetery. This is the same town where he shot the African American man on the street in cold blood and claimed self-defense.

So how do Andy Griffith and Johnny Cash figure into all this? Cash bought the rights to Margaret Anne Barnes's book about the Wallace case, called *Murder in Coweta County*, and got it produced as a made-for-TV movie which aired in 1983.[393] He played the dogged, incorruptible sheriff Lamar Potts, while Griffith played the murderous moonshiner John Wallace. It was one of just a handful of roles in which Griffith portrayed a villain, and he embraced his part with gusto. In the scene where William Turner's body is being burned and the flames are reflecting off Griffith's face, he looks positively devilish. For the final scene in the electric chair, Griffith's full head of silver hair was shaved—or at least appeared to be. The real John Wallace was already bald as a cue ball.[394]

So, then, how does W.D. Upshaw figure into all this? Well, I'm sure the sanctimonious Mr. Upshaw thought John Wallace got what was coming to him for peddling all the demon liquor to the good people of his former congressional district. But Upshaw cast a long shadow. Coweta County did not allow the sale of liquor in package stores until 2021, when county voters approved an ordinance limiting the number of stores in unincorporated areas to three and putting tight restrictions on where they can be located. A similar ordinance was approved by Newnan residents. Within six months, all six licenses were granted.[395]

MURDER MOST FOUL

While researching this book, I stumbled upon a mystery series penned in the 1930s and 1940s by Fulton Oursler writing under the pen name Anthony Abbot. This is the same Fulton Oursler who wrote the flapper fiction novel *Speakeasy Girl* under the pen name Bobbie Meredith and advised Homer Cummings and J. Edgar Hoover on how to build up the reputation of the FBI with publicity stunts.

In the series of seven books, the police commissioner of New York is Thatcher Colt, a wise, witty, immaculately dressed, and relentless law man who can't pass up personally investigating a juicy murder. Anthony Abbot is his private secretary, John Watson to Colt's Sherlock Holmes. The cases are fictitious but probably have some loose basis on crimes Oursler heard about as editor of several popular magazines, including *True Detective Mysteries*. In *The Shudders*, published in 1943, Colt reflects on Gaston Means, "an abominable man—with an air so ingratiating, so deceptively kind, that he might have passed for the favorite nephew of Santa Claus..."[396]

The first books take place while Prohibition is still in place and Thatcher scrupulously adheres to the Volstead Act, but in the post-1933 volumes, Colt and Abbot often enjoy a cocktail, glass of wine, or a highball.

In only one book, *About the Murder of a Startled Lady*, did I find a cocktail described in detail, and it seems to have been Colt's own invention. While mulling over the seemingly intractable case over lunch at the Waldorf-Astoria, Colt orders some cocktails as they wait to be served: "a debonair concoction of old Maryland rye, Cointreau and a dash of Arak—a dizzy thing that the Commissioner calls a 'formidable,' giving it the French pronunciation," Abbot recalls.[397]

That would be "for-me-DAH-bluh," if I remember my high school French correctly.

Arak is the secret ingredient that makes a rye whiskey cocktail formidable. Several were drunk in *About the Murder of a Startled Lady*. Author photo.

continues on next page

They tossed back two of these powerful tipples prior to lunch, and I'll give you the menu just to make you drool: "Maryland oysters on the half shell; bisque d'homard, lobster a la Foyot [with Béarnaise sauce]; then pressed duck done quite as delicately as one eats it at Laperouse [a Paris restaurant]; a light dessert of pears stewed in champagne; and, as a fitting after-clap, a liqueur from Avignon, known by the unprepossessing title of 'The Sweat of the Holy Virgin,' but very soothing and tasty just the same."

They followed this with a *third* Formidable! And then they went back to the police headquarters and quickly solved the crime. These men were formidable indeed!

I took the description and, following the basic recipe for a Manhattan, came up with my own version of the Formidable. I did not seek out old Maryland rye, but I did splurge on a bottle of Arak made in Lebanon, later learning that this licorice-flavored liqueur is comparable to Greek ouzo, French pastis, and absinthe, so if you have any of those on hand, you can substitute. All you need is a couple of drops.

THE FORMIDABLE

- 2 oz. rye whiskey
- 1 oz. Cointreau
- Dash of Arak

Pour in a shaker with ice, shake, and strain into a chilled cocktail glass, or serve over the rocks. (I actually prefer the rocks version, as the melting ice will dissipate some of the sweetness.)

PROHIBITION EXPEDITION: NEWNAN

This charmer of a small city about forty miles south of Atlanta is constantly hosting special events and festivals, and there is non-stop activity around its courthouse square. The **Historic Courthouse** where John Wallace was convicted of murder in 1948 and sentenced to death in the electric chair now houses the probate court.

After a number of visits to Newnan, my favorite places to eat include **Meat and Greet**, 11 Jefferson Street, www.meatngreetnewnan.com, known not only for great food but for its bourbon selection and fabulous Bloody Marys (sold even on Sundays, W.D. Upshaw!) and the **Redneck Gourmet**, 11 N. Courthouse Square, www.redneckgourmet.com, with sandwiches and sides such as a yummy broccoli and cranberry salad but nothing stronger to drink than iced tea.

Be sure and visit the stately **McRitchie-Hollis Museum**, headquarters of the **Newnan-Coweta Historical Society**.

74 Jackson Street • www.newnancowetahistoricalsociety.com

While you are in this neck of the woods, by all means drive down to Warm Springs in adjoining Meriwether County (John Wallace's stomping grounds), where President Roosevelt enjoyed many happy cocktail gatherings, which he called the "Children's Hour"; you can see some of his martini shakers at the **Little White House** and museum. This house, which he built in 1932 and where he died in 1945, is lovingly preserved and run, along with the excellent museum, by the staff of the Georgia Department of Natural Resources.

401 Little White House Drive, Warm Springs
https://gastateparks.org/LittleWhiteHouse

President Franklin Delano Roosevelt used these cocktail shakers for his daily "Children's Hour" gatherings at the Little White House. *Author photo.*

CEMETERY SIDE TRIP

Where in the world is the grave of W.D. Upshaw? Two cemeteries on opposite sides of the country claim him.

Thomasville, near the Georgia-Florida border, was the hometown of Upshaw's first wife, Margaret, who died in 1942. She was buried in Laurel Hill Cemetery in her family plot under a headstone inscribed "Fear Not I Will Hold Thy Hand." Beside it is the headstone of her husband, inscribed, "He Preached to Many Thousands of People." But there aren't any dates on his stone.

W.D. Upshaw's faux grave is in the family plot of his first wife in Thomasville, Georgia. Photo by Andrea Hancock.

Upshaw relocated to California and became a full-time minister after his political career ended, then married Lily Galloway, head of the California WCTU, in 1946. He lived until 1952, dying after a speaking tour that took him to twenty-two states and seven European countries, validating the words on his gravestone. His death was widely reported by newspapers in both Georgia and California, but details of his funeral and burial were never given. The official record of the U.S. House of Representatives says he was buried at Forest Lawn Memorial Park in Glendale, California, which is where his wife Lily was buried after her death in 1965. His grave is indeed listed on the Forest Lawn website, along with Hollywood royalty the likes of actor Errol Flynn. The hard-living Flynn titled his memoir *My Wicked, Wicked Ways* and was said to have been buried with six bottles of his favorite whiskey.[398]

Thanks to my friend and history buff, Dr. Charles "Chip" Hancock of Thomasville, the riddle was solved. Chip went out to the Laurel Hill Cemetery and with the help of the supervisor, "Big Jimmy," found the Upshaw graves. Both gravestones were covered with lichen and almost illegible. Chip cleaned them up and told Big Jimmy about our quandary. Jimmy got a "probing stick," which he drove into the ground to a depth of about four feet, finding Margaret Upshaw's vault. He could not find a vault for her husband. He said often when one spouse pre-deceases the other, two gravestones are purchased and engraved, with space left for the dates of the survivor. Chip's wife Andrea snapped the photo of the newly cleaned marker.

So W.D. Upshaw is most likely buried at Forest Lawn with the Sodom and Gomorrah of Hollywood. Among the other hard-drinking Forest Lawn residents Upshaw would have disapproved of were Clark Gable, Elizabeth Taylor, Bette Davis, Carrie Fisher, Mary Pickford, and Spencer Tracy. Just to name a few. Unfortunately, I do not know anyone in California I could persuade to take a picture of his grave there.

Recommended Reading

Cocktails Across America: A Postcard View of Cocktail Culture in the 1930s, 40s, and 50s (New York: Countryman Press, 2018) by Diane Lapis and Anne Peck-Davis is a must for those who like unusual cocktails with a backstory, as well as fans of linen postcards. (You can tell I am because I have used so many as illustrations, including the delightful one from Anne's collection at the beginning of this chapter.) Anne also posts vintage cocktail recipes illustrated with linen postcards at annepeckdavis.substack.com.

Public Enemies: America's Greatest Crime Wave and the Birth of the FBI, 1933–34 by Bryan Burrough. (New York: Penguin Books, 2004). This highly readable account of the vanquishing of the 1930s gangs, including Bonnie and Clyde, is awash in blood, bullets, and bad behavior. It's great!

Chapter Nine

Whiskey Tourism

WHAT A WORLD WE LIVE IN. The same states that used to send law men into the mountains to bust up stills and haul people to the pokey for making, selling, transporting, and sometimes even buying alcohol are now trying to lure tourists to drink their bourbon, beer, wine, whiskey, and anything else they can knock back that will generate a buzz. Alcohol tourism is big business, enthusiastically promoted by governors, state and local tourism agencies, chambers of commerce and, of course, the beverage makers themselves, individually and under the umbrella of their trade associations.

Take North Carolina, for example. Like other states, it produces a slick tourism magazine with a welcoming message from the governor. The cover picture of the 2022 guide was of Charlotte bartender Justin Hazelton pouring a tall, cool drink from a shaker against a backdrop of bottles. Inside the guide were three pages of "Primo

Bartender Justin Hazelton was featured on the cover of North Carolina's official tourism magazine.

Pairings" that linked such activities as snorkeling, hang gliding, berry picking, fly fishing, and llama nuzzling with beer drinking, wine tasting, and whiskey sipping.

Tennessee's 2022 guide is a little lower key, perhaps fitting for a state that was the first in the country to pass a dry law.[399] Still, it guides visitors to a White Lightning Trail through "a legendary moonshine corridor" and a Jack Trail that includes, naturally, the Jack Daniel Distillery in Lynchburg. We'll visit Jack's place in this chapter.

But nothing is as in-your-face as the 2022 Kentucky tourism guide, with Governor Andy Beshear touting the state's "world-famous bourbon and horse country" in his welcome letter to the Bluegrass State and extolling the pleasures of a mint julep during racing season. Multiple pages of editorial copy and advertisements urge tourists to visit Bardstown, "Bourbon Capital of the World," Elizabethtown, "Bourbon's Backyard," and Franklin, home of "Bourbon, bridles and boutiques." Pages are peppered with photographs of smiling, laughing people with glasses in hand. And I don't mean eyeglasses.

The Kentucky Distillers Association does its part in promoting tourism with two state bourbon trails that guide visitors to eighteen "signature" (i.e. big-ass) distilleries and twenty-four craft distilleries.

I visited one distillery from each trail during a trip to Kentucky to speak to the Whisky Chicks, a women's brown water appreciation group started in 2014 by Linda Ruffenach of Louisville. (She's the author of a book aimed at women drinkers called *How to be a Bourbon Badass*.)[400] The Chicks meet at distilleries, restaurants, bars, museums, and other venues to sample and learn about the many spirits being made today. They learn about the history of the brands and what makes them special, meanwhile having a great time sipping and socializing. Anyone can join for a modest fee of $95 a year, and if you live outside Kentucky, you can Zoom into the meeting and get a drink kit in the mail (complete with liquor if it is legal to ship to your state). At a meeting at Kentucky Artisan Distillery, I spoke about my book *Baptists and Bootleggers*. Kentucky Artisan was founded in 2012 by the late Steve Thompson, who was the president of giant Louisville distillery Brown-Forman for many years. After retirement he wanted to stretch his wings a bit and implement his own ideas for making whiskey.

Kentucky Artisan is housed in a former ice cream distributor's building in Crestwood, about half an hour from Louisville. The company buys all

Kentucky Artisan could be mistaken for a Cracker Barrel restaurant on the outside, with its front porch of welcoming chairs. *Leo Smith photo.*

the grain for its house brands from an adjacent farm. Its own Whiskey Row Bourbon is a pre-Prohibition style spirit that is 51 percent corn (as required by federal law to be called bourbon) and the remainder a mixture of rye, barley, and wheat. Our guide explained that in pre-Prohibition days, there were not such standard recipes for bourbon as distillers make today, and the companies used the crops that were most prevalent in any given year for the other 49 percent of their mash bill. So you might have a rye-heavy bourbon one year and a wheat-heavy one the next. (Someone joked at the meeting that bourbon is actually 51 percent corn and 49 percent bullshit.)

Kentucky Artisan is also a contract distiller for several companies, most notably the Jefferson's Small Batch Bourbon brand. Perhaps you have heard of Jefferson's Ocean, which is literally aged at sea. Thomas Jefferson was chosen as the brand's patron saint because of his interest in innovation and because, an advertising tag on a bottle I purchased says, "Like our third President, this bourbon is complex, elegant and full of sophistication." Never mind that the real Jefferson was a wine lover who described spirits as "poison"![401]

The cocktail we were greeted with that night is made with Kentucky Artisan's own Billy Goat Strut North American Whiskey, a blend of rye and Canadian whiskey. It is named for the alley behind Whiskey Row in downtown Louisville where deckhands who worked on vessels transporting whiskey down the Ohio River gathered to race goats. The races caused such excitement that even the swells in Louisville began attending them. Thus, the label on the bottle shows a dandy billy goat. Incidentally, the billy goat races predate the race Louisville is best known for, the Kentucky Derby.

THE GOAT

- 1-1.5 oz. Billy Goat Strut Whiskey
- 2 oz. cranberry juice
- 1 lime wedge
- Ginger ale or ginger beer

You make this as you would a Kentucky Mule, putting ice in your glass or copper mug, followed by the whiskey and the juice, squeezing a bit of lime juice, topping it with ginger ale or beer, and using the lime wedge for garnish. A light, refreshing cocktail.

The next day, I got a taste of bourbon production on an industrial scale when my husband Leo and I joined Whisky Chick Katie Rixman and her husband Terry on a visit to Bardstown. Bardstown is home to eleven bourbon companies that produce the majority of Kentucky's—and thus the world's—bourbon whiskey. A tremendous amount of this booze is being generated by Bardstown Bourbon Company, a new kid on the block, which has been distilling only since 2016. The founder was Peter Loftin, who was a telecom billionaire before age thirty and had a "deep love and passion for bourbon," said our guide, Samantha Montgomery. Loftin hired as master distiller Steve Nally, who had fifty

The Goat, with a Bourbon Badass hat to wear when you drink with the Whisky Chicks. *Author photo.*

years in the industry under his belt, the last thirty at Maker's Mark.[402]

Bardstown has its own high-end product line, but it is also a "collaborative distiller," working with more than forty companies to make their whiskey. Samantha explained that they can produce custom recipes, from grain sourcing to barrel sourcing, with 500 custom points for tailoring the product. By the time the distilling operation got going, the company had sold out its capacity for the next five years. It is now one of the top ten whiskey producers in the country, running 24/7 and turning out 7.3 million proof gallons a year, with an expansion of another 50 percent of capacity to be in place by the end of 2023.[403]

Bardstown Bourbon's distillery is full of windows. The bar features an awe-inspiring collection of whiskeys, with the company brands on prominent display. *Leo Smith photos.*

Bardstown Bourbon was designed with tourism in mind, styling itself as a "Napa Valley-style destination," according to its website.[404] The gleaming glass distillery building holds a bar with a three-and-a-half-page menu of "vintage" spirits—including the storied 1975 Pappy Van Winkle Gold Wax 16 Years that sells for $2,500 a shot—and an excellent restaurant where we enjoyed a delicious lunch and cocktails with the Rixmans.

After lunch we had time for one more stop in Bardstown, and it was a blast from the past: the Old Talbott Tavern, built in 1779. The downtown tavern has a number of claims to fame. It's said that Daniel Boone slept there. So did a five-year-old Abraham Lincoln, and the exiled king of France, Louis Phillipe (though not together). His royal highness supposedly had murals painted on the walls of his suite that featured birds so life-like that when the outlaw Jesse James stayed there a few decades later, he drunkenly shot at them, imagining the birds were alive. There are bullet holes in the wall as proof. Or not.

The Old Talbott Tavern has welcomed the famous and infamous to Bardstown for almost 250 years. *Photo by Patrick Baehl de Lescure via Wikimedia Commons.*

These factoids were quickly recited by Cal Sherwood, who was manning the cash register for the gift shop at Talbott Tavern, which also claims to be the oldest stagecoach stop in America. And, oh, by the way, it's haunted.

The saying that bourbon is 51 percent corn and 49 percent bullshit certainly applies to the Talbott Tavern, as many of the claims are watered down in its informational hand-out with words such as "legends say" and "it's reported." Nevertheless, it's a charming place to stop for a meal, a drink, or the night, as it still offers rooms to rent. Just bring ear plugs and a sleep mask so you won't be bothered by the ghosts.

All is not well in Bardstown, however, as I learned when the state's legislature convened in early 2023. First, some background about bourbon economics.

Considering the impact of the whiskey industry on Kentucky's economy, it is no wonder Governor Beshear is such a cheerleader for alcohol-based tourism. A study released in 2021 by the Kentucky Distillers Association said the bourbon industry had tripled in size since 2009, pours $9 billion into the state's economy each year, generates more than 22,500 jobs with a $1.23 billion payroll, and pays $285 million in tax revenue. Enthused Governor Beshear, "We all know that Kentucky crafts 95 percent of the world's bourbon and 100 percent of the bourbon worth drinking. But today's news proves that our signature spirit is so much more, and the growth is simply staggering…I'm thrilled Team Kentucky is part of the growth and am glad to help move it forward for the decades to come."[405]

We walked into the Talbott Tavern bar—"the world's oldest bourbon bar"—where an industrious bartender named Alexia fixed the drink she said was a past winner of the Kentucky Bourbon Festival cocktail contest. It's a twist on the sidecar and she had it mixed up in a gallon jug, enough for a spring party with your closest bourbon-loving friends. Here's Terry Rixman's calculation of how to make a batch:

OLD TALBOTT TAVERN SIDECAR

Mix together and then chill for several hours.

A strawberry-infused sidecar sits in front of a bank of bottles in the Talbott Tavern bar. *Author photo.*

- 5 cups Woodford Reserve bourbon
- 3 cups strawberry simple syrup
- 2 cups lemon juice
- 1 cup Cointreau

Shake well before serving in cocktail glasses with sugared rims.

But here's the rub. The whiskey industry, like every industry, thinks it pays too much in taxes. Kentucky is the only state in the country that imposes a property tax on barrels of aging whiskey. To be labeled straight bourbon, the law requires the liquor to age for a minimum of two years in a charred oak barrel. Premium bourbons may age for six to ten years. So a distillery, especially a start-up, could pay taxes for years before they've sold a drop of bourbon. (That's why so many new distilleries sell moonshine, vodka, gin, or rum, because they don't have to be aged.) The Kentucky Distillers Association has been working for years to get the barrel tax removed, arguing that it discourages start-up craft distillers from choosing Kentucky and might even cause some existing distilleries to relocate their barrel houses to other states. Early in 2023, a bill was introduced in the legislature to phase out the barrel tax.

However, the tax, which generated almost $40 million in 2022, supports local schools, libraries, and government operations such as fire departments. In Bardstown, Mayor J. Richard Heaton told television station WKYT, "If this was something that was really killing them, like what was happening back in the 80s when bourbon was out of favor, I could see the need. But I just don't see it at this time. It's not the hindrance that the sponsors of this bill would have us believe."[406] One of the lawmakers criticizing the bill was Rep. Candy Massaroni, who represents Bardstown. "This is a tax cut for a booming industry," she told the Associated Press. "And ultimately, this is going to put more of a tax burden upon my constituents."[407]

Heaton and Massaroni lost. The bill was passed on the last day of the 2023 legislative session and immediately signed into law by Governor Beshear.[408] The final version gave the distillers a state income tax credit equal to what they pay in barrel tax and requires the credit to be invested by the company in its Kentucky operations. It goes into effect in 2026 and the barrel tax is phased out over a period of seventeen years.

Prohibition Expedition: Kentucky

There are two outstanding heritage hotels where I have stayed in downtown Louisville. I chose the **Seelbach** for my *Baptists and Bootleggers* research trip and for this book Leo and I stayed at **The Brown**. Regardless of what my Aunt Susan and I said about the pleasures of The Commonwealth in Richmond, the Brown, built in 1923, is absolutely the most wonderful hotel where I have ever stayed, with lovely rooms, a top-notch staff, piano bar, and a restaurant where I shook off the cold by feasting on the famous Hot Brown open-faced turkey sandwich. Treat yourself to an exceptional stay!

335 West Broadway • www.brownhotel.com

Kentucky Artisan Distillery is one of twenty-four craft distilleries on the Kentucky Bourbon Trail.

6230 Old LaGrange Road, Crestwood • www.kentuckyartisandistillery.com

Bardstown, which claims it has been "aging since 1780" and is the home of the **Kentucky Bourbon Festival** (www.kybourbonfestival.com) is a favorite stop on Kentucky's Bourbon Trail. Among the places bourbon enthusiasts can tour in the area are:

Bardstown Bourbon Company • 1500 Parkway Drive
www.bardstownbourbon.com

Heaven Hill Bourbon Experience • 1311 Gilkey Run Road
www.heavenhilldistillery.com

Lux Row • 3050 E. John Rowan Boulevard
www.luxrowdistillers.com

The **Talbott Tavern** is certainly worth a visit, whether the legends are true or not!

107 W. Stephen Foster Avenue • www.talbotttavern.com

There is also a museum of whiskey history under the auspices of the **Bardstown Historical Museum.**

114 North Fifth Street • www.oscargetzwhiskeymuseum.com

CEMETERY SIDETRIP

You may not be able to afford a bottle of the legendary Pappy Van Winkle bourbon—or even a shot—but it doesn't cost anything to visit his grave. **Julian "Pappy" Van Winkle** is buried at Cave Spring Cemetery in Louisville. He died at age ninety after a lifetime of distilling, just before another massive wave of industry consolidation captured Stitzel-Weller, which he had built into a powerhouse Louisville mainstay known for quality. The Pappy Van Winkle Family Reserve bourbon features a picture of the famous distiller lighting a cigar. Cave Spring is the final resting place of so many distillers that it hosts Bourbon Distillers of Cave Hill Wagon Tours. Other famous people buried there are boxer **Muhammed Ali** and suffrage, abolition, and temperance advocate **Susan Look Avery.** 701 Baxter Avenue. www.cavehillcemetery.com

Pappy Van Winkle Family Reserve has a cult-like following. *Craig L. Duncan via Wikimedia Commons.*

Kentucky's neighbor Tennessee makes a spirit that looks like bourbon and tastes like bourbon but is produced by a slightly different method that earns it the designation Tennessee whiskey. The Tennessee Distillers Guild created a Tennessee Whiskey Trail with thirty-nine participating distilleries spread across the state. The greatest concentrations are around Nashville and the Sevierville-Gatlinburg region, but the granddaddy of those places is certainly the Jack Daniel Distillery in Lynchburg.

Lynchburg, population 6,378, is in rural Moore County, which famously declares itself a dry county, even though it contains ninety-plus seven-story barrel houses, each containing more than a million gallons of Jack Daniel's Tennessee Whiskey. A tee shirt I bought—not authorized by the company—tells the tale.

But wait, there's more to the story. Since 2019, thanks to the loosening of government regulations, you can buy a beer to go with your meal at a Lynchburg restaurant. You can also buy a bottle of wine to go with your meal at the Lynchburg Winery, whose retail outlet is located on the charming town square, and you can even get a liquor cocktail at a tasting room operated by an upstart craft distillery owned by the same people who own the winery. You can buy bottles of whiskey at the Jack Daniel Distillery and enjoy tastings along with your $30 admission ticket.[409] So maybe it's more accurate to say Moore is a damp county than a dry county.

This tee shirt questions the notion of a "dry" county. *Author photo.*

The competition for drinking dollars in Lynchburg is totally one-sided, of course, because the only reason people come to town is to visit Jack Daniel. The distillery was begun by Jasper "Jack" Daniel himself—employees refer to the long-dead founder as "Jack," just like he might walk by at any minute in his Panama hat—in 1875 when he was twenty-five years old (or thereabouts) and came into an inheritance. He learned the art of distilling under Dan Call, a Lutheran pastor who took him in as a farm hand when he ran away from home as a small boy, and an enslaved man working on the Call farm, Nathan Green, known as Uncle Nearest. Following the Civil War, Nearest Green, now a free man, came to work for Daniel at the distillery. He became the master distiller, and Green descendants have worked for the company ever since. Full credit is given to Green's role at the very handsome welcome center a few steps from the heart of Lynchburg that replaced a more modest one in 2000. It contains many historic displays, including collections of bottles and even some of dapper Jack's clothing.

Unlike modern start-up distilleries that have everything on a walkable campus, the Jack Daniel distillery grew organically and is spread out over hills that require walking up and down and even a short bus ride. Before visitors set off, though, they have a photo op in front of a Jack Daniel barrel truck where they are instructed to smile by a photographer shouting, "One-two-three, whiskey!" Photo packages costing $35 can be purchased after the tour. However, you are allowed to take as many personal photos as you want at no extra charge.

When Leo and I visited, we learned that what sets Tennessee whiskey apart from bourbon is a final filtering through crushed sugar maple charcoal chips, which gives it a mellow finish. We were taken step by step

This picture on display at the Jack Daniel's welcome center shows Jack, in white hat and string tie, beside George Green, one of the sons of Nearest Green. *Leo Smith photo.*

through the process by our spritely guide, Maddie, who escorted us to Cave Spring, the source of the water used in making all the Jack Daniel's whiskey in the world. We also visited the modest white wood frame building that was the first headquarters of the company and saw the safe which Jack kicked, injuring his foot, and setting off a lengthy health problem that, complicated by diabetes, would eventually end his life. By the time he died in 1911, Tennessee had passed state prohibition and wouldn't repeal it until 1938. As Maddie said, "We just flat-out had too many churches."

As told in *Blood and Whiskey*, Peter Krass's biography of Daniel, the ownership of the distillery passed to Lem Motlow, the bad-tempered nephew of the unmarried Daniel. Trying to stay in business, he moved most of his stock to St. Louis, where he eventually sold it to the master bootlegger George Remus, then spent the Prohibition years as a mule trader.

Like just about every visitor to the distillery, I had my picture taken with Jack on the Rocks. The real Jack was a diminutive five-foot-two and notably portly. The statue Jack is five-foot-seven. I shared with him a copy of my book *Baptists and Bootleggers*. Leo Smith photo.

To revive his business after Prohibition was repealed, Motlow got elected to the legislature, mostly so he could convince his colleagues to support enabling legislation, and in 1938 the next generation of Jack Daniel's Tennessee Whiskey was barreled. The company had become a moderately successful regional producer by the time Motlow died in 1947 and his sons took over the business.[410]

Back at the distillery, we ended the tour and repaired to a room for an "educational whiskey tasting," the legal designation that enables Jack

Daniel to evade the dry law in Moore County. (The company is also able to sell its booze at a "bottle shop" on the premises because these are "souvenir" bottles. Prior to 2012, visitors had to make do with a glass of lemonade.) Because Leo and I had opted for the high-end Angel's Share tour, we were offered the high-end booze, including a few sips of Sinatra Select, which sells for $150 a bottle.

Maddie explained that entertainer Frank Sinatra was the biggest booster of Jack Daniel's Old No. 7, not as a paid endorser but because he loved the stuff.[411] He was introduced to it by actor and comedian Jackie Gleason in 1947. As the story goes, 1955 was the year that Sinatra brought a rocks glass onstage with him and uttered this magical line: "Ladies and gentlemen, this is Jack Daniel's, and it's the nectar of the gods."[412] The huge jump in sales that followed led to the distillery's 1956 purchase by Brown-Forman for $20 million. Louisville-based Brown-Forman had the muscle and marketing expertise to make Jack Daniel's an international brand.[413] Today it is the best-selling whiskey in the world, and despite the introduction of trendy honey-flavored and Granny Smith-flavored whiskeys by the company, 98 percent of what it sells is Old No. 7.

Sinatra's love of Jack Daniel's whiskey and his own 3-2-1 recipe followed him to the grave. He was buried in 1998 with a bottle of Old No. 7 in his jacket pocket. There is a legend that he also brought with him a pack of Camels and a roll of dimes for calling friends.

What Sinatra was drinking with such relish is not the same whiskey that buyers get today. As Americans' tastes drifted from brown liquor to vodka and gin, mixed drinks like Jack and Coke and Jack and ginger became popular. The company did some blind taste-testing with consumers and learned they were just as happy with Old No. 7 that was 80-proof (40 percent alcohol) as they were with the stuff that was 86-proof (43 percent alcohol). So in 2004 they started watering it down as an economy measure. There were few complaints, and Frank was long gone, though he was no doubt spinning in his grave.[414]

Maddie told us that Jack Daniel, working with the Sinatra family, decided to develop a special whiskey that was more like the stuff Ol' Blue Eyes loved. The result was Sinatra Select, which is 90 proof and aged in barrels that have been grooved to impart an oakier flavor.

SINATRA 3-2-1

In a rocks glass, place three ice cubes and add two ounces Jack Daniel's Old No. 7 and a splash of water. Stir and enjoy.

In a county where sixty to seventy percent of the working population is employed by Jack Daniel Distillery or a related business, Lynchburg is a company town that has to tread lightly with its "benefactor." But that hasn't stopped some residents of an adjoining county from getting riled about the less pleasant aspects of living with millions of gallons of whiskey aging in nearby barrel houses.

A side effect of the aging process is whiskey fungus, a black, mold-like growth that feeds off the alcohol that evaporates from the wooden barrels. (The industry term for this evaporation is the "angel's share.")

There's nothing simpler than a Sinatra 3-2-1. *Author photo.*

Tour guide Maddie pointed out some of this fungus clinging to the branches of trees on the distillery property and assured us it was perfectly harmless. But it does look pretty awful, sort of like Christmas trees that have been flocked in black rather than white, or really dirty snow in New Jersey.

With the company adding even more barrel houses in neighboring Lincoln County, a couple of residents have gotten up in arms about the stuff that clings to their homes, landscaping, and even their cars. The *New York Times* reported in early 2023 that a woman who rents out her historic home as an event venue sued the company over the damage to her property. The company issued a statement that Jack Daniel Distillery "complies with all local, state, and federal regulations regarding the design, construction, and permitting of our barrelhouses." A company representative at a Lincoln County Commission meeting affirmed that the fungus isn't harmful to human life. "Could it be a nuisance?" she asked. "Yeah, sure. And it can easily be remedied by having it washed off." However, she said the distillery could not be expected to do the power-washing because of "liability concerns."⁴¹⁵

As a friend of mine who owned a hog farm once said, "It smells like money to me."

The Jack Daniel story is one of the few whiskey marketing tales that hasn't been greatly embellished or completely fabricated, as Reid Mitenbuler shows in his "pay-no-attention-to-the-man-behind-that-curtain" book *Bourbon Empire*. But it's been less than ten years since the company openly embraced the contributions of Nearest Green. And therein lies another true tale.

UNCLE NEAREST PREMIUM WHISKEY

Nearest Green Distillery • 3125 U.S. 231, Shelbyville
www.unclenearest.com/distillery

A serial entrepreneur named Fawn Weaver was on a business trip to Singapore with her husband Keith in 2016 when Brown-Forman, owner of the Jack Daniel Distillery, acknowledged that Nearest Green had taught the young Jack the secrets of the Lincoln County method. Looking at an old photograph of Daniel seated beside Nearest's son George Green—Nearest was never photographed—Weaver was fascinated and intrigued. Upon returning to the United States, she went to Lynchburg and sought out descendants of Green and others who could help her flesh out the story for a book she planned to write.

In this photograph at the Jack Daniel Distillery, Jack is labeled 1, George Green as 2. *Author photo.*

She dug deep, not only with interviews but in archives, and also bought the former Dan Call farm where Daniel and Green had worked. Her work

continues on next page

Fawn Weaver, left, and Victoria Eady Butler have won numerous awards for their Uncle Nearest whiskey. *Photo Courtesy Nearest Green Distillery.*

drew attention, not only from Brown-Forman, which stepped up its efforts to include Nearest Green in the narratives of its Jack Daniel tours, but from a slew of volunteers who were as fascinated by the story as she was.[416]

In a 2022 interview in *Forbes*, she said, "The crazy part is I didn't recruit anyone. People just kept showing up. To this day, I have counted that I had twenty archivists, archeologists, genealogists, historians that all worked alongside me. Not a single person ever billed me."[417]

By 2017, Weaver, who had no background in distilling but extensive experience in the hospitality industry, decided to release an Uncle Nearest Premium Whiskey. She worked with a Tennessee distilling company at first, but then established her own distillery, recruiting a great-great granddaughter of Green's, Victoria Eady Butler, who likewise had no distillery experience, to work in administration. Perhaps not surprisingly, Eady Butler exhibited a magic palate for whiskey, resulting in her quick elevation to master blender. Weaver and her mostly female team have combined the story and the quality liquor they produce into a powerhouse brand, the fastest growing one in U.S. history and the largest one owned by African Americans. It has also won more than 550 awards, and Eady Butler was singled out by *Whisky Magazine* in 2020 and 2021 as master blender of the year—the first time anyone had received the honor for two years running.[418]

Leo and I made a visit to the Nearest Green Distillery in Shelbyville, about a twenty-minute drive from Lynchburg, on a clear and crisp fall day. Unlike the Jack Daniel Distillery, which has grown organically over more than a century, the 270-acre Nearest Green property, a former Tennessee Walking

The Nearest Green welcome center is located in a renovated horse arena. *Wikimedia Commons.*

Horse farm, was designed with tourism in mind. Immaculate white buildings with Lincoln green roofs sit on lawns encircled by white fences, horses picturesquely grazing on the grass. The welcome center, located in a renovated horse arena, exhibits sepia oil portraits of the Green family based on old photographs, and artifacts uncovered at the former Dan Call farm. It also offers a spectacular array of branded merchandise. The brochure we were given confides, "...if the design of our retail space reminds you a little bit of Disney World, well, that's because it was designed by the former president of Disney Stores Worldwide...and no one merchandises like the Mouse!"

Among the branded merchandise at the welcome center are plush dog toys shaped like whiskey bottles. *Author photo.*

I'll say. The Nearest Green name and logo—a whiskey glass nestled in a horseshoe—is sewn, stamped, engraved and burned on glasses, flasks, and every kind of clothing you can imagine, including Converse sneakers and breast cancer awareness tee shirts (in pink, of course), key chains, cigar cutters, golf balls, baby bibs, and onesies. And don't forget your furry friends at home. There are even Uncle Nearest bowties for dogs and chew toys shaped like bottles of Uncle Nearest Premium Whiskey. I bought an embroidered patch for $6 and a bottle of whiskey and considered myself fortunate to have withstood greater temptation.

continues on next page

Xavier Northcutt conducts a tasting of four Uncle Nearest brands. *Author photo.*

Our tour guide was Xavier Northcutt, a personable young man who had previously worked for Jack Daniel. He guided us around the property, starting at a concession stand and telling the stories of Tennessee-origin foods, such as Moon Pies, cotton candy (originally called "fairy floss" and invented by a dentist who must have been drumming up business), Little Debbie snack cakes, Mountain Dew, and Goo-goo Clusters, and extolled the menu at the Barrel House BBQ cafeteria that would be a handy site for lunch after the tour. (It was, and the food was both decadent and delicious).

In some ways, if you've toured one distillery you've toured them all, but I have to admit I had never been taken into a dry speakeasy at a distillery before. Here, Xavier temporarily turned over the tour group to Erin McBee, who told the intertwined story of temperance and women's suffrage in Tennessee, including the crucial vote ratifying the Nineteenth Amendment passed in August 1920 due to the vote of young legislator Harry Burn. She reminded us that women activists in the late nineteenth and early twentieth centuries brought us not only Prohibition and the right to vote, but also safe water fountains nationwide, industrial schools for women, and battered women's shelters, and convinced male lawmakers to raise the age of sexual consent, which in Delaware had been just seven, to at least sixteen. Eek. There we also watched a short film about Nearest Green narrated by prominent actor Jeffrey Wright, whose noteworthy roles include the villainous Valentin Narcisse in *Boardwalk Empire*.

Xavier guided us by the still house, which was under construction, explaining that all production and barreling was at the time centered in Columbia, Tennessee, but some would be done on site. (Fawn Weaver later expanded on that in an email to me, saying the company is "allocating the still house in Shelbyville for our most exclusive labels.") As with all distillery tours, we wound up in a tasting room, trying the various spirits, Xavier joking, "What looks like sweet tea damn well doesn't taste like sweet tea!" We began with the Uncle Nearest Small Batch 1884—named for the year Green retired—which Xavier described as a good mixer with ginger ale, and the Uncle Nearest Premium Whiskey 1856—named for the year Green perfected the Lincoln County process, which he said was good served straight on the rocks or as the main ingredient of an old fashioned or Manhattan cocktail. These varieties are sold in all fifty states and internationally. The premium 121 proof Master Blend, which we also tasted, is only sold on site.

Since my visit, the Nearest Green Distillery has continued to grow. It now has a full-service restaurant, the world's longest bar, and a performance arena that seats 4,000 people. In an email to me, Weaver wrote, "Our goal is to be within the top three most visited distilleries in the world within the next three years and I have no doubt we'll get there."[419]

THE NEAREST AND JACK-HATTAN

I love Manhattans but I also like a rocks drink I can sip. My favorite for a quiet evening is this one, which combines products from both the Nearest Green and Jack Daniel distilleries.

- 2 oz. Uncle Nearest 1884
- 1 oz. sweet vermouth
- 3 dashes Jack Daniel's Bitters

Put ice cubes in a small rocks glass, add the whiskey, vermouth, and bitters, stir well, and garnish with a maraschino cherry or two. This drink has a nice bite, and if you let it sit too long and the ice starts to melt, you can freshen it with another ounce of Uncle Nearest and more ice.

The Nearest and Jack-hattan is a nice fireside sip. *Author photo.*

PROHIBITION EXPEDITION: TENNESSEE

Lynchburg has worked hard to preserve its bucolic look and most visitors come for day visits because there are so few places to spend the night. However, we were lucky enough to find rooms at the **Lynchburg Country Inn**, a one-star motel with immaculate, comfortable rooms run by an Indian family. The décor was an intriguing mix of elephants and bourbon barrels.

Lynchburg Country Inn • 423 Majors Boulevard,
a short walk from downtown and the distillery • ww.lynchburgcountryinn.com

The **Jack Daniel Distillery** • 133 Lynchburg Highway
www.jackdaniels.com/en-us/visit-us

Downtown Lynchburg is an extension of Jack Daniel's Land, with virtually every shop devoted to selling Tennessee whiskey souvenirs. If you spend a certain amount of money at any shop, you get a complimentary Jack Daniel's shot glass.

After walking around, Leo and I enjoyed lunch at the **Bar-b-que Caboose Café**.

Bar-b-que Caboose Café • 217 Main Street
www.bar-b-quecaboosecafe.com

Lynchburg Distillery produces mostly moonshine and other "white" liquors but offers small-batch whiskey as well. Even in "dry" Moore County, you can buy a cocktail or a bottle there.

Lynchburg Distillery • 30 Hiles Street • www.lynchburgdistillery.com

In Shelbyville we stayed at a charming bed and breakfast, the **Belmont Inn**, located in the renovated antebellum Bailey P. Evans home, where we slept in a beautifully appointed four-poster bed.

Belmont Inn • 422 Belmont Avenue • www.belmontinntn.com

You don't have to pay the admission price to eat at the **Barrel House B-B-Q** at the Nearest Green Distillery. Its specialties include the grilled cheese on crack sandwich that was extolled by tour guide Xavier.

CEMETERY SIDE TRIP

Both **Jack Daniel** and his ornery nephew **Lem Motlow** are buried in the **Lynchburg City Cemetery**, which is dotted with whiskey barrels repurposed into trash receptacles. Writes Daniel's biographer Peter Krass, "After Jack was buried in the family plot, two cast-iron chairs mysteriously appeared next to his headstone—it was said they were for the women who mourned the passing of the county's most eligible bachelor."[420] Cast-iron chairs (probably not the originals) still flank the headstone, though they are turned away from it, all the better for taking selfies while you hoist a shot glass. **Motlow's** grave is marked by a simple, imposing granite slab engraved with his name and birth and death dates. 217 Main Street. www.countyoffice.org/lynchburg-city-cemetery-lynchburg-tn-c59

RECOMMENDED READING

Blood and Whiskey: The Life and Times of Jack Daniel by Peter Krass (Hoboken, N.J.: John Wiley and Sons, 2004) is a lively read. There's plenty about Nearest Green in this book too.

Bourbon Empire: The Past and Future of American Whiskey by Reid Mitenbuler (New York: Viking, 2015) provides a fascinating look behind the marketing, from the American colonial days to the 21st century.

Dead Distillers: A History of the Upstarts and Outlaws Who Made American Spirits by Colin Spoelman and David Haskell (New York: Abrams Image, 2016) also tells you where their bodies are buried, unless no one knows.

CHAPTER TEN

In Search of Sobriety

THIS CRAZY STORY about an alcohol-infused rampage has been traveling around the internet for years, a hoax started on a Facebook page. It was sent to me a few months ago by my son Adam, who is in long-term recovery. He has been attending Alcoholics Anonymous meetings—which he colloquially calls "the program"—and wrote, "After being in the program the willingness for that dude to go through all that doesn't surprise me at all."

As long as there has been alcohol, there have been what we call alcoholics, and virtually anyone reading this book has a bleary-eyed

> 26 SEP 15:
> ABUSE OF PUBLIC ANIMAL, DRUNKEN OR RECKLESS DRIVING
> CAMP PENDLETON, SAN DIEGO, CALIFORNIA
>
> SEP 15: "MALE NAVY ENLISTED FIRST CLASS PETTY OFFICER EXITED A BAR INTOXICATED IN AN ATTEMPT TO DRIVE A POV EQUIPPED WITH A BREATHALYZER INTERLOCK SYSTEM. SUSPECT WAS TOO INTOXICATED TO SUCCESSFULLY START THE VEHICLE, SO HE WENT INTO THE PARK WHERE HE CAPTURED A RACOON RUMMAGING IN A TRASH RECEPTACLE. INDIVIDUAL UTILIZED THE RACOON TO BLOW INTO THE INTERLOCK SYSTEM SUCCESSFULLY, BUT THE RACOON BECAME UNCONSCIOUS FROM BEING SQUEEZED AND WAS DISCARDED ON THE FLOORBOARD OF THE VEHICLE UNTIL A SHORT TIME LATER WHEN THE RACOON REGAINED CONSCIOUSNESS AND BEGAN TO ATTACK THE SUSPECT WHILE DRIVING, CAUSING THE VEHICLE TO CRASH INTO A RESIDENTIAL FENCE. THE VEHICLE CAME TO A COMPLETE STOP IN AN INGROUND SWIMMING POOL. THE SUSPECT SUSTAINED NUMEROUS SCRATCHES AND BITE MARKS TO THE HANDS, FACE, STOMACH, AND ARMS."

It looks real, but it's a hoax. *Courtesy Reddit.*

owl (or three) roosting in the family tree. Some people are able simply to stop, even after years of heavy drinking. For many others, addiction can be impossible to overcome. This book is littered with stories about alcoholics, among them Ethan Allen, Chang Bunker, Adolphus Busch, Jack Daniel, Warren G. Harding, "Machine Gun" and Kathryn Kelly, and Elliott White Springs. The old joke that no great story begins with the words, "I was at a salad bar," has a counterpoint in that a lot of those stories end with a blackout and a bad hangover.

The idea of self-help groups for alcoholics originated in 1840 in a tavern in Baltimore, where six working men signed a pledge to stop drinking. Writes Susan Cheever in *Drinking in America*, "The men came to understand that helping other men get sober actually helped them stay sober themselves."[421] They called themselves the George Washington Society, or the Washingtonians, taking the name of the most ideal man they could think of. (Doubtless, they didn't know about his post-presidential career.) Within a few years, Washingtonian chapters were established in many cities and membership was estimated at half a million men. That's especially remarkable when you consider that the entire U.S. population in 1850 was only 23.1 million people.[422] But the members divided on the issue of temperance legislation—some thought it was a good idea, others that the Washingtonians should be focusing on individuals, not society at large—and they were also criticized by some church leaders for regarding alcoholism as a disease rather than a moral failing. By the time of the Civil War, the organization was on the wane, but its basic concepts would be resurrected in the twentieth century by Alcoholics Anonymous.[423]

AA was founded shortly after Prohibition ended by an alcoholic businessman named Bill Wilson, usually referred to simply as Bill W. He had begun drinking as a doughboy during World War I and, despite great success as a stock trader in the 1920s, by the last years of Prohibition was making two bottles of bathtub gin a day and filching money for beer from his wife's purse. In 1932, he resolved to quit drinking, but found that he couldn't. Even after repeated hospital stays, he would dry out, stay sober for a few months, and go right back to the bottle. Writing in what AA calls the *Big Book*, Bill W. said, "Everyone became resigned to the certainty that I would have to be shut up somewhere or would stumble along to a miserable end."[424]

One day a friend who had been a drinking buddy came to call. He refused the drink Bill offered him and informed him he had quit drinking. "I've got religion," he said simply. Bill writes that he was skeptical, but he listened to his friend talk for hours and slowly realized he could turn his problem over to "a Power greater than myself" and finally get sober.[425]

Once he sobered up, Bill and his wife began enthusiastically reaching out to other alcoholics. AA's birthday is considered to be June 10, 1935, when Bill met an alcoholic doctor, Bob Smith, and helped him stop drinking. He is known within the program as Dr. Bob.

The methods these men devised have evolved into what AA calls the Twelve Steps, beginning with, "We admitted we were powerless over alcohol, that our lives had become unmanageable."[426] They combined an explanation of the steps with personal stories of AA members and published them in the first *Big Book* in 1939. At the time, AA had about a hundred members. In the foreword to the book, the authors explained they had to remain anonymous because if their identities were known they would be so overwhelmed by alcoholics asking for help they could not carry on their professions and occupations.[427] AA members continue this practice, only sharing their first names at meetings. A coded way for one recovering alcoholic to identify another is to ask, "Are you a friend of Bill W.'s?"

The same year the *Big Book* was published, a writer named Morris Markey heard about AA and pitched the idea for a story to Fulton Oursler—yes, the same Fulton Oursler who has popped up over and over in this book—who immediately assigned it to him for the September 30, 1939 edition of *Liberty* magazine, which he edited. Oursler's wife Grace Perkins had suffered from alcoholism for years, and he well knew the misery caused by addiction.[428]

The issue of *Liberty* with the story about AA caused a furor and became a collector's item.

Markey's article, "Alcoholics and God," caused a furor. The magazine received 800 letters from people asking for help, which were turned over to AA leaders. Many letter writers bought a copy of the *Big Book*, and more AA chapters were started around the country. By the time the second edition of the *Big Book* came out in 1955, AA had 6,000 groups and 150,000 members.[429] In 2021, AA estimated it had more than 120,000 groups world-wide, with 1.9 million members.[430] The head count is hard to determine as there are no membership fees or dues, and many recovering alcoholics attend multiple group meetings. "The only requirement for membership," the *Big Book* states, "is an honest desire to stop drinking."[431]

Oursler's wife Grace finally got sober thanks to AA, and he became a board member of the AA Foundation, which raises the money to underwrite the organization's work. Individual AA groups have no paid staff, with each group being self-supporting by passing a hat at meetings. Learning from the Washingtonians, AA does no endorsements and takes no political stands. Its sole mission is to help alcoholics stop drinking.

AA isn't the only path to sobriety, of course. There are even non-anonymous groups like FAVOR—an acronym for Faces and Voices of Recovery—whose vision statement says "The community embraces and celebrates recovery from substance use disorders as a positive, healing force,"[432] and the for-profit addiction "industry" is a tremendous one. For many people who want to stop or drink less alcohol for physical and mental health reasons, a new wave of options has arisen in recent years under the Sober Curious movement. Ruby Warrington's 2018 book by that title became a best-seller,[433] as did *The Unexpected Joy of Being Sober* by Catherine Gray and *Quit Like a Woman: The Radical Choice Not to Drink in a Culture Obsessed with Alcohol* by Holly Whitaker. There's even a name for this genre: Quit Lit.

Around the time these books were published, the world was in for a shock known as the covid-19 pandemic. As people sheltered in their homes, worried about their finances, and feared for their lives, drinking in the United States escalated. (The liquor store where I trade tripled its sales in a matter of months.) Looking back on alcohol-related deaths during the epidemic, a study published in the *Journal of the American Medical Association* in March 2022 found a 25.5 percent increase in alcohol-related deaths due to liver disease in 2020 compared to the previous year. There was a 35.1 percent increase in deaths "with an underlying cause of alcohol-related mental and behavioral disorders." Sharper increases were noted in opioid deaths in which alcohol was a contributing factor.[434]

The study's lead investigator, Aaron M. White, told the *Washington Post* that he was worried that the amount of drinking done during the pandemic would carry over into post-pandemic years. He was especially concerned about the rise in drinking among women.[435]

During this escalation, there was also a surge in the development of products for people who wanted to go to a social event and sip something besides sparkling water and not get drunk on the contents. These faux wines, beers, and liquors are finding their way onto the menus of bars and restaurants, being sold online, and even at non-alcoholic bottle shops. One of these is Sèchey, which opened on Charleston's tony King Street in 2022.

SÈCHEY, 'A MODERN BOTTLE SHOP'

Sèchey, 540 King Street • www.sechey.com

Sèchey (pronounced SE-shay) is a made-up name based on the French word sèche, which means dry, according to Elise Nelson, the company's brand director. Its motto is "Drink Less. Live More." After I was shown around the bright and inviting shop by staffer Emily and served a non-alcoholic cocktail by mixologist Erin, Elise and I settled down on facing gray velvet couches for a chat.

Elise began working with Sèchey's founder and owner Emily Heintz in 2021, when she was selling non-alcoholic products online out of her

Emily Heintz is the proprietor of Sèchey, "a modern bottle shop" in Charleston. *Photo courtesy Sèchey.*

continues on next page

home and delivering them in the Charleston area. Heintz, a veteran of the retail and technology commerce world, did so well that Sèchey progressed to short-term pop-up stores and then opened a longer-term pop-up on King Street near Marion Square. Sèchey moved into the present location at 540 King Street in December 2022.

The shop's offerings include wines and beers that contain no alcohol up to around 0.5 percent (which was the threshold in the Volstead Act, by the way), as well as canned and bottled cocktails and what they call "functional" beverages. These are hemp-based or contain other ingredients that "can take the edge off in a more natural and gentle way," Elise explained. They also sell non-alcoholic alternatives to bourbon, gin, vodka, and rum, which can be used in mixed drinks, either on their own or combined with the real thing to reduce the amount of alcohol in the drink. Rather than the term "sober curious," Elise uses "alcohol flexible," adding, "Our mission is not sobriety but mindfulness."

Elise, a former bartender who no longer drinks, noted that non-alcoholic beverages that mimic alcoholic ones have been around for a long time, but the quality has improved in the past couple of years. "It's not just about alternatives but having good alternatives," she said. On staffer Emily's recommendation, I bought a bottle of Jøyus, a .5 percent alcohol rosè, made in Seattle, Washington with dealcoholized wine and white grape juice concentrate as its primary ingredients. It's a little more fruit-forward than the dry rosè I prefer, but a perfectly acceptable substitute. By reading the label, I also learned that a glass contained just fifteen calories. Elise pointed out that a bottle of wine averages about 600 calories, versus 100 for a non-alcoholic wine.

You can certainly save calories by switching, but you won't save money. The Jøyus sold for $32 a bottle, and the 750 ml bottle of Spiritless Kentucky 74 sold for $40. As a grocery store wine buyer and Jack Daniel's Old No. 7 fan, that was about twice what I would usually spend on comparable bottles.

Nevertheless, there are plenty of people willing to pay the prices, and the best evidence of this is that the giant liquor conglomerates are paying attention. Diageo, which owns 200 brands including Tanqueray Gin, Guinness Beer, Captain Morgan Rum, and Smirnoff Vodka, in 2019 acquired controlling interest in England-based Seedlip, founded in 2015 as the world's first non-distilled spirits company.[436] A 200 ml bottle of its Garden 108 costs $20. ∎

SÈCHEY 75

Sèchey 75 is based on the popular gin and champagne cocktail named for the big gun in the French artillery of World War I. If you wish, you can substitute real champagne for the non-alcohol sparkling Chardonnay listed.

- 1 oz. ISH Ginish Alternative
- ½ oz. RD Naturals elderflower syrup
- ¾ oz. lemon juice

Pour into a cocktail shaker with ice, shake well, and strain into a coupe glass. Top with 1 oz. Noughty Sparkling Chardonnay. Garnish with lemon peel and enjoy.

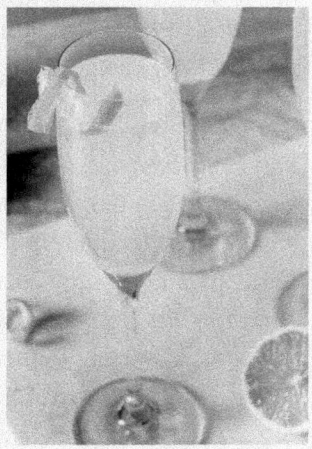

The Sèchey 75 is a nonalcoholic version of the French 75. *Photo courtesy Sèchey.*

Susan Cheever, who I have quoted throughout this book, was the daughter of celebrated writer John Cheever, an alcoholic who got sober through AA, and became an alcoholic herself. Her sharp observations in her book *Drinking in America* are capped by a Q&A in the paperback edition. To the question "Why do you think a middle ground is so difficult to achieve?" she answered, "Other countries drink more than we do in the United States, and other countries drink less, but no other country has our passionate ambivalence about drinking; in 1830 we drank more than most other nations; but by 1930 we had outlawed drinking." She thought Prohibition was a bad idea, by the way.

No one explained this ambivalence better than Noah S. "Soggy" Sweat Jr. He was a Mississippi legislator and judge who probably wouldn't be remembered today except for an extraordinary speech he gave in 1952 while the legislature was debating the repeal of state prohibition.[437] It became known as the "If-by-Whiskey" Speech.

My friends, I had not intended to discuss this controversial subject at this particular time. However, I want you to know that I do not shun controversy. On the contrary, I will take a stand on any issue at any time, regardless of how fraught with controversy it might be. You have asked me how I feel about whiskey. All right, this is how I feel about whiskey:

If when you say whiskey you mean the devil's brew, the poison scourge, the bloody monster, that defiles innocence, dethrones reason, destroys the home, creates misery and poverty, yea, literally takes the bread from the mouths of little children; if you mean the evil drink that topples the Christian man and woman from the pinnacle of righteous, gracious living into the bottomless pit of degradation, and despair, and shame and helplessness, and hopelessness, then certainly I am against it.

But, if when you say whiskey you mean the oil of conversation, the philosophic wine, the ale that is consumed when good fellows get together, that puts a song in their hearts and laughter on their lips, and the warm glow of contentment in their eyes; if you mean Christmas cheer; if you mean the stimulating drink that puts the spring in the old gentleman's step on a frosty, crispy morning; if you mean the drink which enables a man to magnify his joy, and his happiness, and to forget, if only for a little while, life's great tragedies, and heartaches, and sorrows; if you mean that drink, the sale of which pours into our treasuries untold millions of dollars, which are used to provide tender care for our little crippled children, our blind, our deaf, our dumb, our pitiful aged and infirm; to build highways and hospitals and schools, then certainly I am for it.

This is my stand. I will not retreat from it. I will not compromise.[438]

With that, here are two for the road, one with, one without.

Up On the Roof

My friend Trey Boggs, who with his brother Bryan started Palmetto Distillery, the first legal post-Prohibition distillery in South Carolina, came up with this drink and shared it in a text. He dubbed it Up on the Roof "because after a few that's where you end up!"

- 1.5 oz. Palmetto Whiskey
- .75 oz. fresh-squeezed grapefruit juice
- .5 oz. honey
- .25 oz. fresh-squeezed lime juice
- Dash of angostura bitters

Mix all ingredients in a shaker of ice, strain, and pour into a chilled rocks glass, garnish with an orange slice. For an extra special twist, soak a couple of Bada Bing cherries in your whiskey for a few days prior to making the drink and toss them in. Palmetto Distillery is located at 200 W. Benson Street, Anderson, South Carolina. https://www.palmettodistillery.com/

–*Up on the Roof recipe and picture courtesy of inventor Trey Boggs.*

Seedlip Eastside

From the website of the company that makes Seedlip Garden 108 is a refreshing mocktail you can serve in a coupe glass, like this elegant one with a hollow stem.

- 2 oz. Seedlip Garden 108
- ¾ oz. simple syrup (one part water to one part sugar)
- ½ oz. fresh lime juice
- 3 cucumber slices
- 5 mint leaves

Muddle cucumber slices and mint leaves in a cocktail shaker. Add the liquid ingredients and ice to the shaker, shake and double strain into a coupe glass. Garnish with a cucumber ribbon.[439]

Eastside photo courtesy Seedlip.

CEMETERY SIDE TRIP

This one is far outside the South, but a worthy way to end the book. **Fulton Oursler** and his wife **Grace Perkins** are buried under a shared stone in the Garden of Heaven Cemetery in Westchester County, New York. The marker bears their names and birth and death dates, followed by the words "Behold This Dreamer," the title of Oursler's first novel and the autobiography his son, writer Will Oursler, completed after his death. Below that is, appropriately enough, an open book, inscribed with words from Genesis, "—and then it shall appear what…dreams avail."[40]

Married authors share a gravestone with a book as its ornament. *Wikimedia Commons.*

ACKNOWLEDGEMENTS

I POKE A LOT OF FUN at John Wesley, but in fact I was raised in the Methodist church and though I am now an Episcopalian, I worship the same God he did. (Methodists, by the way, have loosened up quite a bit over the years, though they still serve grape juice at communion.) I am grateful every day of my life for the ability God has given me not only to write, but to maintain the focus it takes to finish a book. For a book, even a "fun" book like this one, is a massive undertaking that subsumes not only the writer but everyone in her orbit. So, as always, I am grateful to my husband Leo for accompanying me on several Prohibition Expeditions as my driver, logistics man, luggage carrier, photographer, and fellow drink taster. He also put up with the weeks I spent glued to my desk and computer screen writing and editing and kept reminding me to eat.

As readers now know, I found another travel buddy in my beloved aunt, Susan Yandle Middleton, who was an ideal companion on the George Washington Tour. Two old ladies in a Honda Fit forever!

My daughter, Elizabeth Smith Dowling, and her husband Nick were helpful advisors on the drinking and non-drinking scene in Charleston with their vast contacts in the food and beverage industry. My son, Adam C. Smith, who is in long-term recovery, provided valuable guidance on alcoholism and active recovery. He and my father, Bruce Yandle, kept my underpinnings in the Bootleggers and Baptists theory firmly in place as I explored the policy issues that made Prohibition such a disaster. My mom, Dot, my brothers, Bruce and Eric, in-laws and extended family, and many friends encouraged me along the way by asking, "How's the book going?"

The best thing about being an author is the people you meet as you speak and do research, and I add to my list of friends Bette Hickman, Larisa and Michael Scott, Larry Reed and Mike Brown, who I met in Newnan, Georgia; Katie and Terry Rixman in Louisville, Kentucky; Tim and Tara Boyce in Hendersonville, North Carolina; and Reta Westbury in St. Matthews, South Carolina. A friend I met only through phone calls and emails is Dr. Charles "Chip" Hancock, who did the sleuthing for me at W.D. Upshaw's purported grave in Georgia. It was a joy to finally meet in person cocktail maven and vintage postcard collector Anne Peck-Davis, who provided not only illustrations but her original Silver Slipper recipe. In addition to his kind blurb, author David Pietrusza gave my book a very close reading and prevented me from printing a number of embarrassing mistakes.

As ever, I was impressed with the knowledge and dedication of docents and tour guides at historic sites and museums, many of them unpaid volunteers who do it for the love of history. I was also impressed with the enthusiasm of the many employees of distilleries, bars, and wine shops (both alcoholic and non) who contributed so much to this book.

The staff at Evening Post Books continues to be delightful to work with, and my thanks go to Michael Nolan, now retired, executive editor Elizabeth Hollerith, and editor Alex Lanning. Kim Scott of Bumpy Design, who also designed *Baptists and Bootleggers*, did fine work on this companion volume. My thanks go to Pierre Manigault and John Burbage, who founded EPB, for having the vision for a publishing company "whose accent is Southern."

Photo Credits

MANY OF THE PHOTOS in this book came from the Wikimedia Commons website, where photographs that are in the public domain or whose copyright holders will share them are posted. The links to the appropriate licenses are listed.

Introduction
Lady Mendl: https://commons.wikimedia.org/wiki/File:Elsie_de_Wolfe.jpg

Chapter One
Equal Suffrage League of Richmond: https://commons.wikimedia.org/wiki/File:Equal_Suffrage_League_of_Richmond,_Va.,_February_1915.jpg

Chapter Three
Oglethorpe statue: https://commons.wikimedia.org/wiki/File:General_James_E._Oglethorpe_Statue_in_Chippewa_Square_(4351005904).jpg

Bread: https://commons.wikimedia.org/wiki/File:Piet_Meiners_-_Still_Life_with_Bread,_Bottle_of_Water,_Pipe_and_Mirror.jpg

Stained Glass Windows: https://commons.wikimedia.org/wiki/File:Charles_Wesley,_John_Wesley,_and_Francis_Asbury_(stained_glass_--_Memorial_Chapel,_Lake_Junaluska,_North_Carolina).jpg

Chapter Four
Chang and Eng Bunker and Family: https://commons.wikimedia.org/wiki/File:BunkerFamilies(1865)b.jpg

Bunker Graves: https://commons.wikimedia.org/wiki/File:Bunker_Grave.jpg

Chapter Five
Adolphus Busch: https://commons.wikimedia.org/wiki/File:Adolphus_Busch.jpg

Saloon cartoon: https://commons.wikimedia.org/wiki/File:Woman%27s_Christian_Temperance_Union_Cartoon.jpg

Anti-Saloon League of America: https://commons.wikimedia.org/wiki/File:Golden_Jubilee_and_fifteenth_annual_convention,_the_Anti-Saloon_League_of_America_LCCN2007661749.tif

Chapter Six
Daugherty cartoon: https://commons.wikimedia.org/wiki/File:N-nothin_to_it,_I_tell_you!.jpg

Chapter Seven
Clara Bow: https://commons.wikimedia.org/wiki/File:Clara_Bow_in_Wings_trailer_3.jpg

Chapter Eight
Machine Gun Kelly hideout: https://commons.wikimedia.org/wiki/File:M-gun_Kelly_hideout_1408_Rayner_St_Memphis_TN_03.jpg

Chapter Nine
Old Talbott Inn: https://commons.wikimedia.org/wiki/File:Old_Stone_tavern_in_Bardstown_Kentucky.jpg

Pappy Van Winkle bottle: https://commons.wikimedia.org/wiki/File:Pappy_Van_Winkle.JPG

Nearest Green Distillery: https://commons.wikimedia.org/wiki/File:Nearest_Green_Distillery_(Shelbyville,_Tennessee)_-_exterior.jpg

Chapter Ten
Oursler-Perkins gravestone: https://commons.wikimedia.org/wiki/File:Fulton_Oursler.JPG

NOTES

Introduction

1. Oddly enough, Wesley also wrote a best-selling health handbook which, among other things, recommended holding a warm puppy to an aching stomach. Considering that most medical treatments at the time involved bloodletting, purging and/or application of leeches, it sounds like a pretty good alternative, sort of like using a hot water bottle. https://www.resourceumc.org/en/content/10-fascinating-facts-about-john-wesley-and-united-methodism

2. An economics book is hardly ever fun, but Dad did come up with a pretty cool title and theory. I will explain it a bit more as we go along, or you can tune into an animated video at www.learnliberty.org/videos/bootleggers-and-baptists/ and hear it from the economist's mouth, so to speak.

3. Kathryn Smith, *Gertie: The Fabulous Life of Gertrude Sanford Legendre, Heiress, Explorer, Socialite, Spy* (Charleston, South Carolina: Evening Post Books, 2019), 40.

4. Harry Craddock, *The Savoy Cocktail Book* (Reprint by Mansfield Centre, Connecticut: Martino Publishing, 2015), 124.

5. Frank Maier, *The Artistry of Mixing Drinks* (France: Fryam Press, 1934), 36.

CHAPTER ONE: Travels with My Aunt

6. Readers who want more detail about the enslaved people at Mount Vernon and other places George Washington encountered on his travels may want to read *Travels with George: In Search of Washington and His Legacy* by Nathaniel Philbrick (New York: Viking, 2021).

7. https://www.mountvernon.org/george-washington/the-first-president/george-washingtons-1791-southern-tour/. Washington considered Philadelphia the beginning and end points of his trip. The round trip from Mount Vernon began April 7 and ended June 10, 1791.

8. Terry W. Lipscomb, *South Carolina in 1791: George Washington's Southern Tour* (Columbia: S.C. Department of Archives and History, 1993), 4.

9. https://www.mountvernon.org/the-estate-gardens/the-mansion/

10. Information from tour of distillery and Dennis J. Pogue, *Founding Spirits: George Washington and the Beginnings of the America Whiskey Industry* (Buena Vista, Virginia: Harbour Books, 2011).

11. Pogue, 1.

12. https://www.mountvernon.org/library/digitalhistory/digital-encyclopedia/article/madeira/

13. Susan Cheever, *Drinking in America: Our Secret History* (New York: Twelve, 2015), 40.

14. Pogue, p. 1.

15. Washington, George. *The Writings of George Washington, Vol. 12*, 153, https://oll.libertyfund.org/title/ford-the-writings-of-george-washington-vol-xii-1790-1794.

16. https://twitter.com/lin_manuel/status/556484060244344832

17. There was also an excise tax on snuff.

18. Lipscomb, 2.

19. King, George H.S., "General George Weeden," William and Mary Quarterly, Vol. 20 #2, 245.

20. ibid., 246.

21. Charleston, West Virginia was named for Charles Washington.

22. Rising Sun Tavern, the Mary Washington House, Hugh Mercer Apothecary Shop and St. James' House in Fredericksburg are all owned and operated by the Washington Heritage Museums. The website is www.washingtonheritagemuseums.org.

23. https://www.mountvernon.org/library/digitalhistory/digital-encyclopedia/article/tomb/

24. https://www.historiccolumbia.org/tour-locations/1200-gervais-street-13

25. Frederick Philip Stieff, *Eat, Drink and Be Merry in Maryland* (New York: G.P. Putnam's Sons, 1932), 297.

26. Jos. A. Hoskins, editor, *President Washington's Diaries 1791-1799* (Big Byte Books, 2016), 14.

27. They are, in order, James Madison, James Monroe, William Henry Harrison, John Tyler, Zachary Taylor, and Woodrow Wilson.

28. *President Washington's Diaries*, 13.

29. Ron Chernow, *Alexander Hamilton*. New York: Penguin Press, 2004), 78.

30. Cheever, 67.

31. This is a classic example of the Bootleggers and Baptists theory. The larger, corporate interests were benefited when the small producers were put out of business by the tax.

32. James Thomas Flexner, *Washington: The Indispensable Man* (Boston: Little, Brown, 1969) 315-316.

33. Cheever, 70.

34. https://www.mountvernon.org/library/digitalhistory/digital-encyclopedia/article/whiskey-rebellion/#:~:text=By%201802%2C%20then%20President%20Thomas,true%20challenge%20to%20federal%20authority.

35. https://www.jeffersonhotel.com

36. https://www.jeffersonhotel.com/history

37. I have to admit that, after reading Ron Chernow's biography *Hamilton* I had a complete change of heart. George Washington is my man. Sorry, Martha!

38. If you have no idea who the last three are, don't feel bad. The only one I knew was George Mason, and that's because my son Adam C. Smith went to graduate school at the Virginia university that bears his name. Mason was one of three delegates to the Constitutional Convention who refused to sign the document. Irish-born Andrew Lewis served under Washington in the French and Indian Wars and the American Revolution. Thomas Nelson was a signer of the Declaration of Independence and fought in the siege of Yorktown. Partly obscured by the construction draping were allegorical figures of goddesses representing justice, finance, colonial times, revolution, independence, and the Bill of Rights. http://www.vacapitol.org/washington.htm

39. The women's monument was approved by the Virginia General Assembly, but, unlike the sculpture of George Washington in the capitol, the money to build it was raised privately.

40. https://encyclopediavirginia.org/entries/clark-adele-1882-1983/#heading1

CHAPTER TWO: George Washington Drank Here

41. *President Washington's Diaries*, 17.

42. ibid., 18.

43. Archibald Henderson, *George Washington's Southern Tour, 1791* (Boston and New York: Houghton Mifflin, 1923), 80-81.

44. https://www.mountvernon.org/library/digitalhistory/digital-encyclopedia/article/false-teeth

45. For an extensive discussion of this, see Philbrick, *Travels with George*, 15-18.

46. Cheever, 51-61.

47. Cheever, 65. She takes the Washington quote from Eric Burns's book *The Spirits of America: A Social History of Alcohol* (Philadelphia: Temple University Press, 2004) 16.

48. Flexner, 178.

49. https://ahpcs.org/2021/01/the-road-to-prohibition/

50. https://www.aoc.gov/explore-capitol-campus/art/general-george-washington-resigning-his-commission

51. Stieff, 317

52. https://www.mountvernon.org/library/digitalhistory/digital-encyclopedia/article/society-of-the-cincinnati/

The Society of the Cincinnati still exists, with headquarters in Washington, D.C. https://www.societyofthecincinnati.org/membership-overview/

53. Fans of the Netflix series *Outlander* may remember the palace was used in exterior shots in season six, "The Spark of Revolution," based on the Diana Gabaldon book *A Breath of Snow and Ashes*. The Tryon Palace offers occasional Outlander at Tryon tours.

54. https://www.tryonpalace.org/the-palace-historic-homes/historic-homes/stanly-house

55. Henderson, 89.

56. https://www.ncdcr.gov/blog/2014/03/14/gen-ambrose-burnside-and-the-fall-of-new-bern-1862. Burnside turned up in my *Baptists and Bootleggers* book also. He was stationed in Knoxville, Tennessee in 1863.

57. Henderson, 91.

58. I tried it. It works.

59. https://pepsistore.com/history/

60. https://gracedowntown.church/history/ The church sanctuary building my father attended burned in 1947 and the handsome Neo-Gothic stone structure we saw was completed in 1950.

61. *President Washington's Diaries*, 23.

62. Warren L. Bingham, *George Washington's 1791 Southern Tour* (Charleston: The History Press, 2016), 77.

63. Eliza Pinckney is the subject of several non-fiction books and the novel *The Indigo Girl* by Natasha Boyd (Blackstone, 2014).

64. https://southcarolinaparks.com/hampton#jump. Hampton Plantation stayed in the Pinckney family for almost two centuries. The last private owner was Archibald Rutledge, who served for many years as the South Carolina poet laureate. The house and 271 surrounding acres were purchased by the state in 1971.

65. This charming story has a dark side, as so much of antebellum history does. A sign invites visitors to look high into the branches of the oak tree to find the bell that summoned the enslaved population. So as Susan and I walked up the stairs and across the porch, peering into the windows of the front room with its Prussian blue walls, and then around the grounds, we were always aware that this unnaturally silent place was once home to hundreds of people, most of them living under the control of the Horry family and their descendants. A slave owner himself, Washington had decidedly mixed feelings about the system, believing it was morally indefensible on the one hand, but not knowing how to end it on the other. His diary never mentions the enslaved people he encountered, only the lavish lifestyle they made possible. Philbrick's *Travels with George* goes into great detail about slavery in the South and Washington's lack of action to end it.

66. *President Washington's Diaries*, 25.

67. Bingham, 34.

68. Quote is from signage at The Tavern.

69. The Senator is made by MPG bottled by Proof and Wood out of Bardstown, Kentucky. https://thewhiskeywash.com/reviews/whiskey-review-roundup-the-senator-and-the-ambassador/

70. https://www.scpictureproject.org/charleston-county/bethel-united-methodist.html#:~:text=Bethel%20United%20Methodist%20Church%20is,it%20in%20need%20of%20Methodism

71. Lipscomb, 39-40; https://www.ccpl.org/charleston-time-machine/tail-washingtons-horse. When I saw the portrait in person, city clerk Patrick Carlson told me the people of Charleston were delighted with the portrait and it was a hundred years before a comment was first made about the unseemliness of the horse's behind being so prominent.

72. https://www.hmdb.org/m.asp?m=47791. The sculptor chosen was John N. Michel.

Notes

CHAPTER THREE: An Inauspicious Beginning

73. The recipe for this punch, which has a suspicious resemblance to Fish House Punch, can be found in my book *Baptists and Bootleggers*.

74. Hand-out from The Old Pink House.

75. Because vodka was not sold in America prior to 1933, I don't usually include vodka cocktail recipes in my books. This is the one exception, but if you want to be authentic and try it with gin, be my guest.

76. https://worldpopulationreview.com/us-cities/savannah-ga-population; https://www.savannahchamber.com/economic-development/tourism/#:~:text=The%20Savannah%20tourism%20sector%20suffered,and%206%20million%20day%2Dvisitors.

77. Willie Snow Ethridge, *Strange Fires: The true story of John Wesley's love affair in Georgia* (New York: Vanguard Press, 1971), 58.

78. *Georgia: The WPA Guide to Its Towns and Countryside* (Atlanta: Georgia Board of Education, 1940; Columbia: University of South Carolina Press reprint, 1990), 38.

79. Luckily, the first two names didn't stick. Imagine being a member of the First Bible Bigot Church.

80. Ethridge, 39, 40.

81. ibid., 41.

82. ibid., p. 49-50. Tybee Island became an active center for rum-running during Prohibition.

83. ibid., 18.

84. ibid., 140.

85. Generally, the announcement of a contracted marriage was made in the church on three consecutive Sundays.

86. John Wesley's problems with women continued all his life. He fell in love with another young woman in England and dithered so long about marrying her that she wed another minister. He again behaved badly. Finally, in 1751, he hastily married a wealthy widow he barely knew and soon regretted knowing. They lived apart for most of their marriage and she predeceased him. Sam Wellman, *John Wesley: The Great Methodist* (Uhrichsville, Ohio: Barbour Books, 1997).

87. Cheever, 36.

88. https://worldpopulationreview.com/state-rankings/alcohol-consumption-by-state. Interestingly, Southern states are among the lowest imbibers in the nation, perhaps reflecting the continuing influence of Methodists and Baptists. Florida and Louisiana are the only states that exceed the national average; Arkansas, Georgia, Kentucky, and Alabama rank among the ten lowest imbibing states.

89. Andy Griffith, who we will visit in the next chapter, was a Moravian. https://newhopemoravian.org/tradition.html

90. *President Washington's Diaries*, 31-27.

91. This section on Wesley's ministry in England is drawn from Wellman, 110-141.

92. The current *United Methodist Hymnal* contains fifty-one hymns by Charles Wesley.

93. https://www.crosswalk.com/faith/spiritual-life/john-wesley-continues-to-shape-us-churches-1204980.html; https://www.resourceumc.org/en/content/10-fascinating-facts-about-john-wesley-and-united-methodism

94. https://www.hmdb.org/results.asp?Search=KeywordA&SearchFor=Francis+Asbury; https://www.hmdb.org/results.asp?Search=Series&SeriesID=292; *Dictionary of North Carolina Biography*, 6 volumes, edited by William S. Powell. Copyright ©1979–1996 by the University of North Carolina Press.

95. https://www.hmdb.org/m.asp?m=5447

96. Wellman, 141. I suppose this exception was up to personal interpretation. There wasn't much medicine back then and alcohol was used for pain management and other ailments.

97. https://www.americanprohibitionmuseum.com/? The population of the country in 1850 was about 23 million.

98. Harlan Greene, *The Real Rainbow Row: Explorations in Charleston's LGBTQ History* (Charleston: Evening Post Books, 2022), 12.

99. https://susanb.org/temperance-worker/

100. http://blogs.wofford.edu/from_the_archives/2013/01/30/how-the-methodist-church-split-in-the-1840s/. The denominations reunited 94 years later.

101. https://www.britannica.com/topic/Southern-Baptist-Convention

102. https://timesmachine.nytimes.com/timesmachine/1983/06/11/226524.html?pageNumber=1; https://civilwartalk.com/threads/lutheran-church-and-the-civil-war.80408/

103. https://www.ttb.gov/tax-audit/historical-tax-rates. The Civil War excise tax applied to other "luxury goods" such as tobacco, playing cards, feathers, yachts, carriages, jewelry, pianos, and billiard tables. Additionally, the Revenue Act of 1861 imposed the first federal income tax.

104. Megan L. Bever, "Prohibition, Sacrifice, and Morality in the Confederate States, 1861–1865." *Journal of Southern History*, vol. 85, no. 2, May 2019, pp. 251+. *Gale Academic OneFile*, link.gale.com/apps/doc/A586903115/AONE?u=anon~7fb851fd&sid=googleScholar&xid=c6167073. Accessed 1 Sept. 2022.

105. Frances E. Willard, *Woman and Temperance: The Work and Workers of the Women's Christian Temperance Union* (Hartford, CT: Park Publishing Company, 1883), 20-24.

106. https://en.wikipedia.org/wiki/Catholic_Total_Abstinence_Union_of_America. The Episcopalians also drank wine with communion, but some of their bishops, ministers, and members embraced temperance, which Willard mentioned with great satisfaction in her book.

107. Willard, 122.

108. https://www.chq.org/about/

109. I was scheduled to teach courses on "Franklin Roosevelt and His Women" and "Prohibition: The Only Amendment that Failed" at the 2020 session. Unfortunately, the entire season was cancelled because of the Covid-19 pandemic.

110. https://www.chq.org/blog/institution-news/changes-to-chautauqua-institution-s-sale-of-alcohol-policy/#:~:text=Permission%20for%20beer%20and%20wine,enabled%20by%20policy%20in%202009.

111. Willard, 131.

112. Durant, John and Alice, *The Presidents of the United States* (New York: A.S. Barnes and Company, 1955), 164-165. Hayes, a Republican, was outpolled by the Democrat Samuel Tilden by over 300,000 votes, and also received more electoral votes, but not

enough to claim the presidency. The Republican Congress cut the backroom deal with the last Southern states under military occupation—South Carolina, Florida, and Louisiana—who gave their electoral votes to Hayes in return for the end of Reconstruction. Hayes served only one term.

113. Klapthor, Margaret Brown, *The First Ladies* (Washington, D.C.: White House Historical Association, 1975), 46. https://www.rbhayes.org/news/2016/12/14/general/rutherford-b.-hayes-and-his-religious-views/#:~:text=Throughout%20his%20adult%20life%2C%20however,Christian%20and%20do%20Christian%20work.%E2%80%9D

114. Portrait, Klapthor, 47. The Durants tell the anecdote about the White House servants delivering rum-filled oranges as a banquet course, which wags tagged the "Life-Saving Station." This amused the president, who noted in his diary that the oranges contained rum flavoring, but no alcohol. 165. Mrs. Hayes gave a one-sentence endorsement of a cookbook prepared by prominent Virginia women: "I am very much pleased with it." Yet it contained recipes for making wine from fruit ranging from grapes to tomatoes, and several pages of recipes for punch and cordials. The recipe for blackberry wine was contributed by Mrs. Robert E. Lee. *Housekeeping in Old Virginia* (Louisville, Kentucky: John P. Morton and Company, 1879) also suggested a treatment for a "Weak Back: Two tablespoonfuls finely powdered rosin, four tablespoonfuls white sugar, whites of two eggs, one quart best whiskey. Dose, a tablespoonful three times a day, before or after meals. Excellent also for colds or weak lungs; will stop irritating cough." 494.

115. Willard, 574.

116. Information provided with teapot display at Lanier Library, Tryon, North Carolina, collection of Julie and Kip McIntyre. I found dozens of these teapots on eBay, which indicates to me their wild popularity at one time.

117. Willard, 558.

118. Willard, 566.

119. He was 37. https://www.findagrave.com/memorial/193500270/caroline-elizabeth-merrick?_gl=1*ylgv9o*_ga*MjcxNzk2ODE0LjE2NTczOTg1OTA.*_ga_4QT8FMEX30*MTY2MzA4ODYwOC4xMy4xLjE2NjMwODg5NTQuMC4wLjA.

120. Smith, *Baptists and Bootleggers*, 42. I write extensively about Mrs. Chapin in *B&B*, including the location of her grave in Charleston.

121. Willard, 571.

122. Smith, *Baptists and Bootleggers*, 18. In that book, I focused on WCTU activity in South Carolina, Kentucky, and Tennessee.

123. https://en.wikipedia.org/wiki/Wilmington_insurrection_of_1898

124. https://socialwelfare.library.vcu.edu/religious/womens-christian-temperance-union/

125. Some temperance adherents argued that Jesus was making unfermented wine.

126. http://www.welchs.com/about-welchs/history

127. https://www.christianitytoday.com/history/2017/march/welch-grape-juice-history-temperance-movement.html

128. For specifics on cemeteries in New Orleans, visit https://www.neworleans.com/things-to-do/attractions/cemeteries

CHAPTER FOUR: Mt. Airy and Thereabouts

129. Dr. Victor Tomlinson, a physician I know, became friends with Hal Smith, the actor who played Otis Campbell, after a chance meeting. He told me that Smith was not only a convincing drunk, but a noted voiceover actor whose credits included Winnie-the-Pooh and Owl in the Walt Disney productions. Occasionally he would ask Smith to prank-call a friend, pretending to be Otis. As the head of the radiation oncology department at my local hospital, Dr. Tomlinson strives to create a Mayberry atmosphere of kindness and comfort, even referring to his younger partner as "Barney."

130. A friend who stayed overnight in the former Griffith home said he was surprised to find tourists staring at him through the windows!

131. From observations of site visit and https://www.visitnc.com/story/DvHg/beyond-the-guidebook-mount-airy-the-real-life-mayberry

132. https://www.visitmayberry.com/events/7e454a35-5a39-46e6-8c30-f15a6add142f-moonshine-racers-reunion/

133. It wasn't Griffith's only dark role. He played the cold-blooded murderer John Wallace in *Murder in Coweta County* in 1983 and an alcoholic patriarch in *Under the Influence* in 1986, both made-for-TV movies.

134. Kelly, Richard. *The Andy Griffith Show* (Winston-Salem, N.C.: John F. Blair, Publisher, 1981) 230-280.

135. The Campbells, who were Protestants, fought on the side of the English in the bloody Battle of Culloden in 1746, the last Scottish uprising. There is a Scots saying, "Never trust a Campbell."

136. 1790 Census, accessed through Wikipedia "Scottish Americans"; and "Highland Scots" from https://northcarolinahistory.org/encyclopedia/highland-scots/. Fans of the Starz television series *Outlander* based on the books by Diana Gabaldon will recall that Jamie and Claire Fraser got a royal grant for land in the Upper Cape Fear River region of North Carolina where Jamie does a brisk trade in corn whiskey.

137. Yunte Huang, *Inseparable: The Original Siamese Twins and Their Rendezvous with American History* (New York: Liveright Publishing, 2018), 193.

138. ibid., 197

139. ibid., 207-208

140. ibid., 209

141. ibid., 216

142. ibid., 217

143. ibid., p. 219

144. ibid., 220-222

145. ibid., 238

146. ibid., 224

147. ibid., 237, 285

148. ibid., xiii

149. https://muttermuseum.org/stories/posts/bonded-livers-and-love-chang-and-eng-story

150. Huang, 241-242

151. ibid., p 265

152. ibid., xxiv

153. https://muttermuseum.org/stories/videos/virtual-tour-mutter-museum

154. In more northern climes, such as Virginia and Pennsylvania, rye and barley were the chosen grain for whiskey, but corn grew better as you got further south and dominated whiskey production.

155. Daniel S. Pierce, *Tar Heel Lightning: How Secret Stills and Fast cars Made North Carolina the Moonshine Capital of the World* (Chapel Hill: University of North Carolina Press, 2019), 7.

156. M.L. White, *A History of the Life of Amos Owens, the Noted Blockader of Cherry Mountain* (Forgotten Books reprint, 2012), 18.

157. Smith, *Baptists and Bootleggers*, 122.

158. Pierce, 6.

159. ibid., 27-30.

160. White, 16

161. Pierce, 27

162. ibid.

163. White, 29

164. Pierce, 74-75. I devote a chapter to Carry Nation in my book *Baptists and Bootleggers*, including pictures of her birthplace in Kentucky.

165. Ron Hall, *The Allen Chase: The Search and Capture of the Allen Outlaws as Reported by Period Newspapers* (Hillsville: Carroll County Historical Society, 2016).

166. "Allens Executed; Respite Plan Failed," *New York Times*, March 29, 1913.

167. https://carrollvamuseum.org/museum/courthouse-tragedy/

168. The Baldwin-Felts Agency, based in Bluefield, West Virginia, became notorious for strike breaking in the mining industry. https://www.wvencyclopedia.org/articles/333

169. Sept. 17, 1912, quoted in Hall, 69.

170. https://surrycounty.pastperfectonline.com/photo/4A28061D-4C49-4A13-802E-432337964055

171. Author's site visit.

172. "Last of Allen Clan is Killed in a Fight," *New York Times*, March 19, 1916.

CHAPTER FIVE: The Anti-Saloon Juggernaut

173. Presentation and interview with Joe Hursey at the Piedmont Historical Preservation Society, June 26, 2022.

174. The advent of the steam ship, after the Civil War, cut the time of an Atlantic crossing to just two weeks. Huang, xvi.

175. Daniel Okrent, *Last Call: The Rise and Fall of Prohibition* (New York, Scribner, 2010), 30.

176. "Augusta Brewing Company wasn't city's first, but was last before Prohibition," *Augusta Chronicle*, July 13, 1919; and "Augusta Brewing Company 1888 Augusta, Georgia 1888 The Rise and Fall" by John Douglas Herman, Sr., https://www.scribd.com/document/283474195/Augusta-Brewing-Company-1888-Augusta-Georgia-1888-the-Rise-and-Fall#

177. Okrent, 27.

178. ibid., 30

179. ibid., 26

180. Carry A. Nation, *The Use and Need of the Life of Carry A. Nation* (Topeka: F.M. Steves & Sons, 1905), 70

181. Timmons Pettigrew, *Charleston Beer: A High Gravity History of Lowcountry Brewing* (Charleston: The History Press, 2011), 17-21.

182. Hops are flowers and an oast house is used for drying them.

183. Pettigrew, 28.

184. ibid., 34.

185. https://www.scribd.com/document/283474195/Augusta-Brewing-Company-1888-Augusta-Georgia-1888-the-Rise-and-Fall#

186. Pettigrew, 67-69; https://palmettobrewery.com/about/

187. Or almost the only one. There is a viable argument that the Thirteenth Amendment ending slavery was the first, because it prohibited owning other human beings.

188. Nation, 171.

189. https://2001-2009.state.gov/r/pa/ho/time/ip/108646.htm#:~:text=The%20Progressive%20movement%20was%20a,political%20influence%20of%20large%20corporations

190. Okrent, 54.

191. ibid., 73, 70.

192. ibid., 87.

193. Adam Hochschild, *American Midnight: The Great War, a Violent Peace, and Democracy's Forgotten Crisis* (New York: Mariner Books, 2022). 6-7.

194. ibid., 7.

195. ibid., 83.

196. https://www.washingtonpost.com/nation/2019/02/11/freedom-never-tasted-so-good-how-walter-jones-helped-rename-french-fries-over-iraq-war/

197. Hochschild, 157-158.

198. Collection of the Detroit Historical Society, https://detroithistorical.org/blog/2021-12-01-first-state-and-first-state-out

199. Sources on Upshaw's life include his congressional biography, https://bioguide.congress.gov/search/bio/U000026; and http://www.prohibitionists.org/history/William_Upshaw_Bio.htm

200. "Upshaw Opens Senate Campaign on Monday," *Atlanta Constitution*, March 19, 1918. Upshaw initially planned to run for U.S. Senate but switched to House later in the election season.

201. "Georgia Delegation Will Vote Against Suffrage Resolution," *Macon Telegraph*, May 21, 1919.

202. "South Remains Hope of Nation, Says Upshaw," *Atlanta Semi-Weekly Journal*, December 12, 1919.

203. Burke Davis, *The Life and Times of Elliott White Springs* (Chapel Hill: University of North Carolina Press, 1987), 3.

204. He was a classmate of F. Scott Fitzgerald's, but knew him only casually.

205. Davis, 49.

206. ibid., 51, 54

207. Readers of a certain age may remember that Charlie Brown's beagle Snoopy in the comic strip "Peanuts" imagined his doghouse was a Sopwith Camel and that he regularly dueled with the Bloody Red Baron and his flying circus. It was no joke for the pilots who dueled with the real Baron Manfred von Richthofen. He was the greatest ace of the war on either side, credited with shooting down eighty planes. He died on April 21, 1918, but the pilots of his flying circus continued their rampage under the leadership of Hermann Goring, later head of the Luftwaffe in Nazi Germany. https://www.historynet.com/fighter-pilot-hermann-goring/

208. He referred to D.W. Griffith's second most famous film, after *Birth of a Nation*.

209. David K. Vaughan, ed. *Letters from a War Bird: The World War I Correspondence of Elliott White Springs*. (Columbia: University of South Carolina Press, 2012. 84.

210. Elliott White Springs, *Leave Me with a Smile* (Garden City, New York: Doubleday, Doran & Company, 1928), 133.

211. https://euvs-vintage-cocktail-books.cld.bz/1928-Giggle-Water-by-Charles-S-Warnock

212. Elliott White Springs, *War Bird: Diary of an Unknown Aviator* (New York: George H. Doran Company, 1926), 87-88.

213. Stieff, 291.

214. https://www.hometextilestoday.com/industry-news/after-120-years-in-sc-springs-shuts-plants/

CHAPTER SIX: The Department of Easy Virtue

215. Edwin P. Hoyt, *Spectacular Rogue Gaston B. Means* (Indianapolis: Bobbs-Merrill, 1963).

216. Hoover comment from https://www.ncdcr.gov/blog/2016/07/11/gaston-means-con-man-swindler-and-hoax-artist; Hoyt, 9.

217. https://juliemeanskane.com/# Julie P. Means, *My Life with Gaston B. Means as told by his wife, Julie P. Means*, transcribed and annotated by Julie Means Kane, self-published, 2021.

218. ibid, 9.

219. ibid., 116.

220. Gene Caesar, *Incredible Detective: The Biography of William J. Burns* (Englewood Cliffs, New Jersey: Prentice-Hall, Inc, 1968).

221. Hoyt, 75.

222. ibid., 106.

223. ibid., 143.

224. Okrent, 112.

225. ibid., 189.

226. ibid., 197.

227. ibid., 195.

228. Peter Krass, *Blood and Whiskey: The Life and Times of Jack Daniel* (Hoboken, New Jersey: John Wiley & Sons, 2004), 217-218.

229. Okrent, 112.

230. Smith, *Baptists and Bootleggers*, 169.

231. Roy A. Haynes, *Prohibition Inside Out* (Garden City, New York: Doubleday & Company, 1923), 156-160.

232. "Two Men Jailed in Southport on Murder Charges," *Raleigh News and Observer*, July 31, 1924.

233. "Father and Son Sentenced to Die by Judge H.A. Grady," *Raleigh News and Observer*, October 13, 1924; findagrave.com

234. "Siren of Death Car Sounds as Jury Was Bringing in Verdict," *Raleigh News and Observer*, October 13, 1924.

235. Unpublished diary, author's collection. Henderson Lanham later served as a prosecutor, state legislator, and congressman.

236. Gaston B. Means and May Dixon Thacker, *The Strange Death of President Harding* (New York: Gold Label Books, 1930), 205-207.

237. Hoyt, 158-162.

238. ibid., 147-148.

239. Julie Means, 52-53.

240. Hoyt, 187.

241. Means and Thacker, 247–253. Britton herself had published a book called *The President's Daughter* that revealed Harding was the father of her child and that they had trysted in a White House closet. DNA tests later proved the veracity of her paternity claim.

242. Hoyt, 282. The story was picked up and ran in numerous North Carolina newspapers.

243. Hoyt, 293-306; Julie Means, 71–111.

244. Smith, *Gertie*, 211n.

245. Hoyt, 300–301.

246. https://www.southerngracedistilleries.com/conviction-founders-reserve

247. https://www.nascarhall.com/hall-of-famers/inductees/dale-earnhardt; https://www.espn.com/racing/nascar/story/_/id/30867892/dale-earnhardt-death-daytona-500-revisiting-day-crash; https://www.historicracing.com/driverDetail.cfm?driverID=2785

CHAPTER SEVEN: The Worm Turns

248. "Sousa Says Need of Temperance is Before Country" by United Press, *Athens Banner-Herald*, February 21, 1926.

249. "Testing Prohibition with Straw Votes," *The Literary Digest*, April 3, 1926.

250. ibid.

251. The April 1, 1926, edition of the *Atlanta Constitution* contained a list of faux news stories, one of which involved Wheeler. He admitted that Prohibition wasn't working. "I'm through with it," he declared. "I'm ready to let them belly up to the bar again." In other tomfoolery, W.D. Upshaw had decided to support the legalization of light beer and wine, and the Atlanta City Council had passed ordinances allowing Sunday horse racing, burlesque shows, prize fights, and craps shooting.

252. Okrent, 268.

253. ibid.

254. George Creel, journalist and Democratic politician, quoted in *The American President* by William E. Leuchtenberg (New York: Oxford University Press, 2015), 126.

Notes

255. "Coolidge Orders Probe of Chicago Gangster Rings," *Atlanta Constitution*, February 13, 1926.

256. Moran, born Adelard Leo Cunin, was the son of a French immigrant father and a mother of Canadian descent.

257. Mark Thornton, "Alcohol prohibition was a failure," Cato Institute Policy Analysis Paper, 1991.

258. http://www.encyclopedia.chicagohistory.org/pages/2156.html. How does that compare to today? The FBI statistics for 2019 showed a murder and non-negligent homicide rate nationally of 5 per 100,000, with the rate in the largest cities pegged at 5.7 per 100,000. Unfortunately, there has been a sharp rise in violent crime since then. https://ucr.fbi.gov/crime-in-the-u.s/2019/crime-in-the-u.s.-2019/tables/table-16

259. https://19crimes.com/pages/the-crew

260. Information on Jane Castings comes from the 19 Crimes website, www.19crimes.com, and https://convictrecords.com.au/convicts/castings/jane/7548

261. I wrote at length about Bill McCoy in my book *Baptists and Bootleggers*. The information about the Real McCoy Rum comes from "The Real Bill McCoy," an interview in *Zelda Magazine*, Spring/Summer 2018, and the company website, https://www.realmccoyspirits.com/thestory

262. I also wrote about Lewis Redmond in *Baptists and Bootleggers*. The information about the liquor brand is from the website https://hiltonheaddistillery.com/spirits/

263. George Remus was another prominent player in my book *Baptists and Bootleggers*. Information about George Remus Bourbon is from the company website, www.remusbourbon.com.

264. Lisa McGirr, *The War on Alcohol: Prohibition and the Rise of the American State* (New York: W.W. Norton, 2016), 77.

265. The story comes from "Descendant sets story right in 1926 shootout," *Roanoke Times*, October 10, 2013. By uncovering the truth, Jenny Cooper was able to clear her grandfather's name and get him the recognition he deserved as a fallen law officer.

266. Graves found on findagrave.com.

267. "Drinkers Barred as Dry Enforcers," *New York Times*, September 23, 1926.

268. ibid.

269. Mabel Walker Willebrandt, *The Inside of Prohibition* (Indianapolis: Bobbs-Merrill, 1929), 116.

270. "General Andrews Declines to Reply to Mrs. Willebrandt," *New York Times*, August 9, 1929.

271. Willebrandt, 104.

272. "Facing the Facts About Prohibition," *Atlanta Constitution*, April 4, 1926. The ASL later released a list of its best-paid speakers. Small had been paid $32,654 for one year.

273. "Officers Say Pair Victims of Murder," *Macon Daily Telegraph*, July 13, 1926; "Three Men Arrested in Double Murder Case: Bootleg Farm Discovered at Scene of Crime," *Macon Daily Telegraph*, July 14, 1926.

274. "Glover Pays in Chair for Dual Killing," *Macon Daily Telegraph*, September 10, 1926.

275. "Bars Davis is Found Guilty, Given Life Term," *Macon Daily Telegraph*, September 4, 1926.

276. *Atlanta Magazine*, "The troubled triangle of Scottish heritage, Southern racial politics, and Stone Mountain" by Jim Galloway, October 14, 2021.

277. McGirr, 133.

278. David Pietrusza, "The Ku Klux Klan in the 1920s," https://billofrightsinstitute.org/essays/the-ku-klux-klan-in-the-1920s.

279. McGirr, 134-135.

280. McGirr, 140.

281. "Upshaw is Sponsor for Ku Klux Chief," *Atlanta Journal*, October 13, 1921.

282. "Congressional Investigation of Klan Not Expected as Hearing is Ended," *Atlanta Constitution*, October 18, 1921.

283. "Congressman Upshaw denies 'championing' cause of Klan, saying he only desires fair play," *Atlanta Constitution*, October 11, 1921.

284. Pietrusza, op.cit.

285. https://news.ag.org/Features/This-Week-in-AG-History-Sept-23-1951.

286. "Donaldson, Nemesis of Underworld, Lured to Death in Room of Hotel," *Atlanta Constitution*, July 31, 1926.

287. "Fitchet and Seven Named in Murder Plot Are Indicted for Bert Donaldson Slaying," *Atlanta Constitution*, March 12, 1927.

288. "Jack Lance Held After His Auto Hits Street Car," *Atlanta Constitution*, October 20, 1928.

289. "Donaldson Death Evidences Police Need, Says Jurist," *Atlanta Constitution*, August 1, 1926.

290. Okrent, 270.

291. Smith, *Baptists and Bootleggers*, 141. Johnson was slightly fictionalized as Nucky Thompson in the HBO series *Boardwalk Empire*.

292. "Cost of Prohibition Set at $44,900,000 by Dry Force Leader," *Atlanta Constitution*, July 3, 1926.

293. "Upshaw's Prices for Dry Speeches Are Under Probe," *Atlanta Constitution*, July 3, 1926.

294. Steele again defeated Upshaw in a 1928 match-up but died following a gall bladder operation in 1929.

295. "Election Spooks," *Columbia Record*, September 14, 1926.

296. "Control by Senate of Democratic Party Indicated by Tuesday Election Returns," *Atlanta Constitution*, November 3, 1926.

297. "Two Volstead Extremists," *Chattanooga Times*, January 18, 1926.

298. "Senator Blease Assails Court and Volstead Act," *Chattanooga Times*, January 28, 1926.

299. My thanks go to Professor David W. Earle of West Florida University for enlightening me about Fulton Oursler's authorship of the novel *Speakeasy Girl*. His blog is www.boozehoundsblog.com. I also thank my good friend Dr. Steve Lomazow for introducing me to Professor Earle by e-mail.

300. Oursler/Meredith, *Speakeasy Girl*, 3, 204.

301. Oursler/Meredith, 110.

302. *Single Lady* by John Monk Saunders (New York: Brewer & Warren Inc., 1931) 51–52. The novel was initially serialized in *Liberty*, which Fulton Oursler edited.

303. https://web.archive.org/web/20100528035941/http://www.atlantaga.gov/government/urbandesign_georgianterr.aspx

304. https://web.archive.org/web/20071012133809/http://gtalumni.org/StayInformed/techtopics/sum91/deaths.html

305. The original sculptor, Gutzon Borglum, fell out with the governing organization and went on to work on Mt. Rushmore. https://www.smithsonianmag.com/history/what-will-happen-stone-mountain-americas-largest-confederate-memorial-180964588/; https://stonemountainpark.org/about-us/history-of-smma/#:~:text=The%20figures%20measure%2090%20by,42%20feet%20into%20the%20mountain

306. Findagrave.com.

CHAPTER EIGHT: The Crème de la Crime

307. "Al Smith to Enter Field of Business as Term Expires," *Atlanta Constitution*, January 15, 1926.

308. "Hoover Sweeps Nation to Win by 444 Electoral Votes; Breaks into Solid South," *Atlanta Constitution*, November 7, 1928.

309. "Steele Majority Was 2,389 Votes," *Atlanta Constitution*, September 15, 1928.

310. "Upshaw Out of Town, Jury Postpones Quiz," *Atlanta Constitution*, October 13, 1928.

311. "End Local Drive in College Park," *Atlanta Constitution*, November 5, 1928. Cave Springs is in the congressional district now represented by Marjorie Taylor Greene.

312. Reid Mitenbuler, *Bourbon Empire: The Past and Future of America's Whiskey* (New York: Viking, 2015) 169.

313. Okrent, 286-287.

314. ibid., 293-294.

315. Mitenbuler, 172.

316. McGirr cites a study that found of the 130 murders linked to gangs in Chicago from 1926 to 1927, only 26 went to court. 194.

317. https://journals.sagepub.com/doi/abs/10.1177/1043986213485632

318. "Chicago Gangland Exacts Frightful Toll as Seven Rivals Die in Machine Gun Hail," *Atlanta Constitution*, February 15, 1929.

319. McGirr, 195.

320. Text of Jones-Stalker Act, *Congressional Record*.

321. https://www.presidency.ucsb.edu/documents/calvin-coolidge-event-timeline

322. Smith had been hesitant to sign the law, rightly fearing the consequences if he ran for national office, according to Michael A. Lerner in *Dry Manhattan: Prohibition in New York City* (Boston: Harvard University Press, 2007), 93-94.

323. https://avalon.law.yale.edu/20th_century/hoover.asp

324. I write at length about Sabin in *Baptists and Bootleggers*.

325. Willebrandt had left his administration in mid-1929, disappointed that she was passed over for attorney general or a federal judgeship.

326. McGirr, 195–196.

327. ibid., 202.

328. "'Lone Bandit' Travis Subdued and Hungry Returned to Prison," *Atlanta Constitution*, March 12, 1926. The story of R.L. Travis and the other two "desperadoes" who escaped from the prison camp in a stolen truck kept subscribers of the newspaper riveted for three days. The men abandoned the truck and car-jacked the chauffeur-driven limousine of a prominent Atlanta matron in broad daylight and hid out in the hills until their capture.

329. McGirr, 202.

330. ibid., 203.

331. Smith, *Baptists and Bootleggers*, 159. My chapter "Al Capone Slept Here" tells the story of Capone's time in the South, including his death in Miami Beach in 1947.

332. "Upshaw Turns Dry Scorn on 2 Major Candidates," *Richmond Times-Dispatch*, October 21, 1932.

333. "Dry Candidate Claims Big Vote," Associated Press article in Sumter (SC) *Daily Item*, October 12, 1932.

334. https://www.senate.gov/artandhistory/senate-stories/beer-by-christmas.htm

335. Burrough, 72.

336. ibid., 72-73.

337. ibid., 73-74, 145, 508-509. You sometimes have to take Hoover with a grain of salt when he comments on female criminals. He portrayed Ma Barker as the mastermind behind her sons' gang, when she was actually a fairly harmless old lady who just liked to do jigsaw puzzles, according to Burrough. But he seems to have pegged Kathryn Kelly correctly.

338. ibid., 74.

339. Burrough writes that Kelly had a reunion with his two sons, peeling $20 for each of them off a big bankroll, and told them he was an FBI agent on a secret mission. 129.

340. ibid., 129-133, 547, 548.

341. According to the *Merriam-Webster Dictionary*, the slang term G-man was first used in 1928.

342. Hoover returned the favor by endorsing one of Oursler's Thatcher Colt mystery books, writing, "I was particularly thrilled at the manner in which Anthony Abbot [Oursler's pen name], himself a man well versed in scientific methods of law enforcement, related in detail the method utilized by Thatcher Colt in bringing this case to a logical conclusion."

343. https://www.fbi.gov/news/stories/a-byte-out-of-history

344. McGirr, 220-221.

345. https://www.marquette.edu/library/archives/Mss/FBI/index.php

346. The Twenty-first Amendment was the only one considered by state ratifying conventions rather than state legislatures. Some states, including the Carolinas and Georgia, chose not to convene conventions. https://jackmillercenter.org/eighteenth-twenty-first-amendments/#:~:text=The%20Twenty%2DFirst%20Amendment%20also,its%20popular%20support%20by%201933.

347. https://www.alcoholproblemsandsolutions.org/21st-amendment-repealed-national-prohibition-1920-1933-in-u-s/

348. This agency had several name changes over the years, but we will call it the ATF because that's what people know it as today.

349. *Encyclopedia of Alabama*. http://encyclopediaofalabama.org/ARTICLE/h-4126

350. https://libationlawblog.com/2013/02/21/2013221the-history-of-the-currently-unconstitutional-kentucky-statute-prohibiting-grocery-stores-and-convenience-stores-from-selling-liquor-and-wine/

351. https://www.floridamemory.com/items/show/346664

352. https://constitutioncenter.org/blog/five-interesting-facts-about-prohibitions-end-in-1933

353. https://www.georgiaencyclopedia.org/exhibition/wrestling-temptation-the-quest-to-control-alcohol-in-georgia/#:~:text=A%20crowd%20gathered%20in%20front,transportation%2C%20and%20sale%20of%20alcohol .

354. https://www.alcoholproblemsandsolutions.org/21st-amendment-repealed-national-prohibition-1920-1933-in-u-s/

355. https://libationlawblog.com/2013/02/21/2013221the-history-of-the-currently-unconstitutional-kentucky-statute-prohibiting-grocery-stores-and-convenience-stores-from-selling-liquor-and-wine/

356. https://constitutioncenter.org/blog/five-interesting-facts-about-prohibitions-end-in-1933

357. https://am.aals.org/wp-content/uploads/sites/4/2019/01/AM19ConLawProhibitionInNOLAArticle.pdf

358. https://constitutioncenter.org/blog/five-interesting-facts-about-prohibitions-end-in-1933

359. https://constitutioncenter.org/blog/five-interesting-facts-about-prohibitions-end-in-1933

360. Pierce, 166.

361. https://constitutioncenter.org/blog/five-interesting-facts-about-prohibitions-end-in-1933

362. https://core.ac.uk/download/pdf/347463813.pdf

363. https://www.alcoholproblemsandsolutions.org/21st-amendment-repealed-national-prohibition-1920-1933-in-u-s/; https://www.alcoholproblemsandsolutions.org/prohibition-in-tennessee/

364. https://tennesseeencyclopedia.net/entries/temperance/

365. https://uncommonwealth.virginiamemory.com/blog/2017/11/29/last-call-women-and-the-repeal-of-prohibition/

366. The district attorney is called the commonwealth attorney in Virginia.

367. Charles D. Thompson Jr., *Spirits of Just Men: Mountaineers, Liquor Bosses and Lawmen in the Moonshine Capitol of the World* (Urbana: University of Illinois Press, 2011). Thirty-four were initially indicted but due to guilty or nolo contendere pleas and the murder of the indicted deputy sheriff, only twenty-three were tried.

368. "20 Found Guilty of Conspiracy," *Roanoke Times*, July 2, 1935.

369. Thompson, 112.

370. The former sheriff was sentenced to three years of probation. "Conspiracy Sentences Total 239 Months," *Roanoke World-News*, July 9, 1935.

371. Thompson, 214.

372. "Carter Lee, Attorney, Dies in Rocky Mount," *Roanoke Times*, January 2, 1958

373. Pierce, 189. I guess Pierce and author Thompson will have to duke it out over whether Virginia or North Carolina have the greatest claim to "Moonshine Capital of the World."

374. Pierce, 190. This is the essence of my father Bruce Yandle's Bootleggers and Baptists theory of government regulation. B&B theory argues that regulation is more likely to hold when moral forces and those wanting financial gain work for the same outcome even if for different reasons. The signature example is that Baptists want to ban Sunday alcohol sales because it's a sin to drink on the Sabbath. Bootleggers want to ban it because it gives them a monopoly on liquor sales. To learn more, read Adam C. Smith and Bruce Yandle, *Bootleggers and Baptists: How Economic Forces and Moral Persuasion Interact to Shape Regulatory Politics*, (Washington: Cato Institute, 2014).

375. *Shreveport Times*, February 19, 1943; Mitenbuler, 187.

376. Mitenbuler, 216.

377. Carried by the *New Orleans Times-Picayune*, March 21, 1943

378. Pierce, 187-192.

379. ibid., 196.

380. Thomas R. Allison, *Moonshine Memories* (Montgomery, Alabama: New South Books, 2007), 19.

381. ibid., 20.

382. ibid., 371-372.

383. ibid., 244-251.

384. ibid., 15.

385. Dot Moore, *No Remorse: The Rise and Fall of John Wallace* (Birmingham, AL: New South Books, 2011), 25-26, 34, 43.

386. ibid., 27, 33, 36.

387. ibid., 47-49.

388. ibid., 50-52.

389. ibid., 65. Only White males could serve on Georgia juries at this time.

390. ibid., 68.

391. ibid., 67, 69.

392. ibid., 111.

393. Barnes's award-winning book was published in 1978.

394. A few months after the movie was shot, Griffith married Cindi Knight, the actress who had played William Turner's wife. It was his third and final marriage. He was 56; she was 29. Johnny Cash's wife June Carter Cash also had a role in the movie as the soothsayer Mayhayley Lancaster.

395. Various articles in the Newnan *Times-Herald* in 2021 and 2022.

396. Anthony Abbot, *The Shudders* (New York: Farrar & Rinehart, 1943), 15.

397. Anthony Abbot, *About the Murder of a Startled Lady* (Cleveland: World Publishing Company, 1943), 251-254.

398. Several citations on the internet say this.

Notes

CHAPTER NINE: Whiskey Tourism

399. In 1838, Tennessee passed a law making it illegal to sell alcoholic beverages in taverns and stores. Manufacture of alcohol in the state was banned in 1909, sending the Jack Daniel Distillery to St. Louis, and a bone-dry bill was passed in 1917.

400. I profiled Linda and the Chicks in *Baptists and Bootleggers. How to Be a Bourbon Badass* was published by Red Lightning Books of Indianapolis in 2018.

401. Mitenbuler, 10.

402. https://www.bardstownbourbon.com/steve-nally/ Loftin died in 2019 at age sixty-one and Bardstown now is owned by Pritzker Private Capital.

403. Specifics on clients and capacity came from Brandon Smith, brand manager, in an email on April 10, 2023.

404. https://www.bardstownbourbon.com/plan-a-visit/

405. https://kybourbontrail.com/the-proof-is-here-bourbon-pours-billions-into-kentucky-economy/

406. https://www.wkyt.com/2023/02/28/several-ky-counties-raise-concerns-over-bourbon-industry-tax-bill/

407. https://apnews.com/article/bourbon-barrel-tax-kentucky-fd42c742aac4c257c7548e372310cebc

408. https://apps.legislature.ky.gov/recorddocuments/bill/23RS/hb5/bill.pdf

409. This is the cost of the Flight of Jack Daniel's tour. The Angel's Share tour, which involves barrel tastings, costs $35. There is also a $20 Dry County tour for those who don't wish to imbibe. https://www.jackdaniels.com/en-us/visit-distillery

410. Krass, 215-226.

411. Technically he wasn't paid, but he was given a life-time supply!

412. https://talesofthecocktail.org/culture/frank-sinatra-jack-daniels/

413. Krass, 226.

414. https://talesofthecocktail.org/culture/frank-sinatra-jack-daniels/

415. https://www.nytimes.com/2023/03/01/us/whiskey-fungus-jack-daniels-tennessee.html

416. The large display on Green at the Jack Daniel welcome center gives Fawn Weaver full credit for her discoveries.

417. https://www.forbes.com/sites/dominiquefluker/2022/03/09/how-fawn-weaver-created-uncle-nearest-premium-whiskey-from-hidden-history/?sh=4706a117fea9

418. https://www.prnewswire.com/news-releases/uncle-nearests-victoria-eady-butler-makes-history-winning-first-ever-back-to-back-master-blender-of-the-year-honor-by-whisky-magazine-301492988.html

419. Email from Fawn Weaver via publicist Grace Demeritt, November 14, 2022.

420. Krass, 211.

CHAPTER TEN: In Search of Sobriety

421. Cheever, 93.

422. U.S. Census, 1850.

423. Cheever, 94-95.

424. *Alcoholics Anonymous* (*Big Book*), Fourth Edition (New York: Alcoholics Anonymous World Services, Inc., 2019), 8.

425. ibid, 9-10.

426. ibid, 59.

427. ibid, xiii.

428. The highly collectible issue of the magazine sells for hundreds of dollars online. Fulton Oursler continued to have an eventful life. He became a senior editor of *Reader's Digest* in 1944 and, after accepting Christ and converting to Catholicism, novelized the life of Jesus into *The Greatest Story Ever Told*, which has sold millions of copies and has never gone out of print since its publication in 1949. His wife Grace Perkins became editor of *Guideposts* magazine.

429. ibid., xv.

430. https://www.aa.org/sites/default/files/literature/smf-132_Estimated_Membership_EN_1221.pdf

431. *Alcoholics Anonymous*, xiii.

432. https://favorupstate.org/about/about-favor/

433. Ruby Warrington, *Sober Curious: The Blissful Sleep, Greater Focus, Limitless Presence, and Deep Connection Awaiting Us All on the Other Side of Alcohol* (New York: HarperOne, 2018).

434. https://jamanetwork.com/journals/jama/fullarticle/2790491

435. https://www.washingtonpost.com/opinions/2022/04/19/alcohol-related-deaths-surged-covid-pandemic/

436. https://www.diageo.com/en/news-and-media/press-releases/2019/diageo-acquires-majority-shareholding-in-seedlip-the-world-s-first-distilled-non-alcoholic-spirit

437. The drys won. You may recall that in 1966 Mississippi became the last state in the nation to repeal prohibition.

438. https://rationalwiki.org/wiki/If-by-whiskey

439. https://www.seedlipdrinks.com/en-us/cocktails/eastside/

440. Both "Behold This Dreamer" and the inscription on the book are from the story of Joseph, who was sold into slavery by his jealous brothers, yet became the greatest of them all, just as he had dreamed.

Index

Page numbers in *italic* indicate photographs or other illustrations.

A

About the Murder of a Startled Lady (Abbot/Oursler), 173–74, *173*
Alabama, 6, 62, 95, 113, 138, 141, 162, 165, 167–69, 219n88. *See also names of specific cities.*
Alcatraz Prison, 156, 160
alcohol consumption, 31, 54–55, 59, 153, 204, 204–5, 207, 219n88
alcohol distilling. *See also names of individual distilleries.*
    bourbon of, 180–86
    medicinal alcohol and, 111, *111*, 112, 220n96
    taxes on, 15, 19–21, 54–55, 58–59, 77
    Tennessee whiskey of, 187–90
alcohol tourism, 104, 179–80, 183, 187–88, 197
Alcoholics Anonymous, 57, 201–4, 207
alcoholism, 201–5, 207
Allen Chase: The Search and Capture of the Allen Outlaws as Reported by Period Newspapers, The (Hall), 80–81, 83, 85
Allen, Floyd, 80–83, 81
Allen, Sidna, 82–83, 83, 84
American Medical Association, 111–12, 204–5
American Midnight: The Great War, a Violent Peace, and Democracy's Forgotten Crisis (Hochschild), 96, 105
American Prohibition Museum, 52, 66
Anderson, James, 11–12
Andrews, Lincoln, 134–36
Andy Griffith Museum, 70, 75, 84
Andy Griffith Show (TV program), 69, 70–71

Anti-Saloon League (ASL), 2, 65, 80, *88*, 91, 93–95, *95*, 98, 110, 128, 135, 138, 139, 141, 151, 152, 153, 154
Arkansas, 6, 128, 162, 165
Artistry of Mixing Drinks, The (Meier), 7
Asbury, Francis, 56, 57
Atlanta Constitution, 99, 127, *127*, 129, 135, 140, 140, 142, 152–53, *152*, 226n251
Atlanta, GA, 99, 140–41, 146, 147
Atlanta Federal Penitentiary, 114, 115, 133, 147, 156, *156*

B

Bailey, Thomas, 163–64
Baldwin-Felts Detective Agency, 82, 223n168
Bardstown, KY, 180, 182–87
Bardstown Bourbon Company, 182–83, *183*, 186
Barnes, Margaret Anne, 172
beer and beer-making
    Augusta, GA in, 89, 93
    Charleston, SC in, 92–93, *92*
    gardens, 89, 91, 104
    German-style, 87–93, *90*, *97*, 97
    See also names of individual breweries.
Beshear, Andy, 180, 184, 186
Big Book, 202, 203, 204
Blood and Whiskey: The Life and Times of Jack Daniel (Krass), 190, 199
Boardwalk Empire (TV series), 131, 132, 196
Bootleggers and Baptists: How Economic Forces and Moral Persuasion Interact to Shape Regulatory Politics (Smith and Yandle), 2, 232n374
Bootleggers and Baptists theory, 2, 215n2, 216n31, 232n374

235

Bourbon Empire: The Past and Future of American Whiskey (Mitenbuler), 166, 193, 199
Bradham, Caleb, 36, 38
Brown-Forman, 180, 191, 193, 194
Bruce, Louis, 93
Bunker, Chang and Eng, 71–75, 72, 85, 85, 202
Bureau of Internal Revenue (Internal Revenue Service), 110, 161
Bureau of Prohibition, 110, 113, 114, 134–36, 141
Bureau of Alcohol, Tobacco, Firearms and Explosives (ATF), 161, 163, 167–69
Burns, William J., 108–9, 109, 114, 117, 134, 139
Burrough, Bryan, 158–60, 177, 230n337
Busch, Adolphus, 89, 89, 91, 93, 202

C

Cabarrus County, NC, 109, 118, 121–22, *121*, 122, 167
Call, Dan, 188, 193, 195
Cannon, James, Jr., 95, 153
Capone, Al, 114, 129, 152, 154, 156, *156*, 230n331
Carroll County Courthouse, 75–76, *76*, 80–84
Carroll County Historical Society and Museum, *76*, 83, 84
Cash, Johnny, 170, 172, 232n394
Castings, Jane, 130–31
cemeteries
    Casey's Hill Cemetery, Atlanta, GA, 147
    Cave Spring Cemetery, Louisville, KY, 187
    Colonial Park Cemetery, Savannah, GA, 66–67
    Emmanuel Episcopal Church, Henrico County, VA, 26
    First Presbyterian Church, Columbia, SC, 18, *18*
    Forest Lawn Memorial Park, Glendale, CA, 176
    Garden of Heaven Cemetery, Westchester County, NY, 210, *210*
    George Washington's Tomb, Mount Vernon, VA, 18, *18*
    Laurel Hill Cemetery, Thomasville, GA, 176, *176*
    Lynchburg City Cemetery, Lynchburg, TN, 199
    Metairie Cemetery, New Orleans, LA, 67, *67*
    St. Michael's Episcopal Church, Charleston, SC, 47–48, *47*
    St. Philip's Episcopal Church, Charleston, SC, 47–48
    United Presbyterian Church, Fort Mill, SC, 105, *105*
    Walls Baptist Church, Bostic, NC, 85
    White Plains Baptist Church, Mt. Airy, NC, 85, *85*
Charleston, SC, 39, 41–48, 58, 62, 92–93, 104
Charleston Beer: A High Gravity History of Low Country Brewing (Pettigrew), 92–93, 106
Charleston City Hall, 45, *45*, 47
Charlotte, NC, 55, 64, 80, 164
Chautauqua Institution (Chautauqua Lake Sunday School Assembly), 2, 59–60, *60*, 220n109
Cheever, Susan, 14, 21, 31, 54, 202, 207
Cherry Bounce Festival, 79, *79*, 84
churches
    Bethel United Methodist, Charleston, SC, 44
    First United Methodist, Newnan, GA, 125
    Grace United Methodist, Wilmington, NC, 39
    Memorial Chapel, Lake Junaluska, NC, 57
    Wesley Chapel, Savannah, GA, 56
    See also cemeteries.
Church of England, 1, 51, 53, 56, 57
Civil War, 21, 52, 58, 62, 67, 74–75, 77, 85, 164
Clark, Adèle, 25, *25*, 26, *26*
cocktail recipes
    Aviators' Eggnog, 103
    Bobby Burns, 169, *169*
    Brandy Smash, 103
    Carolina Libre, *36*, 37
    Crystal Strawberry, 86
    Dainty, Unfermented Punch, 65
    Fish House Punch, 17, 19
    Formidable, 173–74, *173*
    French Traveler, 22, *22*, 23
    Goat, The, 181–82, *182*
    Golden Slipper, 144
    Highball, 166, *166*
    Naranja Old Fashioned, 120, *120*
    Nearest and Jack-Hattan, 197, *197*
    Olde Pink House Pink Lady, 50, *50*
    Old Talbott Tavern Sidecar, 185, *185*
    Patty's Boll Weevil, 125, 126, *126*
    Pink Lady, 6–7, *7*

Index

Sèchey 75, 207, *207*
Seedlip Eastside, 209, *209*
Silver Slipper, 144, *144*
Sinatra 3-2-1, 192, *192*
Up on the Roof, 209, *209*
Cocktails Across America: A Postcard View of Cocktail Culture in the 1930s, 40s, and 50s (Lapis and Peck-Davis), 144, 177
Columbia, SC, 18–19, 55
Columbia (SC) Record, 141–42
Commonwealth, The, 22, 26, 186
Concord, NC, 107–8, *108*, 109, 116, 118, 121, 122
Coolidge, Calvin, 115, 129, 134, 136, 146, 150, 153
Congress, 21, 33, 40, 48, 55, 61, 95, 96–99, *98*, 113, 115, 127, 128–29, 139, 141, 153, 156, 157, 220n112
covid-19 pandemic, 3, 37, 65, 132, 204–5
Coweta County, GA, 170–72
crime
    alcohol-related, 77, 79, 83, 112–113, 129–30, 131–33, 136, 142, 152–56, *152*, 158, 170. *See also murders, kidnapping*.
Cunningham, Ann Pamela, 13, 18, *18*

D

Daniel, Jasper "Jack," 5, 188–90, *189*, *190*, 193, 202
Daugherty, Harry M., 109, 111, 114, 115, *115*, 116, 117
Davis, Burke, 100, 101, 106
Dead Distillers: A History of the Upstarts and Outlaws Who Made American Spirits (Spoelman and Haskell), 199
Department of Justice, U.S., 109, 110, 113, 115, 117, 128, 139, 154
Department of Treasury, U.S., 20, 94, 110, 114, 129, 154, 161, 163
Donaldson, Bert, 140–41, *140*, 146, 147
Drinking in America: Our Secret History (Cheever), 14, 21, 31, 54, 202, 207

E

Eady Butler, Victoria, 194, *194*
Earnhardt, Dale, 122, *122*
Eat, Drink, and Be Merry in Maryland (Stieff), 19, 103
Edmund's Oast, 92, 104
Eighteenth Amendment
    introduction of, 95
    description of, 110, 111, 127
    immigration and, 95–96
    minority groups and, 95–96
    passage and ratification of, 94, 98, 109–10
    repeal of, 157
    states opposing, 98
    states supporting, 98
    unintended consequences of, 110, 151–56
    women's suffrage and, 94
    See also Volstead Act.
Ethridge, Willie Snow, 52, 67
executions, 82, 113, 118, 137, 172

F

Face in the Crowd, A (film), 70
Faces and Voices of Recovery (FAVOR), 204
Federal Bureau of Investigation, 109, 114, 117–18, 154, 159–60
Fitzgerald, F. Scott, 6, 111, 143, 224n204
"flapper fiction," 142–45, *143*, 147
Fleming, C. Pridemore, 134
Flexner, James Thomas, 21, 32
Florida, 6, 22, 89, 128, 131, 135, 150, 162, 164, 166, 219n88, 220n112. *See also names of specific cities*.
Foster, William M., 81–82
Founding Spirits: George Washington and the Beginnings of the American Whiskey Industry (Pogue), 14, 27
Franklin County, VA, 133, 163–65
Fredericksburg, VA, 15–17

G

Georgetown, SC, 39, 46, 48
George Washington's 1791 Southern Tour (Bingham), 27
George Washington Society (Washingtonians), 57, 202, 204
Georgia, 1, 6, 51, 54, 63, 65, 71, 98, 99, 113, 125, 128, 135, 136, 137, 140–41, 150, 155, 162, 165, 168, 170, 171, 172, 219n88. *See also names of specific cities*.
Georgian Terrace Hotel, 140, 146, *146*
Great Gatsby, The (Fitzgerald), 111, 143
Great Moonshine Conspiracy Trial, 163–64, *163*, 165, 231n367, 231n370
Green, Nathan "Uncle Nearest," 188–89, 193–97. *See also Nearest Green Distillery*.
Greenough, Mark, 23–24
Griffith, Andy, 69–71, 84, 170, 172, 219n89, 222n130, 222n133, 222n394

H

Habersham, James, Jr., 50, 66
Hall, Ron, 81, 83, 85
Hamilton (musical), 15, 20, 35
Hamilton, Alexander, 15, 20–21, 22, 54

Hampton Plantation, 39–40, *40*, 46, 218n64, 218n65
Harding, Florence, 109, 111, 116
Harding, Warren G., 99, 109, 111, 113, 115, 116, 117, 150, 202, 226n241
Hawkins, Beata, 52, 53–54
Hayes, Lucy, 61, 221n114
Hayes, Rutherford B., 61, 220n112, 221n114
Haynes, Roy A., 113, 114
Heaton, Richard J., 185–86
Heintz, Emily, 205–6, *205*
Henderson, Archibald, 30, 34–35
Heyward-Washington House, 42–43, *43*, 46, 47
Hillsville, VA, 75–76, 80–84
History of the Life of Amos Owens, the Noted Blockader of Cherry Mountain, A (White), 78
Hobson, Richmond P., 95, 141
Hoover, Herbert, 133, 150, 152, 153–57, *154*
Hoover, J. Edgar, 99, 105, 107, 117–18, *117*, 134, 154, 159–60, 173, 230n337, 230n342
Horry, Harriott Pinckney, 39–40, 47–48, *48*, 218n65
Houdon, Jean-Antoine, 24–25, *24*, 30
Hoyt, Edwin P., 107–9, 113–14, 115, 118, 123
Huang, Yunte, 72–74, 85
Hursey, Joe, 88–89

I

immigrants, 87–89, 95–97, 129, 137
Inseparable: The Original Siamese Twins and Their Rendezvous with American History (Huang), 73, 85

J

Jack Daniel Distillery, 112, 180–93, 194, 196, 198, 233n399
Jarvis, Thomas Jordan, 63
Jefferson, Thomas, 15, 19, 21, 22, 23, 24, 54–55, 181, 217n371
Jefferson Hotel, 22, *22*, 23, 26
Jim Crow laws, 125, 137, 172
John Wesley: The Great Methodist (Wellman), 67
Journal of the American Medical Association, 204–5, 219n8

K

Kelly, George "Machine Gun" (George F. Barnes), 156, 158–60, *158*, 202
Kelly, Kathryn, *158*, 159–60, 202
Kentucky, 6, 21, 112, 128, 162, 165, 180–87, 219n88. *See also names of specific cities.*
Kentucky Artisan Distillery, 180–81, *181*, 186
Kentucky Distillers Association, 180, 184, 185
kidnapping, 116–18, 132, 154, 159, 171
Ku Klux Klan (KKK), 79, 93, 99, 136, 137–39, *138*, 146

L

Lanham, Henderson, 113, 226n235
Last Call: The Rise and Fall of Prohibition (Okrent), 90, 105
Leave Me with a Smile (Springs), 102
Leavenworth prison, 155–56, 158, 160
Lee, Cammie Lassiter, 35–36, *35*, 38
Lee, Charles Carter, 163–64
Liberty, 143, 203, *203*, 229n302, 234n428
Lindbergh, Charles and Anne, 116–18, 154
Literary Digest, The, 127
Little White House, 170, 175, *175*
local option laws, 63, 80, 162, 164, 172
Loftin, Peter, 182
Louisiana, 6, 62, 67, 96, 109, 162, *162*, 166, 219n88
Louisville, KY, 181, 186, 187, 190, 191
Lynchburg, TN, 112, 180, 188–93, *188*, 198, 199

M

McCoy, Bill, 110, 131, 133
McGirr, Lisa, 133, 138, 147, 155, 160, 229n316
McLean, Evalyn Walsh, 116–18, *117*
Massie, Thornton L., 81–82
Mayberry Spirits Company, 70, 86
Means, Gaston Bullock, 107–9, *108*, 113–18, *114*, 120, 121, 122, 134, 155, 167, 173
Means, Julie Patterson, 108, 115, 116, 123
Mellon, Andrew W., 110, 111, 115, 154
Mendl, Lady (Elsie de Wolfe), 6–7, *6*
Merrick, Caroline E., 62, *62*, 67
Methodists and United Methodist Church, 59–60, 61, 137, 147, 153, 170
    history of, 1, 39, 44, 51, 55–57, *55*, 58
    leadership in temperance movement by, 1–2, 57, 59, 62, 64, 65, 80, 93, 94–95, 161, 165, 186
Middleton, Susan, 9–10, *10*, 13, 15, 16, 22, 26, 29, 31, 35, 37, 38, 39, 40, 49
Mississippi, 6, 98, 162, 207, 234n437
Mitenbuler, Reid, 166, 193, 199
moonshine
    Alabama in, 167–69
    corruption and, 163–64
    Ford cars and, *161*, 165
    North Carolina in, 70–71, 75–80, *78*, 164–65, 167

Prohibition after, 163–72
South Carolina in, 77, 102, 113, 165, 168
still seizures and, 59, 113, 161, 167–69
stock car racing and, 58–59, 70, *161*, 165–66
tax evasion and, 58–59, 77–78, 114, 154, 163–64, 167
Virginia in, 75–76, 80–81, 133–34
Moonshine Memories (Allison), 167–69
Moore, Dot, 170, 171
Moore County, TN, 188, *188*, 191, 192, 198
Moran, George "Bugs," 129, 152, 227n256
Mt. Airy, NC, 69–76, 83, 84, 85
Mt. Airy Museum of Regional History, 71, 75–76, 84
Mt. Airy Stock Car Racing Wall of Fame, 70, 71, 84
Motlow, Lem, 112, 190, 199
Mount Vernon, 9, 10–14, *11*, *12*, *13*, 17, 18, *18*, 24, 27, 30, 55, 215n6, 216n7
Mullins, James Sherman, 134
Murder in Coweta County (TV movie and book), 172
murders, 63, 70, 75–76, 77, 79, 81–82, 83, 97, 109, 113, 121, 129, 132, 134, 136–37, 140–41, 143, 146, 152–53, 154, 163, 170–72, 173–74, 229n316, 227n258
My Life with Gaston B. Means as Told by His Wife, Julie P. Means (Kane, ed.), 123

N

NASCAR, 63, 122, 165–66
Nation, Carry A., 80, *80*, 91, 94, 128
National Commission on Law Observance and Enforcement (Wickersham Commission), 133, 153–54, *154*, 163
Nearest Green Distillery, 193–97, *195*, *196*. *See also* Green, Nathan "Uncle Nearest."
necessary, the, 42–43, *43*
Newnan, GA, 98, 125–27, *125*, 169–72, 175
New Orleans, LA, 62, 67, 160
New York Times, 76, 81, 83
New York World, 138–39
Newnan-Coweta Historical Society, 169–72, *171*, 175
19 Crimes, 130–31, *130*
Nineteenth Amendment, 25, 58, 196
No Remorse: The Rise and Fall of John Wallace (Moore), 170
North Carolina, 3, 6, 29, 31, 33, 55, 56, *57*, 61, 63, 69–80, 78, 84–85, 96, 98, 113, 122, 128, 132, 150, 155, 162, 164–67, 179–80, *179*, 222n136, 232n373. *See also* names of specific cities.

O

Olde Pink House, 50, *50*, 66
Old Exchange and Provost Dungeon, 41–42, *41*, 44, 47
Old Talbott Tavern, 183–84, *184*, *185*, 187
Okrent, Daniel, 90, 91, 95, 105, 128
Oglethorpe, James, 1, 51, *51*, 52, 54, 66
Operation Dry-Up, 168, *168*
Oursler, Fulton, 143, 160, 173, 203–4, 210, 230n342, 234n428, 234n440
Owens, Amos, 77–79, 85

P

Palmetto Brewing Company, 92, 93
Peck-Davis, Anne, 144, *144*, *149*, 177
Pepsi-Cola, 36, *36*, 37, 38
Perkins, Grace, 203, 204, 210, 234n428
Pettigrew, Timmons, 92–93, 106
Pierce, Daniel S., 164–65, 167
Pinckney, Eliza Lucas, 39–40, 48, 218n63
Pogue, Dennis J., 14, 127
Potts, Lamar, 171–72, *171*
President Washington's Diaries, 1791 to 1799 (Hoskins, ed.), 27
progressive movement, 94
Prohibition. *See Eighteenth Amendment, Volstead Act.*
prohibition (state and local), 162
Georgia in, 63, 98, 172
national Prohibition, after, 162, 164
national Prohibition, before, 63, 93, 109–10
North Carolina in, 63, 80, 164–67
South Carolina in, 93
Tennessee in, 190, 233n399
Prohibition Expeditions
Ale Trails, 104
Atlanta, 146
Cabarrus County, NC, 121
Georgetown to Charleston, SC, 46–47
Kentucky, 186
Mount Vernon, VA, 17
New Bern, NC, 38
Newnan, GA, 175
North Carolina and Virginia Mountains, 84
Richmond, VA, 26
Roanoke and Franklin County, VA, 165
Savannah, GA, 66
Tennessee, 198
Pryor, Bailey, 131
Public Enemies: America's Greatest Crime Wave and the Birth of the FBI, 1933–34 (Burrough), 158–60, 177

R

Redmond, Lewis, 77, 132, 133
Reed, James A., 128–29
Remus, George, 112, 114, 132–33, 166, 190
Remus, Imogene, 132–33
Revolutionary War, 11, 15, 20–21, 31–32, *32*, 35, 39, 44, 47, 48, 56
Reynolds Square, *49*, *50*, *51*, 66
Richmond, VA, 19–20, 22–26, 153, 157
Rising Sun Tavern, 16–17, *16*
Rixman, Katie and Terry, 182–85
Roanoke, VA, 163–64, *163*, 165
Rocky Mount, VA, 163
Roosevelt, Franklin Delano, 150, *151*, 155, 175
Roosevelt, Theodore, 94, 96
rum-running, 110, 131
Russell, Howard Hyde, 93

S

Sabin, Pauline Morton, 153–54, *155*, 157
St. Valentine's Day Massacre, 152–53, *152*
saloons, 89–91, 110. *See also* Anti-Saloon League.
Saunders, John Monk, 144–45
Savannah, GA, 49–54, 56, 66, 99, 113, 114, 135
Savi's Wine Shop, 35–36, *35*, 38
Scots, 71, 81, 137, 222n136
Scott, Michael and Larissa, 126
Sèchey, 205–7, *205*, *207*
Seedlip, 206, 209, *209*
Shreveport (LA) *Times*, 162, 166, *166*
Simmons, William J., 137, 139
Sinatra, Frank, 191–92
Single Lady (Saunders), 144–45, 229n302
slavery and enslaved people, 9, 12, 31, 39, 51, 52, 58, 62, 63, 74, 75, 92, 137, 188, 215n6, 218n65, 224n187
Small, Sam W., 135–36
Smith, Adam C., 2, 201, 211–12
Smith, Al, 149–50, 153, 229n322
Smith, Hilda, 136–37, *136*
Snappy Lunch, 69–70, *69*, 84
South Carolina, 6, 18–19, 25, 39–40, 48, 54, 55, 62, 71, 77, 80, 89, 93, 105, 128, 132, 142, 162, 166, 168, 209. *See also names of specific cities.*
South Carolina in 1791: George Washington's Southern Tour (Lipscomb), 48
Southern Grace Distilleries, 118–120, *119*, *121*
Speakeasy Girl (Meredith/Oursler), 143, *143*, 160, 173
Spectacular Rogue Gaston B. Means (Hoyt), 107, 123
Spirits of Just Men: Mountaineers, Liquor Bosses and Lawmen in the Moonshine Capital of the World (Thompson), 163
Springs, Elliott White, 99–103, *100*, 105, *105*, *161*, 202
Stewart-Parker House, 39, 46
stock car racing, 59, 70, 71, 165–66
Stone Mountain, GA, *137*, 146
Strange Case of President Harding, The (Means and Thacker), 116
Strange Fires: The True Story of John Wesley's Love Affair in Georgia (Ethridge), 52, 67
Sullivan, Leigh-Ann, 37
Sweat, Noah S. "Soggy," Jr., 207–8

T

Tar Heel Lightnin': How Secret Stills and Fast Cars Made North Carolina the Moonshine Capital of the World, (Pierce), 76, 85
Tavern, The, 44, 47
taxes
    alcohol on, 15, 54–55, 58–59, 77–78, 94, 129, 161, 163–64, 184–86
    evasion of, 58–59, 77–78, 114, 154, 163–64, 167–68, 170
    income on, 94, 114, 156
    luxury goods on, 220n103
temperance movement, 3, 25, 32, 51, 57–58, 59, *59*, 61, 63, 80, 87, 91, 94, 95–96, 98, 129, 138, 155, 157, 196, 220n106. *See also* Women's Christian Temperance Union (WCTU), Anti-Saloon League (ASL)
Tennessee, 5, 6, 24, 112, 128, 162, 165, 179, 180, 190, 196, 198, 233n399. *See also names of specific cities.*
Tennessee Distillers Guild, 187–88
Thacker, May Dixon, 114, 116
Thornton, Mark, 129
Tonic Parlor, 36–37
Trumbull, John, 33, 44–45, *45*
Tryon Palace, 33–34, 38, 217n53
Turner, William, 170–72
Twenty-First Amendment, 5, 157, 161, 162, 230n346

Index

U

unfermented wine, 64–65, *64*, 221n125
Upshaw, William David, 98–99, *98*, 127, *128*, 136, 137, 139, 141, 142, 150–51, 157, 170, 172, 176–77, *176*, 224n200, 226n251, 228n294
Use and Need of the Life of Carry A. Nation, The (Nation), 91

V

Virginia, 3, 4, 6, 10, 14, 16, 17, 19, 23–26, 70, 71, 76, 80–84, 95, 98, 133, 135, 150, 155, 162, 163, 165, 217n38, 217n39, 221n114, 223n154, 231n365, 232n373. *See also names of specific cities.*
Virginia Women's Monument, 25, *25*, 217n39
Volstead, Andrew, 110, *110*
Volstead Act, 173, 206
    corruption under, 112–15
    enforcement of, 110, 112–13, 115, 127, 128, 134–36, 141, 153, 170
    loopholes in, 110–12
    modifications of, 153, 157
    newspaper poll regarding, 127–28, 157
    passage of, 110
    Senate hearings on, 128–29, 136, 141
    See also Eighteenth Amendment.

W

Wallace, John, 170–72, *171*, 175
War Birds: Diary of an Unknown Aviator (Springs), 103
Warm Springs, GA, 150, 170, 175, *175*
War on Alcohol: Prohibition and the Rise of the American State, The (McGirr), 133, 138, 147, 155, 160
Washington, George
    abhorrence of drunkenness of, 14–15, 31
    depictions of, *20*, *30*, *32*, *32*, 33, 44–45, *45*, 218n71
    distillery ownership of, 9, 11–12, 58
    drinking habits of, 14, 58
    post-presidency days of, 9–12
    statues of, 19, *23*, 23–25, *24*, *26*, 30, 45
    teeth of, 30–31, *31*
    tomb of, *18*, 18
    Whiskey Rebellion and, 20–21
Washington, NC, 31
Washington Post, 76, 205
Washington's Tour of the South
    Augusta, GA in, 55
    Charleston, SC in, 41–48, 92
    Charlotte, NC in, 55
    Columbia, SC in, 18–19, 55
    Fredericksburg, VA in, 15–17
    Georgetown, SC in, 39, 46
    Hampton Plantation at, 39–40
    meeting with Catawba Indians during, 55
    Mount Vernon, VA at, 9–15, 17, 55
    New Bern, NC in, 29, 33–35, 38
    Richmond, VA in, 19–20, 22–26
    Salem, NC in, 55
    Savannah, GA in, 49, 66
    Tarboro, NC in, 29
    tavern stays during, 10, 29–30
    toasting during, 34–35, 44, 49
    Wilmington, NC in, 39
Weaver, Fawn, 193–94, *194*, 196–97
Welch, Thomas Bramwell, 64, *64*
Wellman, Sam, 56, 67
Wesley, Charles, 1, 52, 53, 54, 56, *57*, 67, 219n92
Wesley, John, 1–2, *2*, 49, 50–57, *57*, 66, 67, 215n1, 219n86
Wheeler, Wayne B., 65, 93, 95, 110, 128, 139, 141, 142, 151–52, 226n251
whiskey fungus, 192–93
Whiskey Rebellion, 20–21, *20*
Whisky Chicks, 180–81, 182, *182*
White, Aaron M., 205
White, M.L., 78
Willard, Frances E., 59, *59*, 59–60, 62, 63, 87, 220n105
Willebrandt, Mabel Walker, 112–14, *112*, 128, 134, 135, 154, 229n325
Wilmington, NC, 39, 63, 113
Wilson, Bill (Bill W.), 202–3
Wilson, E.W., 136–37, *136*
Wilson, Woodrow, 18, 94, 110, 111, 141
Women's Christian Temperance Union (WCTU), 59–63, 67, 80, *80*, *90*, 91, 93, 138, 154, 176
women's suffrage, 25, *25*, 26, *26*, 58, 59, 63, 93, 99, 196
Women's Organization for National Prohibition Reform (WONPR), 154, *155*, 157
World War I, 96–98, 99–103, 108, 117, 134, 145, 202, 207, 225n207
World War II, 166–67
Wright Stanly House, 33–34, *34*, 35

Y

Yandle, Bruce, 2, 39, 215n2, 232n374

About the Author

KATHRYN SMITH is an American history writer. Her non-fiction books include *The Gatekeeper: Missy LeHand, FDR, and the Untold Story of the Partnership that Defined a Presidency* and *Gertie: The Fabulous Life of Gertrude Sanford Legendre, Heiress, Explorer, Socialite, Spy*, which won the Benjamin Franklin Gold Award in biography from the Independent Book Publishers Association. *Methodists and Moonshiners* is a companion to her first foray into Prohibition history, *Baptists and Bootleggers*. She also co-authors the Missy LeHand Mystery Series with Kelly Durham, which features LeHand as the Nancy Drew of the New Deal. Kathryn speaks widely on her books at venues that have included the FDR Presidential Library and Museum and the National World War II Museum in New Orleans as well as to book club, civic club, library, history museum and retirement community audiences. She writes a daily newsletter about the diaries of ordinary Americans in the 20th century at bootleggers.substack.com. Kathryn and her husband Leo live in Anderson, South Carolina and enjoy frequent trips to visit their children and grandchildren.

www.ingramcontent.com/pod-product-compliance
Lightning Source LLC
Chambersburg PA
CBHW070548160426
43199CB00014B/2415